Of God and Man

Of God and Man

*Theology as Anthropology from
Irenaeus to Athanasius*

by
MATTHEW C. STEENBERG

t & t clark

Published by T&T Clark

A Continuum imprint
The Tower Building, 11 York Road, London SE1 7NX
80 Maiden Lane, Suite 704, New York, NY 10038

www.continuumbooks.com

British Library Cataloguing-in-Publication Data
A catalogue record for this book is available from the British Library.

ISBN-10: HB: 0-567-03369-4
PB: 0-567-03370-8
ISBN-13: HB: 978-0-567-03369-7
PB: 978-0-567-03370-3

Library of Congress Cataloging-in-Publication Data
A catalog record for this book is available from the Library of Congress.

Typeset by Newgen Imaging Systems Pvt Ltd, Chennai, India
Printed on acid-free paper in Great Britain by CPI Antony Rowe, Chippenham
Wiltshire

TABLE OF CONTENTS

Foreword   vii
Preface   ix
Acknowledgements   xi
Abbreviations   xii

INTRODUCTION TO AN ANTHROPOLOGICAL THEOLOGY   1
  Defining 'Incarnational'   2
  From Christ to Image   7
  Reading an Anthropological Theology   9
  Methodology   13

Chapter 1
LINKING BEGINNINGS AND ENDS: IRENAEUS OF LYONS   16
  The First Supposition: Humanity Created by God   22
  Re-Thinking the Image   29
  The Incarnate Christ as Iconic Paradigm   34
  The Fashioned Image: The Composite of the Human Person   38
  The Second Supposition: An Intentionally Economic Creation   41
  Characterizing Irenaeus' Anthropology: To Speak of God and Man   51

Chapter 2
IMPATIENT HUMANITY: TERTULLIAN OF CARTHAGE   55
  Controversy in Interpretation   59
  Compositional Elements in the Human Creature   64
  Growing Impatient: The Economic Disfigurement of the One Race   79
  The Salvation of Impatient Humanity: Anthropology
    Grounding Soteriology   88
  Wedded to the Spirit: A Dynamic Anthropology of Growth   98

Chapter 3
A CHANGING PICTURE OF NICAEA   104
  Re-reading Nicaea   107
  Nicaea's Theological Contribution   115
  A Nicene Contribution to Anthropological Theology?   126

Chapter 4

BAPTIZED INTO HUMAN REALITY: CYRIL OF JERUSALEM   128
   What Mystery Immanently Comes? Baptismal Death, Life
      and Enslavement as the Revelation of Human Nature   135
   The Function of the Soul and the Definition of Sin   140
   Who Works This Mystery in Me? From an Economy
      of Sin to a Confession of Redemption   143
   The Role of the Holy Spirit: Bearing the Life of the Son   149
   Joined to the Suffering of Christ   151
   Sacrament and Image: Theology Encountered Anthropologically   154

Chapter 5

MOVING INTO BEING: ATHANASIUS OF ALEXANDRIA   158
   Incorruption, Corruption, Incorruption   162
   The Soul's Movement into Non-existence: Sin as Transformation   174
   Image Renewed: Christ, the Spirit and the Sensibility of Salvation 179
   Becoming Sons and Gods: Athanasius on the Concerns of Nicaea   186

CONCLUSION   190

Bibliography   192
Index   203

FOREWORD

As a research student in Oxford many years ago, I attended a meeting addressed by a Russian monk from Mount Athos, Fr Sophrony, founder of a monastery in England. The discussion was drawing to a close, and the chairman invited one last question. A voice from the back row of the audience said: 'Tell me, what is God?' Fr Sophrony replied briefly: 'Tell me, what is man?'

For the Athonite *starets*, the two questions were inseparable. The mystery of God and the mystery of our human personhood are not two mysteries but one. Created as we are in the divine image, we come to an understanding of God the Trinity through an understanding of our own selves. Authentic humanism and faith in God are interdependent variables. If we affirm the human, we affirm also the divine; if we deny God, we deny also our own humanness.

Such is likewise the primary insight that inspires the present work by the young Orthodox theologian, Matthew Steenberg. He has already become recognized as an expert on Irenaeus through his first work, *Irenaeus on Creation: The Cosmic Christ and the Saga of Redemption*. In this, his second major publication, he has enlarged his scope, so that alongside Irenaeus he includes also Tertullian, Cyril of Jerusalem and Athanasius. In all four of them, in varying ways, he discerns a single master-theme. As he puts it, 'The divine and the human are encountered as one'. All theology must be understood as anthropology, and all anthropology as theology; 'the two can never really be separate'. In patristic writings from the second to the fourth century – at least so far as Dr Steenberg's four chosen authors are concerned – there is what he terms a 'unifying core', and this 'unifying core' is the human person: 'the human creature forms, for all our authors, the framework for articulating theology'.

The inter-connection between the doctrine of God and the doctrine of human personhood – between the two questions 'Who is God?' and 'Who am I?' – is strikingly indicated in two short phrases. 'In his unbounded love', writes Irenaeus concerning Christ the Word of God, 'he became what we are, so as to make us what he is' (*Refutation* 5, preface). Yet more explicitly, Athanasius affirms: 'He was made man, that we might be made God' (*On the incarnation* 54.3). 'He was made man': it is the aim of trinitarian theology and Christology to explore the meaning of these words. '. . . that we might be made God', or 'might be deified': that is the central topic of spirituality and mystical theology. Yet Athanasius unites the two themes in a single sentence, comprising no more than six words in the original Greek. As Dr Steenberg insists, the Fathers did not split up Christian doctrine into separate compartments.

Along with his conviction that theology and anthropology go together, Dr Steenberg develops in this important book a second master-theme; and that is the coherence and continuity of Christian doctrine from the second to the fourth century. The progress of theological discussion during this period, he maintains, 'is marked out by a remarkable spirit of continuity, even as it embraces profound change'. In the past, histories of Christian doctrine often implied that trinitarian theology did not really emerge in a specific way until the fourth century; more particularly, they suggested that an interest in the Holy Spirit only came to the fore in the last decades of that century. Dr Steenberg argues persuasively that already in the second century we find an anthropology that presupposes the coeternal divinity of Father, Son and Spirit. Repeatedly he quotes Irenaeus' words about the Son and the Spirit as the 'two hands' of God the Father, 'who are *always* with him'.

It gives me particular pleasure that Dr Steenberg emphasizes the doctrinal significance of Cyril of Jerusalem, 'one of the great non-Nicene post-Nicenes', as he puts it. Cyril, he says, is 'an understudied voice', who in the past has all too often been 'sidelined', being treated as an author of interest only to liturgical specialists concerned with the sacraments of baptism and the Eucharist. Dr Steenberg shows that, on the contrary, Cyril has much to say about the human person as bearing the image of God and, yet more fundamentally, about the Son's relation to the Father and the Spirit. He is not to be dismissed simply as a 'pastor' and a 'catechist' rather than a theologian, for his *catechesis* is always profoundly theological.

The present work is a creative and original study, closely argued, that requires and repays careful reading. It is based on an exact and detailed knowledge of the patristic sources, but displays also a close acquaintance with contemporary scholarship. It has helped me to look at familiar texts from the Fathers with new eyes, and I am confident that it will do the same for many other readers.

Kallistos Ware
Metropolitan of Diokleia

PREFACE

This book aims to accomplish three interrelated, yet distinct, goals. The first is to explore the connection of an anthropology of the divine image (i.e. humanity 'after the image of God') to the developing articulation of God, confessed as trinity of Father with Son and Spirit, between the second and fourth centuries. The intention here is to investigate how these two realms, anthropology and theology, are co-operatively engaged in the period, and particularly how the former forms the context of the latter. By examining the implications of humanity bearing God's image in key authors from Irenaeus to Athanasius, I hope to demonstrate that what scholars regularly consider doctrinal contributions peculiar to the fourth century – refined conceptions of the trinity, and in peculiar reflections on the Holy Spirit – are current in the anthropological/theological exchange far earlier, and that the character of these earlier discussions provides insights into those later developments.

A second goal is to present the beginnings of a different reading of the history of this period, given expression by these observations on the relationship of anthropology and doctrinal theology from the second century onwards. While it is not my intention to write a history of the era – I will focus primarily on 'case studies' of four key figures, set in the context of the rise of the conciliar age – nonetheless the observations made here present tools for a re-reading of various presuppositions regarding that history.

A third and final goal, which forms a kind of broader setting for the whole project, is to begin to explore the thought of our early patristic sources outside the bonds of customary nineteenth- and twentieth-century systematizations of patristic exegesis, with their pre-conceived notions of doctrinal development through the fifth century. This is the kind of methodology that has told us that the fourth century is about trinity, the fifth about Christology, that doctrines of the divinity of the Spirit are not significantly developed prior to 381, etc. The limitations of such analysis are more widely appreciated in these first years of the twenty-first century, borne witness by the number of books and articles urging a 're-thinking' or 'fresh approach'. A selection of texts from the past few years in particular have begun wide-ranging projects of reading early Christian thought in creative ways, and have been of influence in what follows. My own approach in this regard is explained more fully in the introduction.

These three goals intertwine throughout the volume. When one ceases to read the early centuries as a series of authors writing within the confines of an imposed doctrinal chronology, one discovers developed themes of trinity far earlier than the fourth century, integrated pneumatologies that link the divinity of the Spirit with the fabric of the human creation centuries before Constantinople, and second-century anthropologies that presuppose a co-eternal divinity of the Father, Son and Spirit, imaged in the human creature. Seeing anthropological reflection as the context for addressing theological doctrine, we find, too, the means of addressing some of the abiding historical curiosities of the period, and discover new questions to fuel ongoing interest in early doctrinal study.

M. C. S., 2008

ACKNOWLEDGEMENTS

Much of the impetus to take up the subject of this book, and in this particular way, has come through a series of conversations over the past five years with Fr John Behr, whose works are cited heavily in the pages to follow. To him I owe a great personal debt, as someone who always engages my thinking on patristic matters in the most enticing manner. My interest in the particular subject of this study, namely the relationship of anthropology and doctrinal theology, has been fostered over the years by Metropolitan Kallistos of Diokleia, and for his support and insights I am also very grateful. Special thanks are due to Drs Mark Edwards, Thomas Weinandy and David Gwynn for their assistance with this project – at times directly, by looking through the manuscript and offering comments and corrections, and at others through many conversations and colloquia at which these materials have been refined. Thanks are due to the Fellows of Greyfriars Hall and the Faculty of Theology at the University of Oxford, where this book was begun, and to my colleagues at Leeds Trinity, where it has been completed. Thomas Kraft at T&T Clark has proved invaluable in the tightening up of the manuscript. A portion of the chapter on Tertullian is based on an article I published in *Vigiliae Christianae*, and I would like to express my thanks for the kind permission to incorporate that material here.

ABBREVIATIONS

ACW	Ancient Christian Writers
ANF	Ante-Nicene Fathers
BG	Berlin Gnostic Codex
CCSL	Corpus Christianorum, Series Latinorum
CPL	Clavis Patrum Latinorum
CSEL	Corpus Scriptorum Ecclesiasticorum Latinorum
ETL	*Ephemerides Theologicae Lovanienses*
GCS	Die griechischen christlichen Schriftsteller
GOTR	*Greek Orthodox Theological Review*
Greg	*Gregorianum*
HJ	*Heythrop Journal*
ITQ	*Irish Theological Quarterly*
JECS	*Journal of Early Christian Studies*
JTS	*Journal of Theological Studies*
LCC	Library of Christian Classics
LCL	Loeb Classical Library
NHC	Nag Hammadi Codices
NPNF	Nicene and Post-Nicene Fathers
PBR	*Patristic and Byzantine Review*
PE	*Pro Ecclesia*
PG	Patrologia, Series Graeca
PL	Patrologia, Series Latina
PO	Patrologia, Series Orientalis
PTS	Patristische Texte und Studien
RSR	*Recherches de Science Religieuse*
SC	Sources Chrétiennes
SJT	*Scottish Journal of Theology*
SP	*Studia Patristica*
SVTQ	*St Vladimir's Theological Quarterly*
TS	*Theological Studies*
VigChr	*Vigiliae Christianae*
ZK	*Zeitschrift für Kirchengeschichte*

INTRODUCTION TO AN ANTHROPOLOGICAL THEOLOGY

Who is man, that you are mindful of him? Or the son of man, that you care for him? For you have made him a little lower than the angels, and crowned him with glory and honour.

—*Psalm 8.4, 5*

The human person stands at the centre of Christian reality. At the pinnacle of creation is its formation by the very hands of God. At the opposite pole, at the eschaton, the Christian scriptures proclaim humanity's fulfilment and perfection. Along the way, between these poles of creation and fulfilment, the whole of the economy is focused on this being: that which God fashions, which turns against its creator, for which the creator works correction and redemption, even becoming that which he deigns to save.

At the heart of this historical motion, of the 'economy of salvation' as Irenaeus of Lyons seems to be the first to have called it, stands Christ: God-made-man. This centrality is not temporal, as if it represented some historical 'midpoint' between the pre- and post-incarnational history of the human story. Rather, it is theological: it speaks of Christ not as the midpoint of history, but the central reference of all theological vision. All that comes before and after the historical incarnation in Galilee is centred in the reality of the one there manifest and made known, and has its true meaning and character in the same. The human race, which pre-dates the historical events of the birth, passion and resurrection of Christ, does not pre-date the one thus born, crucified and risen, but from the first to the last takes its reality from the one there seen and touched, yet from all ages known. As Cyril of Jerusalem, speaking on the site of Golgotha, would remind his hearers in the middle of the fourth century, the one who died 'here' was he who 'was begotten by the Father before all ages, eternally and inconceivably'.[1] The one who took flesh, who revealed fully the true image of God, is the one who from the foundation of the cosmos has been divine Son of the Father.

The starting point of the Christian confession is this Jesus Christ, whose eternity was revealed through the cross and empty tomb, and subsequently explored within the heritage of scripture. As Paul wrote to the young Church at Ephesus, 'in former generations this mystery was not made known to humankind, as it has now been revealed to his holy apostles and prophets by the Spirit' (Ephesians 3.5).

---

1   Cyril, *Cat.* 4.7. See below, pp. 128–57.

The mystery existed, but was not fully known. That which is provided in Galilee is a new means of encountering the mystery that was real in the past, revealed in the present – provoking Tertullian to quip, 'O Christ, even in your novelties you are old!'[2] Summarizing this mystery, the epistle to Timothy notes, 'Remember Jesus Christ, raised from the dead, a descendant of David – this is my gospel' (2 Timothy 2.8). The one who has died is the one come from David, the one 'of the scriptures', known from the tomb, who walked among humanity 'in the flesh'. At the height of its message, Christianity thrusts human reality to the dignity of the divine, for it confesses that the Son of God 'became flesh and dwelt among us', that the divine has condescended to the stature of its human handiwork. The heart of Paul's gospel – that the 'mystery of Christ' is of the descendent of David raised from the dead – is inherently concentrated on the human creature 'fashioned from the dust', descended to David and to Christ as much as to Paul himself. The one known as Son of God is proclaimed the descendent of his human creature. The divine and the human are encountered as one.

It is this union of the divine and human that frames in the focus of this study. The one descended from David is not simply 'God', but Son of God, Son of the Father. So from Peter's initial confession, 'You are the Christ, the Son of the living God' (cf. Matthew 16.16), articulation of the incarnate Saviour has involved discussion not only of the union of man and God, but of man's union with a God *who has a Son*. Moreover, this is a Son who sends a Spirit, also called the Father's, by whom he is himself anointed. To speak of Jesus Christ as incarnate Son of the Father is intrinsically to speak both of the nature of humanity (the anthropology of the Son) and a triadic understanding of the divine (the nature of the Son as Son of the Father, united with the Spirit). The interconnection of these realms of anthropology and theology, or rather, the fact that both form a single subject of exploration in the single subject of Christ, is the focus of the present volume.

Defining 'Incarnational'

The basic confession that Christ is the Son-made-man provides Christianity with its label, 'incarnational'. It is theological, inasmuch as it deals with the divine – the Son of God in relation to his Father and the Spirit; but it is also anthropological, inasmuch as it deals with the human, which the Son takes up in the virgin birth and makes his own in his offering and resurrection. Indeed, as scholarship from time to time reminds us, Christianity is as much anthropology as theology, for the *anthropos* and *theos* of these categories are understood to meet in the single person of Jesus Christ. Feuerbach pronounced the connection in his famous observation that all theology should be understood as anthropology, an idea supplemented by Jenkins' later insistence that 'this is so only because all anthropology

2 Tertullian, *Adv. Marc.* 4.21.5.

must be understood as theology'.[3] From the perspective of the incarnation, the two can never really be separate.

Nonetheless, and for all its centrality to the Christian message, the terminology of 'incarnation' is used loosely in scholarly discourse. With the definite article, as 'the incarnation', it usually refers to the actual (physical) act of the annunciation and virginal birth. Without the definite article, 'incarnation' tends to imply the general concept of God-becoming-man. Used adverbially, 'incarnationally' might mean 'as justified by the physical enfleshment of Christ', or 'according to the concept of divine enfleshment'. No such definitions are entirely inaccurate. Nonetheless, they are usually employed in a manner that has little precedent in early patristic testimony. Almost always they foster a type of chronological understanding of the divine by indicating a specific 'period' in the eternal existence of the Son: that 'phase' in which the Word is enfleshed, exists as man, offers the sacrifice of his life and death so as to rise in glory in the defeat of death. The one who 'before' existed 'pre-incarnationally' as Word and Son of the Father, 'in the incarnation' exists as man on earth before returning to his Father, the newly 'incarnate one' ascending whence he came. And so, to study the incarnation is to study a before, a during, an after.

The main problem with such a way of speaking of the incarnation, at least to one interested in early patristics, is that it has little precedent in the expression of the early Church. There the one spoken of is not the Word known first, who has become incarnate, but Jesus Christ first and foremost as encountered person, known in that encounter as eternal Word. This distinction, between God understood as coming to be man, and a man coming to be understood as God, constitutes an important confession of the one who *is* Word and Son in the flesh, and how he is known as such. It is Jesus Christ, the one of Galilee, the one 'descended of David', who is, in this very humanity, understood to be the Word 'in the beginning with God' (John 1.1). The starting point is not a dogmatic confession of the Son followed by a description of his human becoming, but the human Christ, who *from* and *in* his humanity is identified with the eternal Son of the Father. One does not begin with the eternal Word, later to take flesh. One begins with the flesh and bones of Jesus of Galilee, and sees in him the eternity of the divine Son.

This is an inversion of what is, by far, the normal manner of speaking of our subject. To speak of 'incarnation' in these terms is to begin with the cross and the resurrection, and to find, in the human experiences of the descendent of David, encounter with the eternal Son. Rather than starting with a confession that there is a divine, eternal Word who at a moment in history becomes incarnate as Jesus Christ, this approach is grounded instead in the centrality of the encountered and

---

3   D. E. Jenkins, *The Glory of Man: Bampton Lectures for 1966* (London: SCM Press Ltd., 1967). The same idea was the focus of Dodd's work in Cambridge at roughly the same period; see C. H. Dodd, 'Man in God's Design According to the New Testament', *Studiorum Novi Testamenti Societas* (1952).

confessed Christ of Galilee. It is not with an abstracted concept of 'God' that
the Christian Church starts, thereby extrapolating how Jesus can be 'Son of God'
and 'God' himself, but *with the person of Jesus Christ* and none other. Paul's
gospel is not of 'the divinity made flesh', nor of the 'Father who has a Son who
took flesh', but of 'Jesus Christ, raised from the dead'. To abstract the Son, or
the divinity of the Son, from the person of Jesus Christ – as, for example, the eternal reality or person that 'became' Jesus Christ – is to disfigure the language of
Christianity's earliest testimony.

To re-focus incarnational language on indicating how this human Jesus Christ is
the eternal Son of the Father, rather than how the Son of the Father has become
this human Jesus Christ, is to take a step away from many usual methods of reading incarnational theology. It is, however, a more authentic means of reading the
incarnational language of early Christendom, and in particular the texts of the
early patristic corpus, with respect to their own vocabulary, methodology and
intention. It is only in this context that Christianity's unique anthropology – its
approach to who and what the human creature really is – finds merit and coherence within its larger theological confessions. This is so precisely because the
starting point of those confessions is not 'the Father who is divine and has a
Son who is divine, who takes to himself the human', but the very human Jesus
Christ who is, *as the human Jesus Christ*, known to be Son of the Father. Incarnational anthropology is not about a divinity that comes to relate to and embrace
humanity, but the experience of the divine in the human. It is the human reality of
Jesus Christ, the 'anthropology' of the Son, that begins the Christian endeavour
of theology, which is therefore not only superficially, but intrinsically and necessarily, a work of anthropology.

If, in modern discussions, anthropology is generally divorced from theology
as a unique entity, even if the purpose of this divorce is in the end to compare
and relate, this must be redressed with an eye towards earlier discussions. The
question posed by the psalmist, 'What is man?' has summed up for over two millennia questions on 'self' and 'personhood' (to use two particularly modern terms)
that are today seen so often as natural to 'human self-consciousness'. These
modern terms being less than helpful for understanding the past, perhaps, they
nonetheless reveal an age-old curiosity: one longs to know the nature of her being,
to understand the character of that which is 'my nature' as human person. Thrust
into the context of human relation to the divine, the question becomes weightier
still. 'What is man', if he is – in any sense – the work and heir of God? Christian
confession may describe God in terms of absolute transcendence, yet it is this
selfsame God who is in Christ encountered humanly, possessing fully human
attributes – so does Jesus eat and sleep, weep and die. How is this relationship
between transcendent creator and finite creation to be understood, as it is experienced and beheld in Christ? How are the limitations of humanity to be examined
in light of the limitlessness of its creator, and how can the limitless creator be
known from this context? These questions are not intrinsically bound up in the

fifth- and sixth-century Christological debates over Christ's natures and wills, in which context they are most often raised. They are more broadly related to the whole scope of anthropology, understood as the approach to the human as created being, fashioned by the limitless God and met most fully in this God's incarnation.

And yet, it is not merely in Christ that one encounters both the divine and human, but in all the human race created by God, related to God as creature to its creator. The stature of the creation, with regard to its generation, nature and future, can be understood only with reference to its fashioning and fashioner. It is only in the interrelation of human and divine realms that there is ground to reflect on the kinds of questions that have always captured the attention of Christian thinkers. Such questions are exemplified in a third-century author, from a group much lamented of early Christian theologians, in what has become a classic pericope of anthropological self-interrogation:

Who were we? What have we become? Whence have we arrived, and where have we been cast? Whither are we hastening? From what have we been delivered? What is generation, and what is regeneration?[4]

This particular set of questions, cast in the midst of a debate on anthropology, cosmology and the complexities of human suffering that consumed much of the Church's attention in the second and third centuries, loosely and inaccurately lumped together in modern study as 'Gnosticism', met with responses attempted precisely in the realm of doctrines of the divine, of God. Questions about man are answered with doctrines about God. While the Church would come to reject firmly the fundamental convictions of the various groups marked out today by the 'Gnostic' title, the questions they posed were as much of concern to those theologians canonized as orthodox as they were to the followers of Valentinus, Ptolemy, Marcion or Marcus. Explored from the confessional starting point of the incarnate passion and resurrection of Christ, how is the Christian person to answer, or even pose, questions of anthropology?

The challenge of responding properly to anthropological questions comes, at least in part, from the false separation of 'anthropology' from 'theology' occasioned by an inverted reading of incarnation. To begin with the doctrine of God as 'divine godhead', one of whose members 'later' takes flesh, not only challenges logical presuppositions of eternity, but requires at the very outset the formation of a rift between theological and anthropological discourse. The former can be seen to have relevance distinct from the latter; and discourse on *theos* can be held in distinction from discourse on *anthropos*. Man must always be addressed in terms of comparison, contrast and relation to God. Not only does this explain how it is

---

4   Recorded in Clement, *Ex.Theod.* 78.2 (SC 23: 202).

possible to separate the study of God from the study of man, it in fact creates a divide whereby the two *must* be apprehended separately, if the notion of their relation is to be understood properly. Human nature can only be understood for its 'createdness' once God is understood distinctly for his uncreatedness. A picture of God *qua* God must come before a picture of man *qua* man.

If, however, the starting point of incarnation is not the godhead who condescends to human stature, but the encountered Jesus Christ, the descendent of David, who through the cross and resurrection reveals that 'I and the Father are one' and thus establishes Peter's confession that he is 'the Christ, the Son of the living God', the analytical separation between *theos* and *anthropos* becomes posterior, not anterior, to incarnational discussion. That which Christianity confesses as the truth and reality of God is known humanly, in and through Jesus Christ. This is the strong sense of 'incarnation' as it resonates in the early Church: in beholding the Son of Mary, one beholds the Son of God. In the life and acts of Jesus of Galilee, one beholds the nature of the divine. God is revealed in the incarnate Jesus Christ, as he himself says: 'he who has seen me has seen the Father' (John 14.9).

Such an approach inextricably links humanity and divinity in Christian reflection, for it is in humanity (Christ's humanity) that divinity is known (Christ's, but known and confessed to be the divinity of the Father). Jenkins' 'anthropology must be understood as theology' provides a summation, some 2,000 years after these questions first began to be posed in a Christian context, of the realm of response to which the Church would come in its reflections on the human person. That which stands at the heart of Christianity, namely the incarnate Son, serves to bind together God and man in theological articulation as much as they are confessed to be bound together in the life of Christ himself. So the psalmist's 'What is man?' is joined, in Christian exposition, to the correlated 'Who is God?' – a connection periphrastically drawn already by the author of Hebrews in the first century:

Therefore we must pay greater attention to what we have heard, so that we do not drift away from it [. . .] It was declared at first through the Lord, and it was attested to us by those who heard him, while God added his testimony by signs and wonders and various miracles, and by gifts of the Holy Spirit distributed according to his will. Now God did not subject the coming world, about which we are speaking, to angels. But someone has testified somewhere, *'What is man that you are mindful of him? or mortals, that you care for them? You have made them a little lower than the angels and have crowned them with glory and honour, subjecting all things under their feet.'* Now, in subjecting all things to them, God left nothing outside their control. As it is, we do not yet see everything in subjection to them – but we do see Jesus, who was made a little lower than the angels, now crowned with glory and honour because of the suffering of death, so that by the grace of God he might taste death for all. (Hebrews 2.1–9; cf. Psalm 8.4, 5)

The salvation offered in Christ is offered by one whose life is expressed here in the scriptural language of human stature. The reality the psalm describes as human existence, is ascribed in the epistle to the Son. To know the nature of the one who 'tastes death for all', one must know the 'all' that he is confessed incarnationally to be, for it is in this context that his being is disclosed. There is a relation established between God and humanity, such that the author can reflect more acutely, 'the one who sanctifies and those who are sanctified have one Father' (Hebrews 2.11).

FROM CHRIST TO IMAGE

The deliberate interchange with which the author of Hebrews can take the words of Psalm 8, which speak of human nature, and apply them to Christ, speaks to a relation between 'the human' in general and 'Christ' in particular. This relation is central to Christian thought, encapsulated in language of the 'image of God'. There is from the first a firm Christian confession that the relationship between the divine and human in Christ is not accidental or contrived at the historical moment when he begins to gestate as human in the womb of the Virgin, but that this relationship is foundational to the natural reality both of Christ the Son and every human person *qua* human.

In speaking of how the man known through the resurrection to be also God, is in fact God and true God, John would proclaim 'the Word became flesh and dwelt among us' (John 1.14), perhaps the most famous of all incarnational passages in the Gospels. It is a text that speaks to the same divine-yet-human reality encountered in Hebrews, in a manner that unites the theological and the anthropological in Christian discussion ever after. But while this passage on incarnational theology has served as the bedrock text for many an exploration of doctrinal development from the second to the fifth centuries, the fact that its short contents speak twice of humanity ('flesh' and 'us') and once of the Word's relation to it ('dwelt among', or more literally 'tabernacled among us') has often been of secondary significance to commentators who speak primarily of the theological implications of God's 'becoming', as pertain to trinitarian and Christological realms of discussion. Yet long before Christian authors were debating the implications of the incarnational becoming on the nature of God as transcendent and immutable, they were offering considered reflections on the being and life of the human being this passage proclaims Christ to be. John's prologue is not chiefly an excursus on the eternal nature of the Logos as Logos, whom he then explains as transformed into the human. That Jesus Christ 'became flesh and dwelt among us' is for the evangelist a statement of the obvious – the common knowledge of experience which he feels no need either to explain or justify. What is key in the prologue is the demonstration of how, and to what effect, this flesh-and-blood Christ *is the Word*, is God. Its aim is to make clear that what Christ is *as us*, as human, he is *as Word*, as Son of the Father. His main point of reflection is how this man is divine, with and as the divinity of the Father ('. . . and the Word was with God, and the Word was God . . .') – how the experienced *anthropos* is at once *theos*, and how the theanthropic reality of Jesus Christ represents a 'coming to his own' (cf. John 1.11). The object of John's consideration, then, is how this 'flesh' which is ours, which is the very nature of man, is mysteriously the flesh of the eternal Son.

Since the earliest written Christian testimony, reflections on this question were framed in the iconic context of 'image'. The humanity beheld in the one who 'dwelt among us' is seen, in itself as natural reality, as related iconically to God. In this, Christianity calls on much older language. That the human creature is formed 'after the image and likeness of God' is established in the first chapter of the first book of scripture (cf. Genesis 1.26–28), though set out most poetically in the second- or third-century BC book of Sirach:

> The Lord created human beings out of earth and makes them return to it again. He gave them a fixed number of days, but granted them authority over everything on the earth. He endowed them with a strength like his own, and made them in his own image. (Sirach 17.1–3)

This ancient currency of humanity as divine image is taken up in the nascent Christian confession in correlation to the one who 'became flesh'. Again, this is not an accidental or secondary correlation, as if there is first a developed Christian vision of the *imago Dei* that is then applied to the humanity of Christ. Rather, and more centrally, it is *in Christ* that the Christanization of the ancient scriptural language of the divine 'image' is accomplished. What it means for humanity to be 'after the image and likeness of God' is apprehended in the one 'who dwelt among us', the very Word of the Father. Paul speaks of Christ directly as the image, more specifically the 'image of the invisible God' (Colossians 1.15), and connects the terminology of 'image and likeness' to human relationship to this Christ: 'Just as we have borne the likeness of the earthly man, so shall we bear the likeness of the man from heaven' (1 Corinthians 15.49). The scriptural declaration of the divine image encountered in humanity, is assigned to Christ as pointing to Christ. As realized in Christ, it becomes for Paul the means by which the whole race comes to resemble, to 'bear the likeness', of the crucified and resurrected saviour.

Paul's language offers insight into John's. The 'flesh' which the Word became is the flesh which, in him as full and true image, is known to be the flesh of 'the image of the invisible God' – the image who is Jesus Christ. Christ as image reveals the full nature of that which is 'after' the image. The one after whose image humanity is fashioned, is the one who *is* the Image in flesh in Galilee. To confess Christ as 'Word made flesh', and to discover in the human Word the antitype of the image typified in the fabric and being of every human person, is to provide an authentic context for anthropological discussion. The context of what defines human as human, is tied together inextricably with what defines God as God – and more particularly, with what defines Christ as Son of the Father and the means of vision and encounter with him. To speak of humanity as the Son's 'image' makes this linkage direct, establishing the comprehensive scope of humanity's existence as in some sense 'imaging' the existence of the eternal Christ. It is the divine Son of the Father, descended of David, who not only reveals but *is* the very image after which all humanity is fashioned. Thus to know the nature and reality of man, to articulate a truly Christian anthropology, is at one and the same time to articulate a truly Christian theology: a doctrine of God known in and through Christ, the Father's incarnate Son.

READING AN ANTHROPOLOGICAL THEOLOGY

Our aim in the present volume is to explore this interrelation of humanity as 'after the image of God' to the Church's developing articulation of its doctrine of God. Precisely because the chief anthropological doctrine of the Church is one that defines humanity in terms of a reflection or image of the divine, it is only within the scope of an articulation of God that Christian anthropology can rightly be understood. And yet, it is in and through its anthropological considerations – that is, reflections on the Son of God as human – that this doctrine of the divine finds the grounds of its own articulation. One is compelled to treat the two together: to explore the discussion of human reality in concert with that of divine reality, as these develop and are refined in the course of the Church's early history. This task is inherently Christological, as it is in the encounter with Christ that there is articulated a Christian 'doctrine of God' (which, especially in the early centuries, almost always means a doctrine of God the Father, whom the Son of this God reveals). But more broadly than a rigid Christology, the task is also trinitarian, if by that term we refer not to a presupposed post-Nicene trinitarianism, but mean that the Son's revelation of the Father reveals also the reality and activity (and is further understood as being revealed *by* the reality and activity) of the Holy Spirit, received by the incarnate Christ at his baptism and sent by him upon the Church at the Pentecost. Indeed, as will become apparent in the pages ahead, the pneumatological confession of earliest Christendom is central to its anthropological discussion. A developed doctrine of the Spirit is today often taken to be primarily a fourth-century phenomenon, an outgrowth of the groundwork laid at Nicaea and fleshed out at Constantinople, not something to figure heavily in the thought of the earliest centuries. Yet what is conspicuously consistent in the second and third centuries both, is a confession of the humanity redeemed by the

Son, of the *imago Dei* revealed in his person, framed within consideration of the Spirit in relation to the Son and Father. To articulate anthropology as primarily iconic, as 'in the image', is for our principal second-, third- and fourth-century sources, tied up in an increasingly nuanced articulation of Father, Son and Spirit in eternal and, economically, temporal co-relation.

To suggest that the development of Christian anthropology in the early period is grounded in a refined articulation of the Son of the Father, imaged in the Spirit's relationship to the creature, requires a certain re-assessment of key periods in that history. Too often, the field of historical theology is content to explore the early Church in rather forced categories – matters trinitarian, matters Christological, matters polemical, matters anthropological – each of which is assigned its own position on the timeline of early Christendom. The timeline that results almost always sees the fourth century as 'trinitarian', the fifth as 'Christological', and so already stands at odds with what we have outlined above. Twenty-first-century scholarship is still feeling the effects of Grillmeier, of Quasten, of Hanson, all of whom contributed profoundly to our knowledge of early Christianity, yet all of whom, to various degrees, expounded that Christianity in the very categorical terms we are today seeking to overcome. Fortunately, the present day is witnessing important efforts to revisit such readings of Christian history, to take the wealth of historical data unleashed in the nineteenth and twentieth centuries, and explore it in terms and contexts more authentic to its origins. Since Bauer's inversion of the 'branch theory' of early Christendom in the early 1930s, the hares have been set running.[5] Such static and often ill-defined categories of thought as 'Gnosticism' and 'Montanism' have been relegated to the realm of inverted commas, not because the principles that ground the old distinctions have been done away with, but because we are coming to understand more authentically the fluidity and amorphism of the various groups these titles are used to represent.[6] The same is true with the most current work on Arius and 'Arianism'.[7] And while careful scholars set about clarifying the details of such labels and arenas of thought, others are engaged in broader re-assessments of the whole historical scope in which these issues are staged. Here the recent and ongoing work of John Behr is of significance, with his *Formation of Christian Theology* series, still in progress, an expansive effort at synthesizing the massive corpus of early Christian

---

5   See W. Bauer, *Orthodoxy and Heresy in Earliest Christianity*, tr. R. Kraft (Philadelphia: Fortress Press, 1971); originally published in German (Tübingen: Mohr, 1934).

6   For the challenge to such terms as 'Gnosticism' and 'Gnostics', see the seminal study by M. A. Williams, *Rethinking 'Gnosticism' – An Argument for Dismantling a Dubious Category* (Princeton: Princeton University Press, 1999); we will have more to say on this in our chapter on Irenaeus. For the best treatment to date of 'Montanism', see C. Trevett, *Montanism: Gender, Authority and the New Prophecy* (Cambridge: Cambridge University Press, 1996).

7   See D. M. Gwynn, *The Eusebians: The Polemic of Athanasius of Alexandria and the Construction of the 'Arian Controversy'* (Oxford: Oxford University Press, 2006).

scholarship into a developmental portrait, reflecting the early Church's own scriptural matrix of doctrinal reflection.[8]

It is in concert with such efforts that we seek in the present text to explore afresh the question of 'image' as related to the doctrinal articulation of God, as it advances and develops in the early Church. This is a project only possible through the re-assessment of that doctrinal articulation put forward by the scholars mentioned above, among others. In light of early doctrinal discussion authentically considered, how are we to understand the vision of the human person expressed in early Christianity? How are we to see humanity as 'image' from the framework of an increasingly refined articulation of Father, Son and Spirit witnessed in scripture through the life, death and resurrection of Christ, and simultaneously see the incarnationally driven anthropology of this era as the context for framing these theological articulations?

It is my increasing conviction that the anthropological confession of the *imago Dei* is advanced in Christian thought in precise correlation to the increasingly nuanced articulation of the divine, and itself forms the context in which divine reality is explained more and more articulately as Father, together with his Son and Spirit, co-existing, co-relating, as trinity. Far from suggesting adherence to a type of developmental doctrine that sees the Church progressively inventing or even newly discovering theological and anthropological realities from one century to the next, the early patristic corpus reveals instead a development of articulation: the mystery encountered in the person of Jesus Christ, especially from the vantage point of this Christ died and risen and ascended in glory, is understood as the mystery of the 'faith once for all delivered to the saints' (Jude 1.3), on which the Church has reflected since the first among the first twelve confessed it fully, yet was rebuked for not proclaiming aright that which he had received.[9] The task of doctrinal theology, as it came to be understood and practiced in the early Church, was not perceived as creation or discovery, but preservation of the mysterious faith of an incarnate Son through new and constructive articulations of what that mystery entails, drawn from a reading of the scriptures it is created to fulfil. G. L. Bray, in a masterful though not unproblematic study of Tertullian, with which we shall engage more directly in Chapter 2, made this point succinctly:

To the Fathers of the Church, Christian theology was the work of the converted mind seeking to get to grips with the teaching of Scripture. Compared

---

8 See J. Behr, *The Formation of Christian Theology, vol. 1: The Way to Nicaea* (New York: St Vladimir's Seminary Press, 2001); *The Formation of Christian Theology, vol. 2: The Nicene Faith* (New York: St Vladimir's Seminary Press, 2004). See also his *The Mystery of Christ: Life in Death* (New York: St Vladimir's Seminary Press, 2006), which lays particular emphasis on the questions of right approaches to understanding incarnation.
9 So Jesus' rebuke of Peter following the latter's confession of him as the Christ and Son of God (see Matthew 16.16). Jesus' foretelling of his passion provokes Peter's 'Far be it from you, O Lord; this shall not happen unto you', met with Christ's rather emphatic 'Get behind me, Satan!' (Matthew 16.21–23).

with ancient philosophy, it contains little in the way of speculation, and even less diversity of approach. However different Antiochenes and Alexandrians, Apologists and Cappadocians may appear to us, to their non-Christian contemporaries they spoke as one voice. Later generations drew upon the work of earlier ones not as imperfect specimens of theological activity which required substantial revision in light of subsequent reflection, but as models to be revered and imitated, even as they were expanded and developed further.[10]

There is immense diversity in the patristic corpus, but diversity of a common scope. The post-enlightenment critical project has been keen to categorize and classify its patrimony with discreet historical labels; but these, while coherent each in their own right perhaps, have in application served by and large to transform the early fathers into nineteenth- and twentieth-century scholars rather than strive to orientate modern academic exploration to their way of thought. But perhaps because the preceding generation had done so with such vigour, scholars of the mid- to late-twentieth century have proved keen to explore alternative visions. Bauer's work, already mentioned, which successfully questioned and then inverted the 'branch theory' of single-articulation origins in earliest Christianity, met with enthusiastic embrace and refinement in the pen of J. Dunn, and within a few decades an English translation of B. Lonergan's *The Way to Nicaea* was reframing doctrinal considerations in a manner consonant with their readings.[11] Yet the process of re-envisaging the 'how', even the 'why', of early Christian thought has proved a challenging task. The clear, yet nonetheless false, categories to be overcome pose the heady challenge of being precisely that: clear, concise frameworks of address. How to speak without them? Few would agree that Lonergan's model of a move from 'undifferentiated' to 'differentiated consciousness' suffices, though it makes a step in the right direction. One finds there a clear perception of the process of unfolding articulation, without suggestion of creation of substance, and in this his theory is appealing. But one senses in Lonergan that the old preference for succinct categorizations is still in play, that we are still attempting to read ancient history from the standpoint of modern philosophy – or in his case, modern psychology. Is there a way to read this history of thought that accommodates the reality of fodder for centuries of intense, engaged analysis, without at once giving rise to anachronistic claims that later modes of thought secretly inspired their forebears?

Such questions have been the focus of the most current scholarship. If the central thesis of Behr's reading, that the questions boil down to one question, Christ's 'Who do you say that I am?' (Matthew 16.15), seems at first impossibly

---

10   G. L. Bray, *Holiness and the Will of God – Perspectives on the Theology of Tertullian* (London: Marshall, Morgan and Scott, 1979) xi.

11   See G. D. Dunn, *Tertullian* (London: Routledge, 2004); B. Lonergan, *The Way to Nicaea* (London, 1976).

simple, it is perhaps a sign that we have lost today a full sense of the complexity of this question and its centrality to Christian life and thought. To articulate authentically the mystery of the Christ encountered in Galilee and known in the scriptures, is a project that extended through seven ecumenical councils, indeed far beyond – and, as some of the fathers themselves would argue, will carry on so long as it continues with legitimacy to be an articulation of encounter with a God transcendent of complete description. It is precisely in this sense of coming to articulate more fully that which is encountered wholly in the first moment of confession, that a fresh exploration of early discussions on anthropology holds the potential to reveal the manner in which they form part of that larger project of developing doctrinal articulation. By consequence, it also holds the potential to reveal more genuinely the full scope of what is meant by calling the human person God's 'image'.

What we discover in such a reading of early Christian discussion, is an explicit linkage of image-anthropology to what will come, by the fourth century, formally to be referred to as trinitarian theology. As the confession of Father, Son and Spirit in relation is refined, so the human person bearing God's image is confessed – with ever greater precision – to be a being joined to this life of relation through the working of its persons in the substance and economy of human life. The effect is not simply to articulate some manner of link between the human creation and its God confessed as trinity, but through such a linking to understand the nature of the dynamic qualities of that creature. This context of 'dynamic' characteristics, by which we mean that in which a being cannot be defined in static terms, but must be understood as interconnected with something beyond itself, which relation is prone to change and advance, is critical to understanding the thought of our era. To see the person as one in receipt of God's presence, and by that presence borne up into increasing relation to the life of the Father with his Son and Spirit, will be to understand ever more clearly the necessarily economic reality of human existence. Static categories of human composition do not hold together coherently in a definition of that composition as the image of a dynamic God – that is, of a God who relates eternally and fully to his two hands – and this becomes ever more clear as articulation of that relation advances.

METHODOLOGY

My approach in what follows is to explore this interrelationship of 'anthropology' and 'theology' primarily through a series of sequential case studies from various key stages in the doctrinal discussions from the first to the fourth centuries. This methodology requires some justification. In a sense, any 'case by case' approach risks artificially separating a given patristic source's thought from the larger dynamic of Christian discussion taking place around him – of treating Church fathers in isolation in precisely the manner we have suggested above needs to be overcome. This is a risk, and one of which we must be aware. Yet it is possible to be authentic to the sense of progression and interrelation of Christian thought in the early period without requiring that every book on patristic matters be an exhaustive synthesis of all authors in every era. Moreover, this approach allows one to see the manner in which various patristic sources engaged in their task in a personal, unique manner, very much voices unto themselves even as they are voices in common tradition. Tertullian is not a copy of Irenaeus, nor Cyril of Jerusalem a mirror of Athanasius. An interest of the present study is precisely the manner in which common conceptions of an interrelationship between economic anthropology and a dynamic doctrine of God, arise in authors with little direct relation one to another. The key voices selected for this task – Irenaeus of Lyons, Tertullian of Carthage, Cyril of Jerusalem and Athanasius of Alexandria – have been chosen because they mark out various interconnected periods in the articulation of doctrine in the early era, but also because they are *not* voices in direct succession. The rhetorically, rationally structured arguments of Tertullian are of distinctly different voice from the more eclectic exegesis of Irenaeus; and Cyril of Jerusalem not only speaks in a different voice than Athanasius – that of catechesis rather than treatise – but he grounds his teaching in a different creed than that used by the great, though controversial, bishop of Alexandria. I hope the chapters as I have designed them will allow a detailed look at certain representative figures to indicate the larger stream of thought that unites them in their diversity. Reference is made in each to various other individuals not treated in so thorough a manner, but I have chosen to focus primarily on the main figures of address in each chapter. This helps to show that the larger point of a correlation between image-anthropology and refinements of articulation of the doctrine of God should not be construed as an academic concept, created by a forced synthesis of varied voices, none of whom speak of it directly, but as clearly a point of direct address in each.

Given that our central assertion is of a correlation between anthropological development and refined articulation of trinity, it seems natural that this study should terminate in the era of most intense trinitarian discussion, namely the fourth century AD. However, I have intentionally not concluded with the council of Nicaea in 325, nor that of Constantinople in 381. The notions of 'all things pointing toward Nicaea', or that the rise of Nicene trinitarian doctrine finds its terminus in the Cappadocians at Constantinople, are aspects of the historical misreadings that modern scholarship is working to overcome. The ecumenical council of 325 does figure in these pages, but as a kind of fulcrum rather than a terminus. I have situated it between chapters on Irenaeus and Tertullian on the one hand, and Cyril of Jerusalem and Athanasius on the other. The fact that, at the very time that Athanasius is beginning to pen his most pro-Nicene documents, Cyril can speak of the matters under investigation whilst not once mentioning Nicaea or its creed, speaks volumes to the historical situation of the mid-350s, and will be explored at length in due course. It seems pertinent to show in these pages that Nicaea does not represent either a terminus of reflection on the trinitarian and anthropological matters to hand, nor a radical 'new beginning', nor an immediate force of univocality to reflection on the same.

*   *   *

This is a book primarily on anthropology, on the discovery of the human through the refinements in articulation between the formative second and fourth centuries of the Church's life. But it is also a book on theology, on trinity, precisely because an exploration of anthropological reflection in the early Church reveals the two realms to be fundamentally interrelated. It is in its tendency to separate the two, to study early theology apart or as distinct from early anthropology, that scholarship has at times been hindered in its understanding of both. But to work within an authentically incarnational context – a confession that in the human Jesus, the Image after which humanity fashioned, the divine Son of the Father is encountered; who makes that encounter transformative by receiving and sending the Father's Spirit – is inherently and necessarily to connect these realms. To speak of God or man is always to speak of God *and* man, for early Christendom is unwilling ever to start from any point other than the witness of Christ, who, though being in the form of God, 'took flesh and dwelt as man among us'.

Chapter 1

LINKING BEGINNINGS AND ENDS:
IRENAEUS OF LYONS

The present chapter will explore the connection of anthropology and theology in Irenaeus of Lyons, commonly appreciated – at least since the 1940s[1] – both for his extensive anthropological discussion and his 'nascent trinitarianism', or development of what is essentially an 'economic trinity'.[2] I will argue in what follows that, despite the popularity of such themes in Irenaeus, his thought is still not well understood. Irenaeus' trinitarianism is not 'nascent' (there is an intrinsic anachronism to such language in any case) but markedly well developed; and despite dwelling extensively on economic matters, is nonetheless eternal and 'immanent', to borrow for the moment that later term. The challenge to determining an authentic Irenaean trinitarianism and anthropology comes partly through the habit of staging exegesis in just these terms: Irenaeus speaks of neither as such, but always of the experienced reality of the incarnate Son as Saviour. It is in speaking about Christ's salvation of creation that he presents, as integrated aspects of his Christological discussion, an articulation of the Son as eternal hand of the Father who, in the baptismal anointing of the Spirit, unites the creation of his own fashioning to the God after whom this creation is imaged. The ancient confession of humanity as 'in the image and likeness of God' is used by Irenaeus to reveal the means through which this union is made real in the life of the created person: through a compositional fashioning that joins the creature to the creator, in a relation that images the Son's eternal communion with the Father and Spirit.

*   *   *

To say the word 'theology', and more especially 'anthropology', in the same breath as 'the second century', serves immediately to conjure up the name of Irenaeus of Lyons. Not a few handbooks on early Christianity speak of him as

---

1 The publication of G. Wingren, *Man and the Incarnation: A Study in the Biblical Theology of Irenaeus*, tr. R. Mackenzie (Edinburgh: Oliver & Boyd, 1959) (originally printed in 1947 in Swedish) was perhaps the key monograph in renewing scholarly appreciation for Irenaeus in the past century.
2 See D. Minns, *Irenaeus*, ed. B. Davies (Outstanding Christian Thinkers; London: Geoffrey Chapman, 1994) 7–38.

the Church's 'first theologian', and standard studies of image-anthropology take him as the first voice of the patristic age to consider it at length. His stance against Valentinus and 'the Gnostics' widely appreciated, his positive valuation of the body as part of the totality of humanity in God's 'image' stands him in good stead for such assessments. Yet for all the popularity of Irenaean study in the twentieth and now twenty-first centuries, he is still a mysterious figure, one whose thought continues to challenge modern analysis. He was, for a time, dismissed outright as insignificant, a writer whose theological contribution could be summarized in a paragraph or a page, anything longer usually couched in harsh terms, at times edging on vitriol.[3] More recently he has come to be valued to the other extreme as one who speaks of nearly everything, whose thought is addressed in books and articles of microscopic focus. Finding the fullness of Irenaeus' vision, however, as well as his position in the larger arena of early Christian reflection, remains challenging, and for all the variety of extant studies, the definitive book on Irenaeus has yet to be written.

The challenge of discovering the full character of Irenaeus' contribution finds its first hurdle in the questions surrounding his textual witness. An oddity of our knowledge of the second century, and more precisely of our receipt of textual material from that century, is how it consolidates in its latter decades around his person. The relatively voluminous body of epistolary writing from the immediately post-apostolic age carries forward into the early and mid-second century, from which we have a variety of voices at our disposal in the works of such fathers as Justin and Theophilus and others known most often as 'the apologists'. These we may extend to the latter decades of the second century with reference to Athenagoras, though with less material in preservation. Between AD 165 and 190, during which period Tertullian is just coming of age in Carthage to produce his first written tracts, Clement readying himself to succeed Pantaenus at the 'school' in Alexandria (c. 190) and Origen but a young boy about to face the outbreak of persecution in that city, the scene to the north is largely dominated in the historical record by the voice of our Irenaeus, writing in Lyons.[4]

That Lyons should spontaneously become the centre of Christian thought for a spattering of decades in the late second century is an absurdity, and but the first of many observations that make the dominance of Irenaeus in our library for this

---

3   See A. V. Harnack, *Philotesia zu Paul Kleinert zum LXX – Geburtstage dargebracht* (Berlin, 1907) 1–38; W. Bousset, *Jüdisch-Christlicher Schulbetrieb in Alexandria und Rom: Literarische Untersuchungen zu Philo und Clemens von Alexandria, Justin und Irenäus* (Göttingen: Vandenhoeck und Ruprecht, 1915); and, expanding on these, F. Loofs, *Theophilus von Antiochien – Adversus Marcionem und die anderen theologischen Quellen bei Irenäus* (Leipzig: Hinrichs, 1930). A summary of their views and a note on the shift in appreciation for Irenaeus is found in K. M. Tortorelli, 'Some Notes on the Interpretation of St Irenaeus in the Works of Hans Urs von Balthasar', *SP* 23 (1989), 284; and more extensively in M. A. Donovan, *One Right Reading? A Guide to Irenaeus* (Collegeville: The Liturgical Press, 1997) 10–11.

4   There is the exception of Melito of Sardis (fl. c. 170s), but our possession of almost nothing of his corpus is rather a case in point.

period something of a curiosity. From his own perspective, Irenaeus considers his posting in Gaul to situate him in the middle of nowhere, despite the fact that Lyons had by the second century become an important Roman outpost and centre for trade, and the churches of Vienne and Lyons had already a reputation for sanctity in the face of intense localized persecution.[5] It is clear that there was a bustle of ecclesiastical activity in the air. The persecutions there in 177 are connected in Irenaeus' person to the Quartodeciman controversy that arose in the years following, in which context he was sent to pacify pope Victor, whose fierce stand-point went against that of Irenaeus' own teacher, Polycarp.[6] This was not the only controversy to rack Roman Christianity in the era, and the closing decades of the second century form the context of ferment that would give rise to the disputes surrounding Victor, Hippolytus and a host of others. The relative gap in our source-text reception does not correspond to a period of stillness.

A further question mark over our receipt of Irenaeus is occasioned by the curious matter of his reception – or, rather, lack of reception – in the decades and centuries following his life. While he seems today a kind of principal voice from the late second century, Irenaeus appears to have been a voice familiar to few in the third, fourth and beyond. A Latin translation of the *Refutation* was read by Augustine,[7] and there are continuing hypotheses as to whether Athanasius might at times have lifted axioms from the document in its original Greek;[8] but rarely do we hear Irenaeus' name mentioned in the increasingly historically minded dis-courses of the fourth and fifth centuries. There is argument for an Irenaean influ-ence on Tertullian put forward by such scholars as Tränkle, Quispel, Moreschini and Waszink, repeated more recently in the work of Bray and Osborn; yet again such influence, if it existed at all (and this cannot be proved, though it seems hard to deny) was fairly secondary.[9] Others would see his influence in Origen, though

---

5   On Irenaeus' attitude towards living in the hinterlands, see *Ref.* 1.Praef.3. See M. C. Steenberg, *Irenaeus on Creation: The Cosmic Christ and the Saga of Redemption* (Vigiliae Christianae Supple-ments; Leiden: Brill, 2008) 16 n. 47 on the various hypotheses that have been put forward for his move there.

6   See *Ref.* 3.3.4; *Eus. HE* 5.20.4–8; cf. 5.5.8–9, 5.24.16–17. Cf. E. Osborn, *Irenaeus of Lyons* (Cambridge: University Press, 2001) 5–6.

7   Who mentions it for the first time in AD 421. Speculation over dating the Latin edition had not found unanimity when Wingren commented on it in 1947, and it still has not today; see Wingren, *Man and the Incarnation* ix–x; A. D'alès, 'La date de la version latine de Saint Irénée', *RSR* 6 (1916), 133–3. There seems little grounds for being more emphatic today on either an early dating, or one closer to the fifth-century, than was d'Alès almost a century ago.

8   Vis-à-vis his comments at *DI* 54.3: 'God became man that man might become God'; cf. Irenaeus *Ref.* 3.18.1; 4.38.4. On the question of whether Athanasius read Irenaeus, see K. Anatolios, 'The Influence of Irenaeus on Athanasius', *SP* 36 (2001), 463–76.

9   See H. Tränkle, *Q.S.F. Tertullian's Adv. Ind.* (Wiesbaden, 1964); G. Quispel, *De bronnen van Tertullianus' Adv. Marc.* (Lieden, 1943); C. Moreschini, 'L'*Adv. Marc.* nell'ambito dell'attività lettera-ria di Tertulliano', *Ommagio a E. Fraenkel* (1968); J. H. Waszink, *Quinti Septimi Florentis Tertul-liani, De Anima* (Amsterdam: J. M. Meulenhoff, 1947) 13*. More recently Bray, *Holiness and the*

this seems less likely. Despite this vague situation, however, we know his texts travelled, and travelled quickly. The Oxyrhynchus papyri locate a copy of at least a portion of the *Refutation* in Egypt during Irenaeus' own lifetime.[10] Presumably his texts travelled because they were being read, but this only makes more intriguing the lack of reference and reflection evident in the later corpus. Epiphanius (d. 403) would prove happy to lift whole passages from the *Refutation* for insertion into his own heresiological *Panarion*, but this function as sourcebook for information on various sects and schools of thought seems to be his only use for Irenaeus. The closest we come to any considered reflection on his life and thought by a patristic source in the centuries immediately to follow is located in the *Ecclesiastical History* of Eusebius of Caesarea (d. c. 341), a critical document for our knowledge of Irenaeus, containing several of his letters and imparting nearly all our scant bibliographical data on the man.[11] Yet even in Eusebius' sweeping survey of the Church before Constantine, Irenaeus holds no special pride of place. Eusebius seems to have admired him, but does not make any great deal of his theological articulation. Irenaeus is no giant in the eyes of his successors, no *sphragis pateron*, 'seal of the fathers', as Cyril of Alexandria would be remembered after his death.

So we have in Irenaeus something of a mystery. We cannot make too much of it, for citation of secondary sources is hardly a second-century phenomenon, but there is room for curiosity all the same. Perhaps this is part of the appeal he represents to scholars today. Among these he is often taken to stand out, to represent a new way of thinking in relation to the apologists before him, to be 'the first biblical theologian' of catholic patrimony.[12] There is something of a truth here.

Will of God; E. Osborn, *Tertullian, First Theologian of the West* (Cambridge: Cambridge University Press, 1997).

10   *Oxyrh. Pa.* 3.405, dating from before the close of the second century, contains the earliest known fragment of the *Ref.* (3.9.2–3); see R. M. Grant, *Irenaeus of Lyons*, ed. C. Harrison (The Early Church Fathers; London: Routledge, 1997) 6–7. By the end of the sixth century his smaller work, the *Epid.*, had been translated into Armenian; see A. Rousseau, *Irénée de Lyon: Démonstration de la prédication apostolique – introduction, traduction et notes* (SC 406; Paris: CERF, 1995) 20.

11   Irenaeus' letters, cited at *Eus. HE* 5.20.1, are *On Schism* (to Blastus in Rome); *On the Sole Sovereignty* or *That God is Not the Author of Evils* (to Florinus); and *On the Ogdoad* (also to Florinus); as well as a letter to Victor in Rome (quoted at *Eus. HE* 5.24.11–17), a treatise *Concerning Knowledge* (written against the Greeks, mentioned in 5.26); and an unnamed 'little book' on Hebrews and the Wisdom of Solomon. The 'Letter from the Churches in Gaul' (recorded in *Eus. HE* 5.1–2) is also rightly ascribed to Irenaeus; for further details, see Steenberg, *Irenaeus on Creation* 10 n. 24 and 19–20.

12   See Y. de Andia, *Homo vivens: Incorruptibilité et divinisation de l'homme selon Irénée de Lyon* (Paris: Etudes Augustiniennes, 1986) 24 n. 138. See also R. Seeberg, *Lehrbuch der Dogmengeschichte* (Second Edition edn., I; Leipzig, 1908) 290. Cf. J. Lawson, *The Biblical Theology of Saint Irenaeus* (London: The Epworth Press, 1948) 24, 115; L. S. Thornton, 'St. Irenaeus and Contemporary Theology', *SP* 2 (1957), 318, 20; and G. May, *Creatio ex Nihilo: The Doctrine of 'Creation out of Nothing' in Early Christian Thought* (Edinburgh: T&T Clark, 1994) 164.

One does sense, when turning from the apologists to Irenaeus, that one hears not just a new voice, but a new way of speaking – there is something fresh in his tone and tenor. But to take this variation in style to imply a new kind of Christian endeavour, a new 'phase' of Christian thought or a 'first theology' following pastoral and apologetic modes of address, is to divorce Irenaeus from his own avowed heritage. He is nothing if not the disciple of Polycarp, and few voices are of such determinative influence on his discussion as Justin and Theophilus.[13]

The difference to previous writers comes not so much through his mode of approach as genre or category, but through interaction with his collocutors. Irenaeus must be understood as a man in rhetorical dialogue with Valentinus, even if his works are later and not addressed to him directly. The impetus for Irenaeus' discourse is what he sees as non-apostolic scriptural exegesis in the voices to which he responds. Valentinus, like others Irenaeus mentions (Saturninus, Simon Magus, Carpocrates, etc.), reads the scriptures no doubt, but Irenaeus is convinced that one cannot locate in his exegesis a 'demonstration of the apostolic teaching', or the exegesis the apostles themselves would have offered. This Irenaeus then sets as his task: to exegete those same scriptures, particularly around the points raised by the groups in question, but to do so after a manner he considers authentic to the reading and exegesis of apostolic heritage. So will he give the title 'a demonstration of the apostolic preaching' (ἐπίδειξις τοῦ ἀποστολικοῦ κηρύγμα–τος) to his smaller text, which is neither about the apostles nor missionary kerygma, but a reading of the Septuagint after the manner of these chief Christian exegetes.[14] In this task he acutely feels himself part of the tradition before him – a tradition exemplified in Polycarp, in Justin – which he frames in as the community

---

13 On the influence of Justin on Irenaeus, see J. A. Robinson, *St Irenaeus: The Demonstration of the Apostolic Preaching* (London: SPCK, 1920) 6–68; R. A. Norris, *God and World in Early Christian Theology* (New York: The Seabury Press, 1965) 71–72; M. Slusser, 'How Much Did Irenaeus Learn From Justin?', *International Conference on Patristic Studies* (Oxford, 2003). The latter has posited that Irenaeus may have known Justin personally.

I have been arguing for at least the past five years that Irenaeus knew the text of Theophilus' *Ad Autolycum*, given the clear coherence of themes between them and, more specifically, their modes of interpreting the Eden narrative of Genesis; see detailed analysis of the relationship of both Justin and Theolphilus to Irenaeus throughout Steenberg, *Irenaeus on Creation*, esp. at 16–19. This seems today to be more widely accepted in Irenaean scholarship, though it remains impossible to establish concretely due to the lack of named mention in the corpus. See R. M. Grant, 'The Problem of Theophilus', in R. M. Grant (ed.), *Christian Beginnings: Apocalypse to History* (London: Variorum Reprints, 1950/1983) 196; Loofs, *Theophilus* 44–80.

14 By assigning this project the title of an exposition of the *kerygma* of the apostles, Irenaeus identifies that *kerygma* with the exposition of scripture in its Christological interpretation. This implicit clarification of the nature of the *kerygma* is reinforced by his discussion at *Ref.* 3.3 and 3.4.1, where the nature of the apostolic office is primarily the handing down of an authentic Christological understanding of scripture, such that should the scriptures themselves be lost, the preaching (*kerygma*), which is a handing down (*traditio*) of its message, would suffice to ensure the preservation of its message.

of exegetical continuity with the apostles (so, in his detailed treatment of apostolic succession in *Refutation* 3, does he describe the unity found in this succession as grounded in the common faith and reading of the scriptures[15]). His grounding-point, which he repeats time and again – namely that there is one God who created heaven and earth, and that this one God has in Christ saved the human race[16] – is no different in either form or focus from that seen in the writers before him. If he can be seen to address in a more detailed manner the questions of anthropology and the Father in relation to his Son and Spirit, it is because his articulation of the Christian confession is made in response to groups he perceived as errant prima-rily in these regards.

It is in this context that we explore Irenaeus' thought. While neither of his extant texts, the heresiological *Refutation and overthrow of knowledge falsely so-called* and 'catechetical' *Epideixis* or *Demonstration of the Apostolic Preaching*, is prop-erly an anthropological treatise (nor, it would seem, were any of his other works, since lost to history), his considerations in each treat of the human creature to such an extent as to foster an academic fondness for Irenaeus as among the chief early theologians of the human person.[17] His anthropological views centre round two apparently simple, fundamental suppositions, each raised in opposition to variant exegetical hypotheses laid out by those with whom he engages: first, that it was God himself who created the human person in Eden; and second, that God did so intentionally, with purpose and as part of a larger *taxis* or economy. Both will require exploration in the pages ahead, but it is essential to note already at this juncture that each is in some sense a protological pronouncement, framing discus-sion from a Christological focus on cosmic beginnings. That, on the one hand, God creates the human formation, and on the other creates it intentionally into a fore-ordained economy, are both statements on beginnings, defining the character of the human person in large part through the perspective of the first moments of its existence, explored retrospectively from the witness of the incarnate Christ.

---

15 See *Ref.* 3.2–4.

16 See *Ref.* 1.10.1, 1.22.1, 2.1.1, 2.2.3–5, 3.11.1, etc.

17 I am increasingly convinced that the common abbreviation of Irenaeus' longer text as 'Against heresies' is misleading, polarizing his language and focus in a way inauthentic to his style. It additionally leaves out the emphasis on right and wrong knowledge that the proper title, 'The refuta-tion and overthrow of knowledge falsely so-called', makes central, a contributing factor in continuing mis-use of the term 'Gnostic' as applicable to this era and to Irenaeus' aims. Throughout, I refer to Irenaeus' main work as the *Refutation* (abbreviated *Ref.*). Whether the first term in the title, ἔλεγχος, ought to be translated 'refutation' or 'detection' is debatable; both preserve something of the intention of the writing and the meaning Irenaeus wished to convey, but certain internal evidence – such as the apparent usage of the same term at 3.2.1 to speak of the heretics being 'refuted (*arguuntur*, in SC's Greek translation as ἐλέγχωνται) from the scriptures'– grounds my favouring of the former. An argument could be made for the latter from 5.Praef., where Irenaeus speaks of 'exposing (*traductis*, translated by SC as ἐλεγχθέντων) all the heretics'; but he uses *manifestatis* later in the same sentence, which would indicate he did not mean quite the same thing with *traductis*.

This protological approach to anthropology, and indeed to theology as a whole, is typically Irenaean. Moreover, in this protological orientation towards anthropological discussion, Irenaeus comes – through his discussions of the human – to refine his articulation of the divine. The human handiwork discloses its creator.

THE FIRST SUPPOSITION: HUMANITY CREATED BY GOD

The first step in assessing Irenaeus' contribution must be to explore his insistence on God as the creator of man. The protological orientation of both suppositions outlined above, locates the foundation of his anthropology in creation, but as we shall see in this section, it is a particularly Christocentric reading of human creation, grounded in the Son's creative union with the Father, that supports this. By rejecting the concept of multiple creative agents, Irenaeus will articulate the immediate working of the Father through his Son, who is not an external mediator but a 'hand' of the Father himself. Taking note of how this anti-Valentinian clarification establishes the Son, together with the Spirit, as eternally active with the Father, we shall proceed to explore how the methodology of Christocentric interpretation grounds Irenaeus' reading of 'image', which we shall explore more fully in the subsequent section.

Irenaeus' first anthropological conviction is outwardly straightforward: the human formation, wrought first from the dust in Eden, was created and fashioned by none other than God himself. Each aspect of this claim as we have stated it is important. Taking the final point first, Irenaeus is insistent that it was God and only God that created humanity. Substantial ink is spilt across his polemic in defence of this confession against those who would claim otherwise, who most often boil down for Irenaeus to the Ptolemaean Valentinians (in the vast majority), the Marcosians, Ophites, Basilidians and Barbeliotes, though there is some cause for supposing he was at least passingly familiar with certain strands of philosophical (i.e. 'Philonic') and apocalyptic Judaism he would characterize similarly – groups that structured their principal hypotheses in the form of detailed exegesis and ornate mythologies, built around fairly exacting commentaries on scriptural books.[18] In what is a peculiar strength of Irenaeus' approach, and a trait that has thrown scholars off for centuries, he does not meet such commentary with a correction of the same. Despite several passages of extended treatment, there is no 'commentary on Genesis' in Irenaeus' corpus, aimed to refute the commentaries on that book that he encountered in others. His response takes the form of challenging the root suppositions of his opponents, which may take the form of calling on Genesis here, the Apocalypse or the parables there. This has called forth perennial lamentations of Irenaeus as 'disorganised' and 'inconsistent', but

---

18   On the influence of Jewish sources on Irenaeus, see Steenberg, *Irenaeus on Creation* 19–20.

the apparent lack of commentative structure is not accidental, and discerning a 'method to the madness' is perhaps more critical in his case than in many others.

It was P. Bacq who in 1978 first suggested – through a study on book four of the *Refutation*[19] – that there is in Irenaeus a discernible and well-defined methodology, but one that does not accord with most types of academic categories popular in Bacq's day. It is not a scientific analysis of scriptural or historical data, through means of successive verse-by-verse or even theme-by-theme commentary, that is the primary criterion for authentic theological reflection, but coherence of Christological centring and perspective, of the confessional hypothesis used in exegeting Christian truth from the scriptural witness set forth by the apostles. In other words, it is not what one reads in scripture, but how one reads it, that forms the basis of Irenaeus' methodology. This insight was taken up in the elaboration of M. A. Donovan who, in her 1997 *One Right Reading?* explored further refinements and showed its presence across the whole of the *Refutation*. While the work of both scholars has been well received, the full implications of their offerings have taken time to set in. They demand not only that we see in Irenaeus a methodological coherence regularly denied by past generations, but in fact that we fundamentally alter the way we approach not simply Irenaeus' texts, but the vision of Christian theologizing they exemplify. To synthesize his works to provide commentary or analysis of twentieth-century design, is to wrest from Irenaeus the very insight of his non-synthetic approach. This cause has been taken up most recently by J. Behr as part of his larger project of re-visioning early Church thought, and it must inform us here.[20] It is not the scientific anthropology of Valentinus and others that most upsets Irenaeus, but the underlying framework or hypothesis on which they ground their anthropological exegesis of the scriptures. It is the principle of theological vision, enshrined in specific interpretive details which are thus always ancillary, that is skewed and which Irenaeus seeks to correct.

This constitutes one of the most important principles for reading Irenaeus authentically; namely, that his task of responsorial exegesis is not structured around what today would be considered critical analysis of textual traditions, but around the theological re-orientation of the reader to a new and (to Irenaeus' mind) more authentic hypothesis of interpretation. Rather than analyse a set of texts to draw from them a collection of conclusions, Irenaeus approaches scripture from the antecedent question of a base framework or reference point, which to his understanding of Christian patrimony must always be the witness of the incarnate Jesus Christ. What today seems the project of exegesis proper, for example,

---

19   See P. Bacq, *De l'ancienne à la nouvelle alliance selon s. Irénée: unité du livre IV de l'Adversus Haereses* (Paris: Editions Lethielleux, 1978).

20   See Behr, *Way to Nicaea* 111–33 (and more broadly the whole of the volume), as well as his earlier *Asceticism and Anthropology in Irenaeus and Clement* (Oxford: The University Press, 2000) and 'Scripture, the Gospel, and Orthodoxy', *SVTQ* 43 (2001).

reading Genesis 2 (on the creation of the human) in its context and structure to
provide information on the nature of the human composition, was to Irenaeus
the second stage of exegetical reading, which has to begin with the revelation
of Christ's incarnation upon the text in question. So he can approach Genesis
2.7 with reference to Christ's healing of the man born blind (cf. John 9.6), con-
cluding that Christ's healing via mud 'indicates the original fashioning of man'.[21]
What the early text might mean 'on its own', apart from the testimony of the life
of Christ, interests Irenaeus little. Moreover, it is just this kind of reading 'opposed
to the tradition' of Christological exegesis received from the apostles, that he suggests is the cause of heresy and discord.[22] Divergent readings of specific texts
arise as the natural fruit of an improper 'root vision' of what scripture presents to
a Christian reader.

With regard to the groups mentioned, the perversion of this root vision is
seen most clearly by Irenaeus in a frequent insistence on a specific idea: that the
creation of the cosmos and its human inhabitants is ultimately the working of
multiple creative agents. The speculative mythologies of these groups lie beyond
our current scope, save for the assertion of one detail: that in at least a few of the
systems known from the second century, the anthropogonic work of such agents
is bound up in attempts at exegeting the chief Old Testament verse on an anthropology of image, Genesis 1.26. In the voices of others, Irenaeus encounters the
connection of image-anthropology to the doctrine of God in clear terms. So for
Basilides, whom Irenaeus attacks directly, the human creature is fashioned by
angels, mediating between the transcendent God and his finite creatures.[23] Philo,
who may be of a more abstracted or secondary influence on Irenaeus, argues
similarly:

> 'Come, let us go down and confuse their tongue there' (cf. Genesis 11.7)
> makes clear that he is conversing with some persons whom he treats as
> his fellow-workers; and we find the same in an earlier passage of the forma-
> tion of man. Here we have, 'The Lord God said "let us make man in our own
> image and likeness"' (Genesis 1.26); where the words 'let us make' imply

---

21   See *Ref.* 5.15.2.

22   See *Ref.* 3.2.2.

23   See *Ref.* 1.24.3, 4.

24   *De.Conf.Ling.* 168–69, 179. The strong parallels between Philo's discussion here and the
systems attacked by Irenaeus (see below) are evidence more of the relationship between Judaism
and the development of certain 'Gnostic' cosmological systems than they are of a direct influence
of Philo on Irenaeus; see J. E. Fossum, 'The Origin of the Gnostic Concept of the Demiurge',
ETL 61.1 (1985), 142–52, building upon the important treatment of G. Quispel, 'The Origins of the
Gnostic Demiurge', in P. Granfield and J. A. Jungmann (eds.), *KYRIAKON: Festschrift Johannes
Quasten, 1* (1; Münster: Verlag Aschendorff, 1970) 271–76. Cf. the critical study of P. Bilde, 'Gnosticism, Jewish Apocalypticism, and Early Christianity', in K. Jeppesen, K. Nielsen and B. Rosendal
(eds.), *In the Last Days: On Jewish and Christian Apocalyptic and its Period* (Denmark: Aarhus

plurality. [. . .] He delegated the forming of [the lower part of man] to those with him.[24]

For Philo, the function of the angels explains the plurality of 'persons' in the scriptural account, and has the theological function of separating the transcendent and good God from the lower, base aspects of the created order – a separation that speaks of the relationship of things made 'after the image' to the one imaged. God creates what is pure and holy (those things in accordance with his own reason, λόγος); intermediaries fashion that which is not harmonious with divine purity (i.e. all reality that is ἄλογος). An exegesis of humanity created 'after the image' of God is connected to a doctrinal assertion of God's being as λογικῶς; but the confession of God as transcendently and immutably λογικῶς in turn demands that the creature 'after the image' must have its lower aspects fashioned by another, since the purely λογικῶς would not fashion something ἄλογος.

Irenaeus objects to this conception, not on grounds that the 'image' exegeted from scripture is misconstrued, but that this conception of image is grounded in a flawed doctrine of God the Father as creator. The root hypothesis of approach fails to account for this creative character of the Father. The linkage to 'image' is direct: it is because the broader issue of the nature of the Father is articulated inaccurately, that specific exegesis of the divine image fails. As such, he frames his rebuttal in the shape not of a counter-commentary on Genesis 1.26–28 on the created image, but of a corrected proclamation of the creative Father:

When we obey him, we do always learn that there is so great a God, and that it is he who by himself has established, fashioned, adorned and does contain all things – and among the 'all things', are both this world of ours and our own selves. We also, then, were made, along with those things which are contained by him. And this is he of whom the scripture says, 'and God formed man, taking dust of the earth, and breathed into his face the breath of life' (cf. Genesis 2.7). It was not angels, therefore, who made or formed us, nor had angels power to make an image of God, nor any one else except the true God, nor any power remotely distant from the Father of all things. For God did not stand in need of these [beings], in order to accomplish what he had determined with himself beforehand should be done, as if he did not possess his own hands. For with him were always present the Word and Wisdom, the Son and the Spirit, by whom and in whom, freely and spontaneously, he made all things, and to whom he speaks, saying, 'Let us make man after our image and likeness', taking from himself the substance of the creatures formed and the pattern of things made, and the type of all the adornments of the world.[25]

University Press, 1994) 9–32. For a survey of the issue in Irenaeus, cf. Steenberg, *Irenaeus on Creation* 22–32.
25 *Ref.* 4.20.1.

The Basilidian and Philonic vision of angels taking part in the creation of the human person, even if (perhaps especially if) they do so to protect the transcendent God from the lowliness of what is earthen and corruptible, equates for Irenaeus to a more problematic denial of the power of God to act with immediacy in and for his creation, which is where the testimony of a redeemed humanity forces Christian theology to begin. The Father fashions always directly, always with his two 'hands' – the Word and Spirit – an image which in this passage is as much intended to provide for the conceptualization of such direct activity as it is meant to be a commentary on the relationship of the Father, Son and Spirit one to another. Not only will Irenaeus argue that an angelically mediated or fashioned creation stands unsubstantiated by any scriptural evidence, but that it distorts what scripture clearly proclaims, rending from the Father the actual formation of the cosmos and its inhabitants.[26] For the followers of Ptolemy, the 'mediation' of creation took what Irenaeus considers a more sinister turn: not only were 'spiritual' agents responsible for the formation of the human creature, but these were according to most interpretations fallen entities acting apart from or opposed to the benevolent wholeness of the Pleroma – agents not only distinct from, but in purpose against, the true God.

In light of such views, of which numerous variations are presented in the *Refutation* and others known from external sources, Irenaeus' insistence that God himself, and he alone, created man takes on a particular potency. By it he establishes his method of correcting anthropological claims, chiefly as establishing their connection to right discussion of the Father's creative nature. The human, as handiwork of the divine, can be conceived of only in terms of right correlation to its divine maker. The various theological and philosophical voices vying for influence in the first and second centuries seemed, to Irenaeus' mind, to wander dangerously far from the foundation stones on which the Christian faith is laid: the one God the Father, creator of heaven and earth, known from scripture through the apostolic witness of the incarnate and resurrected Christ. To claim, as did Philo, that God formed only the 'higher parts' of the human creature while angels fashioned the 'lower', or more drastically the Valentinian line that 'God' proper was not involved at all, but humanity was the work of a demiurge opposed to divine order, is to fly in the face of three scriptural confessions that shape Irenaeus' reading, though the texts themselves are used in unique ways:

'In the beginning, God created the heavens and the earth'. (Genesis 1.1)

'And the Lord God formed man, taking dust of the earth, and breathed into his nostrils the breath of life'. (Genesis 2.7)

'All things were made through him [the Word], and without him was nothing made that was made'. (John 1.3)

---

26   His comments on the theme are numerous (see 5.1.3, 5.15.4, *Epid.* 55, etc.).

The first, which it would seem logical to assume Irenaeus would quote and discuss at every opportunity given its direct relevance and protological stature as the opening phrase of scripture, is in fact used in his corpus only once.[27] This is neither an oversight nor evidence of a lack of influence, which is undisputable. It is, rather, evidence that Irenaeus does not desire to refute his collocutors with a counter-commentary of the creation narrative: if they could read Genesis 1.1 in one way, he could read it in another, but this would in the end do little to establish any solid grounding for the exclusive rectitude of either interpretation. The real question is not what texts one reads, but how one reads the texts. Simply quoting passages back at his foes will do little to influence their overarching approach. They must be made to see creation from the perspective of Christ, of the incarnation, of the resurrection; to change the underlying mode of approach, or 'hypothesis' (to use Irenaeus' term) by which they approach the themes represented in the texts.[28]

Given this need to assert a right hypothesis, Irenaeus is more inclined to exegete the creation of humanity from the Gospels, using Genesis as a support and verification rather than a foundation. John 1.3, rather than Genesis 1.1, is his key text, and it is quoted in his corpus more times than bear counting. The confession that 'all things were made through him, and without him nothing was made' provides the lens through which the matrix of the earlier scriptures is clearly defined as Christological in focus.[29] The apostolic witness of Christ as eternal Son, the Word who was with the Father 'in the beginning', offers the clarity needed by the Christian to unlock what otherwise might remain only a partial truth contained in the ambiguous anthropological statements in Genesis. The Father, who 'has always with him his Word and Wisdom' (by which Irenaeus means explicitly Son and Spirit) is, by this retrospective approach to scripture, known to be the creative actor in human creation – no other. As such, when 'God formed man, taking dust from the earth', the apostolic witness as Irenaeus reads it declares this involvement with the 'dust' and 'earth' was the direct and immediate working of Father by means of his Son and Spirit, and not of angels, a demiurge, 'nor any power remotely distant from the Father of all things'. This is made known through the Septuagintal book, but only as its witness is received into the Church's confession of the crucified and resurrected Lord. Genesis 2.7, which speaks more specifically of the manner in which humanity is fashioned, is similarly understood from the perspective of the incarnation: it is the same Jesus who spat into the dust and by the mud healed the man born blind (cf. John 9.1–12), who at the dawn of creation

---

27   At *Ref.* 2.2.5. Quotation of the text at 1.18.1 is a description of Marcosian use of the passage. *Epid.* 43 relies on the text, but does not quote it. See *Irenaeus on Creation* 221 (Appendix 2) for a full analysis of Irenaeus' use of Genesis 1–11.

28   On the importance of 'hypothesis' to Irenaeus, see Behr, *Asceticism and Anthropology* 19, 32–34.

29   For the language of 'scriptural matrix' and 'texture', I am indebted to Behr's terminology in various articles and texts; for example Behr, *Nicene Faith* 1, 203.

took up the dust to fashion humanity, who previously had created the dust itself.[30] For Irenaeus, the Valentinian misunderstanding of the human person is a side-effect of the fact that they do not employ scripture after the manner of the apostles, whose 'method' is always to read the sacred texts from the starting point of their confession of Christ.[31] The culmination (Christ) effects the beginning (Adam) – a retrospective and recapitulative theology that will be of influence across Irenaeus' reading of the human person and human history.

Irenaeus' first anthropological conviction is thus one taken from the earliest pages of scripture, but only as read from the standpoint of the apostolic proclamation of Christ as incarnate Lord. In view of this, the simple statement that 'God created humanity' is transformed from a basic affirmation of divine action and power into a revelatory statement on the character and nature of man, precisely because it articulates more fully the reality of the Father as creator with and through his Son and Spirit, who together fashion the creature. By fleshing out this conviction first of all through an exegetical proclamation of God the Father creating by his two hands, Irenaeus imbues it with implications for the stature of the human formation. First among these is that the creative activity of the good God – the one who allowed Jonas to be swallowed, not for destruction but edification and growth;[32] the one who in Christ suffered for his creation;[33] the one who in the Son forgave his tormentors on behalf of the human race;[34] all of which are read by Irenaeus as acts of beneficence grounded in love for the creation – implies the intrinsic worth and goodness of that which he has created. Irenaeus has little time for those who regard the human creature as the 'fruit of a defect', the deficient embodiment of corrupt materiality.[35] He will not allow that the sinfulness of humanity, or even the power and influence of Satan, indicate or impose a deficiency in the human formation proper. As the human person is the handiwork of God, that which is constitutive of human being is, as the fruit of the Father's activity in the Son and Spirit, 'good', as scripture, and particularly Genesis, repeats in canticle-like refrain.

But more than simply defining humanity as 'good' because it is created directly by a good God, Irenaeus has also drawn together discussions of human attributes and those of the divine. His emphasis on 'image' comes to its strength here. That which constitutes the human person as 'good' is her iconic participation in the spring of goodness, the proper quality of none but God himself. Moreover, as the goodness of this imaging is disclosed in the Christological testimony of the incarnate Son, one of the Father's 'hands', so the human person created after the image of this Son-made-human, becomes a means for understanding and approaching God himself.

---

30 See *Ref.* 5.15.2.
31 Cf. *Epid.* 3.
32 *Ref.* 3.20.1.
33 *Ref.* 1.9.3.
34 *Ref.* 3.16.9.
35 See *Ref.* 2.19.9, 3.25.5.

RE-THINKING THE IMAGE

When Irenaeus writes of the human person as in the 'image' of God, it is important to remember that he does not do so solely as a reflection on the obvious
scriptural comments at Genesis 1.26, 27 and 9.6. While the former passage
will eventually become the grounding-point for his detailed consideration of the
matter, his impetus for dwelling so strongly on the question of 'image' comes not
from a spontaneous exegesis of scripture, but from the nature of his confession of
the incarnate Christ, specifically in response to the mythologies of Ptolemy and
Valentinus. The same responsorial project that framed in his insistence on the Son
and Spirit as eternally co-active and co-creative with the Father, is the context of
his expansion on this anthropological theme. Further, just as the method of his
reaction to claims of multiple agents in creation was not to counter-exegete protological texts, but to re-orientate cosmological questions into the framework of
the eternal relation of Son to Father and Spirit, so his reaction to skewed image
anthropologies – and we will see in what follows that Irenaeus' focus on image is
explicitly reaction – is again to re-orientate the discussion, rather than simply
countermand individual points. To appreciate this, we have first to engage authentically with the reading to which he reacts, a project that must involve approaching
and re-assessing so-called 'Gnostic' anthropologies of image; then exploring the
manner in which Irenaeus' conviction of God's direct activity in human creation
establishes a counter-reading of 'image' grounded in the relation of Son and
Father. The present section will consider the intersection of these themes, delin-
eating the means by which Irenaeus comes to consider 'image' from the perspective of Christ as iconic paradigm, which we will explore in the subsequent; and to
find in the baptized Christ the means of articulating the Spirit's role in humanity's
bearing 'the image of God'.

We have already seen that Irenaeus' forceful statements on the Father as creator,
through and in his Son and Spirit, were made in corrective opposition to alternative readings of the 'Let us create . . .' statements of scripture. The same responsorial context is present when he considers the divine 'image', and in direct
correlation; for the groups which took the 'let us' of Genesis 1.26 to imply multiple creative agents, explained humanity's formation after the 'image' of the divine
as grounded in this multiplicity. To connect humanity as 'in the image' to confessed doctrines of 'God' is not Irenaeus' invention – it is the common practice of
second-century speculation to which he reacts. The *Nag Hammadi Codices* preserve an example of precisely this:

The whole aeon of the chief archon trembled, and the foundations of the
abyss shook. And of the waters which are above matter, the underside was
illuminated by the appearance of his image [of the heavenly Man, the aeon
Anthropos] which had been revealed. And when all the authorities and the
chief archon looked, they saw the whole region of the underside which was
illuminated. And through the light they saw the form of the image in the water.

And he said to the authorities which attend him, 'Come, let us create a man
according to the image of God and according to our likeness, that his image
may become a light for us'. And they created by means of their respective
powers, in correspondence with the characteristics which were given [in the
reflection of the image]. And each authority supplied a characteristic in the
form of the image which he had seen in its natural form. He created a being
according to the likeness of the first, perfect Man. And they said, 'Let us call
him Adam, that his name may become a power of light for us'.[36]

Such testimony ought to give serious pause for thought. The explicit exegesis
of creation after the image in a source text from the period substantiates the
degree of focus on image-anthropology in the era, and begs the question of how
much we actually know of the groups against which Irenaeus wrote. It is in this
arena that the most recent work in the field of 'Gnostic' studies helps inform
our understanding of the philosophical and theological phenomena with which
Irenaeus was faced, and the framework within which his response was constructed.
M. Williams' seminal *Rethinking 'Gnosticism': An Argument for Dismantling a
Dubious Category* (1999), paved the way for a reformation in the field; but as with
Bacq and Donovan's contribution to Irenaean studies, the full effects of Williams'
critique are still *fully* appreciated by too few. He has not merely (though he has
successfully) forced subsequent writers to locate the word 'Gnostic' in inverted
commas; he has more profoundly challenged the association of 'Gnostic' groups
with characterizations based on questions of *gnosis*, or knowledge, as has been
standard practice for generations. H. Jonas, like so many to follow, described
'Gnosticism' in the following terms:

> The emphasis on *knowledge* as the means for the attainment of salvation, or
> even as the form of salvation itself, and the claim to the possession of this
> knowledge in one's own articulate doctrine, are common features of the
> numerous sects in which the gnostic movement historically expressed itself.[37]

Such definitions can no longer be defended. That which might unite the various
groups called 'Gnostic', which are in a proper sense hardly homogenous at all, is,
if anything, their attitude towards creation and not their conception of knowledge
vis-à-vis redemption. Williams suggests 'biblical demiurgical traditions' as a
more authentic category, and while we may express some reservations with this
wording, his primary observation is surely correct.[38]

---

36   *Ap. John*, NHC II, 1.14.24–15.13; ed. J. M. Robinson, *The Nag Hammadi Library in English* (San
Francisco: Harper, 1991) 113.
37   H. Jonas, *The Gnostic Religion: The Message of the Alien God and the Beginnings of Christianity*
(Third edn.; Boston: Beacon Press, 2001) 32, first written in 1958.
38   See Williams, *Rethinking 'Gnosticism'* 51–53. My reservation towards his proposed terminology
rests primarily in the use of the term 'biblical', given that ample sources from the period make little

This re-definition helps explain Irenaeus' obsession with refuting such groups, documented in a five-volume treatise that not once speaks of their principal flaw as a type of gnosiological soteriology. Ironically, it is Irenaeus himself who wishes to emphasize the importance of right knowledge, rather than false 'so-called knowledge', as the proper title of his longer work attests.[39] It is creation, not salvation, that his rhetorical foes exegete eschew, on the grounds, states Irenaeus, that they do not know the true Saviour truly. To Irenaeus' mind, he is dealing above all with falsifiable knowledge of anthropological and cosmological truth, a 'knowledge falsely so-called' of God and his creation.

In this light, the kind of image-anthropology encountered in the *Apocryphon of John* becomes important in understanding Irenaeus' line of discourse. As we noted above, it bears similarities in textual detail to the words of the Genesis account on which it is based; but there are notable differences, even at the surface level, between such image-anthropologies and Irenaeus' reading of the same. In the example of the *Apocryphon*, the image borne by man is pleromatic, but only partially so. It is the image of one aeon only – one attribute of the fullness, the Pleroma, of the divinity. Moreover, and more importantly, it is a wanting image. The demiurge, fallen from communion with the Pleroma and itself a pseudo-material 'abortion' generated in passion, fashions the human creature as a sham copy of the higher divinity from which he resentfully finds himself separated, yet nonetheless longs to re-approach. The image is a false image, corrupt, an attempt at copy which fails and therefore has no iconic connection to its prototype. The creature fashioned by the demiurge is lifeless, barren, dead. Even within the mythos of *Apocryphon* it is understood as a contrived imitation, redeemed only by the interjection of divine power, the participatory knowledge of which lies behind the very title 'gnostic' that scholarship so improperly applies to the scheme (interestingly, Irenaeus makes no mention of knowledge in refuting this anthropological model).

Irenaeus seems to have known such systems of thought fairly well. Whether Lyon and Gaul were the hotbeds of Valentinian adherence that the fact of Irenaeus writing against them from that location might suggest, is disputable; but Irenaeus had come to Gaul from Rome, where Valentinus had first begun to teach and eventually found himself ousted from the Roman Christian community (c.160). That the *Refutation* is a work addressed to a distant recipient has puzzled Irenaean scholars for centuries: was he writing to the communities in Asia Minor from which he had come in his youth? Or to fellow Christians in the Roman metropolis? The latter seems more probable, given the attention paid to Roman forms of cosmologically speculative thought – Valentinian and Ptolemaean in particular.

---

to no use of biblical imagery and language. Whilst it may be true that many if not most do, Williams' own attempt to break apart popular categories of false homogenization seems best served by preventing this adjective from giving rise to another.

39   Irenaeus calls this knowledge 'false knowledge', and its possessors are not 'Gnostics' but 'falsely-called Gnostics' (*falso nomine Gnostici*, as at *Ref.* 2.35.2, 4.35.1, etc.).

But whatever the case for his intended recipient and audience may be, the text of the *Refutation* makes clear that Irenaeus had been, and perhaps continued to be, confronted with the type of speculations recounted in the above passage, and that such speculations formed the polemical context in which his heresiological work was composed. It is only with such a contextual framework in mind, together with its assertions on what is meant by 'God' and 'image', that we can understand how Irenaeus read the apostolic confession of humanity as 'in the image' both confessionally and reactively. This he does draw in large part from the actual text of Genesis 1.26, 27:

> God said, 'Let us make man in our image and likeness (κατ᾽ εἰκόνα ἡμετέ ραν καὶ καθ᾽ ὁμοίωσιν); let them have dominion over the fish of the sea, the birds of the air and the cattle, over all the earth and every creeping thing that creeps on the earth'. So God created man; in the image of God (κατ᾽ εἰκόνα θεοῦ) he created him; male and female he created them.

Keeping in mind the content of Irenaeus' first anthropological conviction, that God himself creates humanity, and that this 'God' is the Father with his two hands, his reading of the words in this text demand a considerably different conception of the 'image' than that expounded by the Valentinians. The Father speaks in the first person, 'Let us' – a single word (ποιήσωμεν) that has intrigued theologians for millennia, and which we have already seen inform the various attempts at exegesis that Irenaeus refutes. Beyond the suggestive implication of the plural form of the statement, however, it is important to recognize what is implied for Irenaeus by the first-person usage. The image in which humanity is fashioned is not an attempt at ethereal reproduction of the divine, wrought by external agency, but the work of the Father to fashion, through the Son and the Spirit, a creature after the image of *his own life* in relation to these two hands. In the recounting of the Nag Hammadi codex, the demiurge is ultimately powerless to create an image of God, and as such he produces only lifeless, material objectifications of his personal defect. We have already seen Irenaeus comment on this, stating in no uncertain terms that a demiurgic fashioning of the divine image is not a possibility, 'nor had angels power to make an image of God, nor any one else except the true God'. In the scriptural text, however, it is precisely the 'true God' who does fashion the creature, and who does so as an iconic manifestation of his own being. The same God who had the power to create the cosmos, not from previously existing matter but *ex nihilo*, out of nothing (the chief witness of his omnipotence), is he who now fashions the human person in his own image – and the witness of that first creation from nothing is the assurance that God has the power to realize the iconic creation to which he here betakes himself.[40]

---

40 On Irenaeus' employment of a doctrine of creation *ex nihilo* as primary evidence of his power to achieve salvation, see *Epid.* 4, *Ref.* 2.14.4, 2.28.7. The most famous text is that at 4.20.2, where

At one level, then, the fashioning of the human person 'in the image of God' comes to bear on Irenaeus' battle against speculative dualism. His conviction that God fashioned humanity, drawn together with the further point that he so fashions 'in his own image', comes as a counter to any anthropology that would separate the divine realm from the human and deny qualitative goodness to the latter. One can say 'the human formation is good' because one can say – one must say – that God is good, and humanity bears his image and reflects his goodness. Just as the Son is the image of the Father, and as the filial image makes visible the goodness and glory of the Father ('for the Father is the invisible of the Son, but the Son is the visible of the Father'[41]), so does the human person, made according to the Image which is the Son, participate in and manifest the goodness and glory of the Father thus made visible.

Thus far, however, Irenaeus' proclamation of the *imago Dei* has primarily a symbolic reality. That humanity is good because it is the image of the good God is a statement valid on an entirely logical or aesthetic level, without necessarily implying anything ontological to the human formation. One is left wondering if there is anything to the confession of humanity's formation 'in the image' that represents an integral aspect of its existence – an actual, foundational element of its being. In point of fact, it is in an examination of its constitutive value for human life that a study of Irenaeus' anthropology of image becomes most rewarding, for what is discovered is that it stands not only as a reality, but *the principal ontological reality* of human existence, the very thing that makes humanity the 'living being' breathed to life by God. Further, it is on this account that man 'after the image' becomes a venue for discovering God who is imaged.

As with his other theological convictions, Irenaeus takes his theology of the image from the starting point of the incarnate Christ. This Christ, as perfect image of the Father, the 'visible of the invisible' who declared that 'he who has seen me has seen the Father' (John 14.9), is the living paradigm for an anthropology of the image. It is not Adam, as too many scriptural commentators assume. Adam is, in point of fact, prohibited from being the full example of the image and likeness, for, as Irenaeus makes clear in the last lines of the *Refutation*, the perfected image is an eschatological, not a protological reality.[42] It is known and realized only in the Incarnate One who stands as the full human 'adult', whereas Adam had been a 'child', however we may understand that analogy.[43]

Irenaeus quotes *Herm.*, Mand. 1. The importance of creation *ex nihilo* to Irenaeus, and the clarifications he makes to its meaning, are still not fully appreciated; cf. Steenberg, *Irenaeus on Creation* 44–49.

41 *Ref.* 4.6.6.

42 See *Ref.* 5.36.3.

43 See M. C. Steenberg, 'Children in Paradise: Adam and Eve as "Infants" in Irenaeus of Lyons', *JECS* 12.1 (2004), 1–35.

For Irenaeus to build his theology so solidly on the retrospective and recapitulative framework of Christ as 'new Adam', who heals and makes whole at the
pinnacle of the economy that which was wounded and corrupted at its beginning,
demands that the vision of the initial formation – that which preceded the wound-
ing of the race – can be obtained only by looking to Christ. What one sees, in
examining the full image of the Father who is the incarnate Son, is an image of
human life lived as the dynamic recipient of the life and action of the Father in the
Spirit. Christ realizes the Father's will through his obedient relationship as Son
and through the sanctifying chrismation of the Spirit. The stature of the image is
not merely the human life of the Son (an impossibility for Irenaeus, who argues
at length against those who would separate his humanity from his divinity[44]), nor
even the divine-human life of the eternal Word-made-man; rather, it is the human-
divine life of the eternal Son-made-man, lived in harmony with the will of the
Father through the grace of the Spirit. The paradigm for an anthropology of
image, disclosed in the Image encountered in his humanity, is one of triadic relationship between the Father, Son and Spirit who fashioned man according to this
image at the creation in Eden.

THE INCARNATE CHRIST AS ICONIC PARADIGM

To understand what Irenaeus means in his paradigmatic vision of the Son in
relation to the Father and Spirit as true image for all humankind, one must understand first of all what he means in his description of the encountered person, Jesus
Christ. Here we must be attentive not to read back into Irenaeus' 'Christology' the
developments in Christological thought that would take place centuries after
his death, especially in the fourth and fifth; but we must also not let trepidation
for anachronism blind us to what are genuinely Irenaean insights into the person
of Christ, which in many ways anticipate those later discussions. It is by these
Christological refinements that he is able, as we shall explore in this section, to
coordinate Christ's active relation to the Father, and particularly the Holy Spirit,
with the concept of the 'image' into which humanity is created, since this Image
is conceived as the Son anointed by the Spirit to bring about the Father's will for
creation.

First, it is to be noted that Irenaeus presents a clear and well-defined doctrine of
two natural realities in Christ, though he never employs the terminology of
'nature', primarily because he does not think of divinity and humanity as abstract
concepts. What is of consequence are not categories of existence, but the basic
assertion that Christ is both God and man. Irenaeus is shy about neither, calling
Jesus both *anthropos* and directly *theos* on multiple occasions.[45] The proof of this

---

44   See for example his discussion at *Ref.* 3.21.4, and the whole of 3.22.
45   See *Ref.* 3.6.1, 3.16.7, 3.19.2.

dual-reality comes from the 'two generations' by which he comes to exist as man: the heavenly, eternal generation from the Father, and the material, temporal generation in the cosmos from Mary the Virgin. What is born of God must be God, and what is born of man must be man; thus Christ, born of both, is himself each.[46] The one who lives and acts as 'new Adam' lives and acts as man and as God – the eternal Son existing humanly as single, unitary being.

The Son who lives and acts as incarnate Word-made-flesh (there is no distinction in Irenaeus between the terminology of 'God-made-man' and 'Word-made-flesh' that would be problematic in a later era), thereby expresses in all his actions a union and communion of the divine and human. Moreover, this union is expressed always in conformity to the will of the Father. Christ is above all the 'obedient one', he who became 'obedient even to the point of death' (cf. Philippians 2.8), who undid the transgression of Eden 'by the obedience of the tree'.[47] In commenting on a passage in Isaias, Irenaeus takes special note of this:

> The Son calls himself the servant of the Father, because of [his] obedience to the Father, for also among men every son is a servant of his father. (cf. Isaias 49.5, 6)[48]

The same Son who, as creative 'hand' of the Father must be confessed as pre-existing the created order, with whom the Father 'conversed' before his human birth (as Irenaeus relates earlier in the same passage), is incarnate in the cosmos as 'servant of the Father' inasmuch as he is obedient – not passively, but actively expressing, manifesting and conforming himself and those around him to the Father's will. As such, the incarnate Christ is not defined solely by reference to the man born in Bethlehem, yet known as Son and thus encountered as God-and-man, but through the ongoing, relational existence of this incarnate Son to his Father. Christ is the image of the Father inasmuch as he is ever and always – most importantly in the incarnation but similarly from all eternity – the living actualization of the Father's will.

This dynamic character of the incarnate Christ, as reflecting a relational union of Father and Son, is elevated further when Irenaeus considers the presence of the Holy Spirit in Christ's incarnate life. The Spirit is the unction, the anointing, by which Christ, who is joined in filial obedience to the Father, receives in his incarnate existence the grace of the Father's Spirit, uniting in the temporal, material order the two 'hands' of the Father which eternally co-exist in harmony of will and act. The eternal relation of Father, Son and Spirit is expressed in the temporal order in the incarnate reality of the Son, which is his human existence in perfect

---

46   See M. C. Steenberg, 'The Role of Mary as Co-recapitulator in St Irenaeus of Lyons', *VigChr* 58 (2004), 123–24.

47   *Epid.* 33; cf. 34, 37.

48   *Epid.* 51; cf. 50.

concord with the Father and the Father's Spirit. This Irenaeus expresses most directly in a passage on the baptism of Christ which has often puzzled interpreters. It is lengthy, but repays full consideration.

> Furthermore, in regard to his baptism Matthew said, 'The heavens were opened, and he saw the Spirit of the God descending like a dove and alighting upon him; and lo, a voice from heaven saying, "This is my beloved Son, with whom I am well-pleased"' (Matthew 3.16, 17). For it was not then that the Christ descended into Jesus; nor is Christ one person and Jesus another. The Word of God, who is the Saviour of all and the Sovereign of heaven and earth, who is Jesus, as we have shown before, who also assumed flesh and was anointed by the Spirit [sent] from the Father, is become Jesus Christ. To this Isaias, on his part, testifies, 'There shall come forth a shoot from the stump of Jesse, and a branch shall grow out of his roots. And the Spirit of the Lord shall rest upon him; the Spirit of wisdom and understanding, the Spirit of counsel and might, the Spirit of knowledge and godliness. He shall not judge according to appearance, nor condemn according to hearsay; but he will render justice to the poor, and convict the haughty of the earth' (Isaias 11.1–4). [. . .] For the Spirit of God rested upon the Word of God, and he [the Word] was anointed to announce the Gospel to the poor, inasmuch as he was man from the stump of Jesse, and the son of Abraham. [. . .] So the Spirit of God descended upon him, the Spirit of him who through the prophets had promised that he would anoint him, that we might be saved by receiving from the abundance of his anointing.[49]

What Irenaeus means by stating that, at the baptism, the Word of God 'is become Jesus Christ' lies at the root of scholarly fascination with this passage.[50] A. Orbe's question posed in 1984, '¿San Ireneo adopcionista?', summarizes the main concern: does not Irenaeus describe an adoptionist conception of what makes Jesus 'the Christ' – namely, that he is anointed by the Spirit for this rôle (a point further emphasized by Irenaeus' language at *Ref.* 3.19.1, where he speaks even more directly of Christ 'receiving adoption')?[51] One must look carefully at his nuance. Irenaeus' point is not to claim that without the unction of the Spirit, Jesus is not Messiah; rather, that without the Spirit the incarnate Son is not fully redeemer,

---

49 *Ref.* 3.9.3.

50 For general investigations of baptism in Irenaeus, see A. Houssiau, 'Le baptême selon Irénée de Lyon', *ETL* 60 No 1 (1984), 45–59; A. Orbe, 'El Espiritu en el bautismo de Jésus (en torno a san Ireneo)', *Greg* 76.4 (1995), 663–99.

51 A. Orbe, '¿San Ireneo adopcionista? En torno a *adv. haer.* III,19,1', *Greg* 65.1 (1984), 5–52. The matter of Irenaeus' potential adoptionism was taken up again more recently by D. A. Smith, 'Irenaeus and the Baptism of Jesus', *TS* 58 (1997), 618–42; with a response issued by K. McDonnell, 'Quaestio disputata: Irenaeus on the Baptism of Jesus', *TS* 59 (1998), 317–19.

since he who redeems recapitulatively does so by uniting humanity to the full life of God, which is only and ever the life of 'the Father with his two hands'. Should the incarnate Christ be only the Son in obedience to the Father's will, and not also recipient of the Spirit's anointing, the 'new Adam' would convey to human existence the likeness of only a portion of the divine life. The eternal relationship of the Son and Spirit, Word and Wisdom, is not brought wholly to bear in a recapitulative economy that does not include the entirety of this relationship. Moreover, the Spirit as 'wisdom and understanding, counsel and might, knowledge and godliness' (cf. Isaias 11.1–4), the 'sanctifier' who accustoms humanity to bear the fullness of divine life, would remain absent from the scene of humanity's salvation. Thus is the incarnate Son in receipt of the Spirit's anointing at his baptism in the Jordan, becoming completely the recapitulative saviour – Jesus Christ the Lord – manifesting the interrelated life of the Father, Son and Spirit. It is *this* life, then, that comes to bear on all humans joined to Christ 'by receiving from the abundance of his anointing'.[52]

'God himself created humanity', Irenaeus' first anthropological supposition, is properly understood only from the perspective of an awareness of Christ's incarnate life – a life manifesting in the cosmos his divine unity with the Father and Spirit, offering the fullness of this life to the human race recapitulatively by joining it to his being as incarnate Son. To be created in the 'image' of this God-made-incarnate (and Irenaeus is clear that humanity is created not in the image of God generally, but in the image of the Son who is known incarnationally as the living Image in its fullness[53]), is to be made an iconic representation of, and thus an active participant in, this full divine life of God as Father with his Son and Spirit. The goodness of humanity's formation, of the nature or character of human reality, lies in its substance as image of this trinity. It approaches to greater or lesser degree its likeness through union with Christ the Recapitulator, by means of the Spirit's anointing and accustoming of the human to the divine, and divine to the human. What it means for man to be 'like' God – that is, the 'likeness' of 'image and likeness' – is explained through the linking of ontology and economy in Irenaeus' overall presentation. Being and act are as distinct as creation and history, which, while interconnected, are nonetheless separate. This is the whole focus of Irenaeus' response to groups who would ontologize evil or sin and give it material stature. As the distortion of the created order must be understood in economic terms, as a disfigurement or departure from creation as fashioned into history by God, so renewal and rapprochement must be understood as economy in

---

52   So Behr, paraphrasing Irenaeus: 'Jesus, at his baptism, was anointed by the Father with the Spirit so that man might share in the abundance of his Unction which made him Christ' (*Asceticism and Anthropology* 67).

53   This Christological reading of the *imago* pertaining to the incarnate Son specifically, is brought out in J. Fantino, 'Le passage du premier Adam au second Adam comme expression du salut chez Irénée de Lyon', *VigChr* 52.4 (1998), 424, based on *Ref.* 5.16.2; cf. *Epid.* 22.

relation to ontology. To be 'in the image' is to speak of the fabric of creation; to be 'in the likeness' is to realize economically the life that creation enables – the likeness of the incarnate Son, in obedience to his Father through the Spirit.

THE FASHIONED IMAGE: THE COMPOSITE OF THE HUMAN PERSON

How is the human person, created after the image of God, joined to the life of Father, Son and Spirit? Here Irenaeus' theology of image comes to deal with the more precise definitions of anthropological substance. 'What is man?' is answered in reference to the dust of which he is fashioned, the image of Christ into which this dust is formed, and the vivification of the Spirit offered to this image-bearing dust, which leads the human person, through divinizing likeness to the Son, to an obedient, filial relationship with the Father.

The fabric of humanity is the earthen, material creation joined to the life of the Father by his two hands. This Irenaeus establishes through a discussion on the various constituent 'parts' of the human formation: body, soul and spirit. This emphasis on composite being is built on the framework we have explored above: the paradigm of the incarnate Son, Word-made-flesh, indicates (especially in his baptism) a distinction-yet-connection of the material and the spiritual in man. The present section will explore his understanding of what precisely constitutes each of these three 'parts' of man; and by identifying the soul in particular as means of reception of the Spirit of the Father, will lead into Irenaeus' second great anthropological supposition, that the fashioned creature is necessarily economic, and in its economy of growth further reveals the unchanging attributes of the God into whose image it grows.

The first two component parts – body and soul – Irenaeus identifies in a discussion on their relationship in the experience of human life, contained in a passage of no little oddity of language:

> The body is not stronger than the soul, since indeed the former is inspired, vivified, increased and held together by the latter; but the soul possesses and rules over the body. It is retarded in its velocity in exactly the proportion that the body shares in its motion, but it never loses the knowledge which is its own. For the body should be compared to an instrument, while the soul possesses the reason of an artist.[54]

Irenaeus here speaks of the human person as a 'body', made of the earth and in some sense an 'instrument [. . .] inspired, vivified, increased and held together' by

---

54 *Ref.* 2.33.4.

the soul. His language is unique, especially in his imagery of the 'velocity' of the soul as hampered by the physical constraints of the body – a spatial conception that reaches its pinnacle in his assertion that the soul has a 'shape', the same as that of the body which it animates.[55] His basic point, however, is simply to categorize the assertions of scripture: that God fashioned man from the dust, and breathed into his face the 'breath of life' (cf. Genesis 2.7). These claims demand recognition on the one hand of the material element in the human person; and on the other the 'spiritual' or 'soulful', though there is little expansion in the scriptural narrative as to what this latter might be in a concrete sense. Irenaeus ponders this in some detail, spurred on by his reflections on resurrection. If, as the scriptures proclaim, the human formation will at the end be raised from the dead, even as Christ was raised from the tomb, what does the experienced (in the life of Christ) and awaited (applicable to all others) resurrection have to tell us of the constitutive relationship of the 'parts' of the human creature? Those against whom Irenaeus' polemic is aimed argued that that the resurrection must be 'spiritual' rather than physical, for the material is the product of corruption and bound to corruption. Predictably, Irenaeus reads the situation differently.

> What, then, are mortal bodies? Can they be souls? But souls are incorporeal when compared to mortal bodies, for God 'breathed into the face of man the breath of life, and man became a living soul (*animam viventem*)'. Now the breath of life is an incorporeal thing; but certainly they cannot maintain that the very breath of life is mortal. [. . .] What, therefore, is there left to which we may apply the term 'mortal body', unless it be the thing that was moulded, that is, the flesh, of which it is also said that God will vivify it?[56]

Here Irenaeus identifies the soul with the 'breath of life' recounted in Genesis 2.7, the force by which the dust becomes a living being. It is a gift directly from God, an actualizing (Irenaeus' preferred term is 'vivifying') power, reflecting or transmitting his own divine attributes, for it is incorporeal and immortal, each of which are attributes of God alone. This soul, through union with the body, brings the 'thing moulded' – the flesh wrought of the dust – from inanimacy to life. Irenaeus' intention is to show that the soul, thus defined as properly incorporeal and immortal, cannot be the object of the resurrection 'from the dead', given that death is not an event applicable to the immortal force in man. That which dies, which consequently can be brought back to life, must be the body. Yet the two – body and soul – are one in the actualization of human personal reality. Irenaeus' peculiar language of the soul's 'shape', of its relation in 'velocity' to the body, is meant above all to demonstrate the intimacy of their union. In this light, his conception

---

55 'Souls themselves possess the figure of the body in which they dwell, for they have been adapted to the vessel in which they exist', *Ref.* 2.19.6.
56 *Ref.* 5.7.1.

is not in fact as peculiar as it may at first seem: the same thing is said, and for the same reasons, by Theophilus before him and Tertullian after.[57]

Framed in this way, one is left wondering whether the soul, as the breath of life, is thus itself an eternal principle of human existence. In other words, does the proclamation that the soul is 'immortal', and thus not the proper object of resurrection, imply that the human creature is 'naturally immortal' at the level of its ensoulled existence? Our passage from *Refutation* 5 might tend towards such a conclusion; but already Irenaeus' comments on the soul's immortality, paired with his proclamation earlier in the text that God is 'alone immortal, alone eternal', suggest otherwise. He in fact qualifies his remarks in an important way:

> As the body animated by the soul is certainly not itself the soul, but has fellowship with the soul as long as God desires, so also the soul herself is not life, but partakes in the life bestowed on her by God. Wherefore also the prophetic word declares of the first-formed, 'He became a living soul', teaching us that by participation in life the soul became alive. Thus the soul and the life which it possesses must be understood as separate existences.[58]

The soul which gives life to the body, and the life which the soul thus transmits, are not one and the same. Ultimately, the 'life' which the soul grants the human frame is the life of God, and more clearly the life (or Life) that is the Spirit of God the Father.[59] Through means of the soul, which is a constitutive yet immaterial component of humanity's being, the person receives the life of the Holy Spirit, given in token as the 'breath of life' first granted in Eden, yet fully borne into human experience only when man is united to the divine life through the incarnation. Through this means, the Son and the Spirit are united in their full glory to the handiwork fashioned by the former and sanctified by the latter. As such, to frame this point in the words of Behr, 'the Spirit is essential to Irenaeus's understanding of man, yet is not a "part" of his constitution [. . .] The Spirit itself is not a man, nor even a part of a man, but is itself given to man in such a manner that it can be legitimately described as his Spirit'.[60] Categories of 'bi-partite' and 'tri-partite', which scholars of theological anthropology often assign to a given author's perception of the human creature, are challenged by Irenaeus' reading. The human person is two 'parts' in composition (body and soul), yet three in actualization (body, soul and Spirit). Already in its formation it is both material and immaterial,

---

57 See Theophilus, *Ad Autolycum* 1.5; Tertullian *DA* 5–9, esp. 7.1, 9.4. So too earlier in Justin Martyr, though he suggests only that souls retain sensation after death (cf. *1 Apol.* 18, 20). Cf. E. Osborn, *The Emergence of Christian Theology* (Cambridge: University Press, 1993) 235. We shall have more to say on this in subsequent chapters.

58 *Ref.* 2.34.4. In this Irenaeus almost exactly mirrors Justin's comments at *Dial.* 5.

59 See *Ref.* 5.1.3.

60 Behr, *Asceticism and Anthropology* 99–100.

but this composite being of body and soul has *life* – true and full life – only when these exist in communion with the vivifying Spirit of the Father.

That the soul is not life, and certainly not itself eternal life, but that which transmits God's life to the person, defines human existence from the outset as a dynamic of relationship between the creature and its creator. Humanity 'lives' only in communion with its creator, enabled most fully by the incarnate Christ and perfected through the accustomization of the Spirit in whose life it takes part. This relationship of human and divine, of man and God, is dynamic not only in reference to the need for relational communion between them; it is so too in the necessary implication of maturation and development – themes for which Irenaeus is rightly well known, though with regard to which he is often not well understood. Irenaeus' discussion at *Ref.* 4.38.1–3, where he strikes off by asking 'Could not God have created man perfect from the beginning?' and concludes by noting that though God can do anything, humanity could not bear the full glory of the divine life until such time as it had matured in Christ, has its relevance precisely here. The formation of the human person is that of a material, fleshly body in possession of an immaterial soul, which bears in its frame the life of God. This confession defines the reality of human existence as a dynamic of growth into an ever fuller reception of this divine life. The human person as created in the image of God is, at the moment of its formation in Eden, one that awaits the experience of being 'profoundly enriched and transfigured'[61] through the incarnation of the Son – a transfiguration expressed most potently in human history through that very incarnation, but which in its apprehension by man awaits the eschatological hope promised in the Spirit.

THE SECOND SUPPOSITION: AN INTENTIONALLY ECONOMIC CREATION

At the outset of this chapter it was suggested that Irenaeus develops his anthropological discussion around the basis of two fundamental suppositions. The first, that God himself (and he alone) creates humanity, we have examined in some detail, exploring in turn the implications for humanity's essential goodness grounded in the image of the Son, anointed by the Spirit, together realizing the Father's creative will. This is an image that is 'dynamic' inasmuch as it is the *receipt* of the Spirit that enables the incarnate Son to *actualize* the Father's will for salvation. The second supposition, that humanity is so created intentionally and as part of a larger *taxis* or economy, takes its grounding from this dynamic character of the image in its human realization. The human person in its nature as image of

---

61 The language of *And the Word became flesh and dwelt among us, full of grace and truth*; published in *GOTR* 46.1–2 (2001) 167.

the Son, is created from the outset to progress along a given *oikonomia* of development and growth, such that in due time 'the Son might yield up his work to the Father' and the handiwork might at last become 'a perfect work of God'.[62] So where the convictions that ground the compositional assertions of Irenaeus' anthropology are protological – on God the Father creating through his Word and Wisdom (cf. Genesis 1.1, 1.26–28; John 1.1–3), on material and spiritual aspects to the human formation (Genesis 2.7), on the fundamental principle of the image (Genesis 1.26–28; 9.6) – the economic conviction of his anthropology is fundamentally eschatological, orientated towards the future. The question is not properly what the human person is, but what she is becoming in Christ by the power of the Spirit to bring about filial adoption to the Father. This constitutes what is certainly Irenaeus' most important contribution to the Christian understanding of image, which as connected to the Son *in relation to the Spirit and Father* becomes the principle for understanding not only creation and composition, but history and salvation in recapitulative terms. In this regard, much of what Irenaeus has to say is still unexplored. Our task, in what must necessarily be a longer section than those previous, will be first to explore the eschatological dimension of the protological image, then to show how these dual dimensions of protology and eschatology ground Irenaeus' focus on history and salvation as 'recapitulation'. We will structure this reading on the means by which Irenaeus sees the Spirit as uniting humanity in Christ as 'one race', which thus lives and acts in its antitype, Christ; and the salvific life of this antitype brought to its fullness and perfected on the cross, where the disunion of sin is met by a sacrificial offering of forgiveness that restores human union in the image of Christ.

From protology to eschatology

The connection of protology and eschatology is expressed with greatest impact through the manner in which Irenaeus draws to a conclusion his great polemical text. Having spent the better part of the fifth book detailing the reality of the resurrection and the eschatological hope of the millennial kingdom, Irenaeus returns at the end to his final definition of human existence in its economic perspective. His entire project of combating speculative cosmological dualism culminates in a confession of God's supreme power as creator to fashion a creature bearing his image, which one day shall bear fully and completely his glory.

> And in all these things [i.e. Irenaeus' argument throughout the *Refutation*] and by them all, the same God the Father is manifested, who fashioned man and gave promise of the inheritance of the earth to the fathers, who brought the

---

62 *Ref.* 4.39.2.

[human] creature forth [from bondage] at the resurrection of the just and fulfils the promises for the kingdom of his Son; subsequently bestowing in a paternal manner those things which neither the eye has seen, nor the ear has heard, nor has [thought concerning them] arisen within the heart of man. For there is the one Son, who accomplished his Father's will; and one human race also in which the mysteries of God are wrought, 'into which the angels desire to look', and they are not able to search out the wisdom of God, by means of which his handiwork, conformed and incorporated with his Son, is brought to perfection; that his offspring, the first-begotten Word, should descend to the creature, that is, to what had been moulded, and that it should be contained by him; and, on the other hand, the creature should contain the Word and ascend to him, passing beyond the angels, and be made after the image and likeness of God.[63]

The full stature of the human handiwork 'made after the image and likeness of God' is here relegated to the eschaton: it is that which humanity is becoming, which from the first it has been destined to become, which the incarnation was ever foreseen to enable fully. The likeness to God, which for Irenaeus is the personal appropriation of the divine image that is the foundational principle of human existence, is brought about only through the anointing of the Holy Spirit which the incarnate Christ received at his baptism, precisely so to be able to pass it on to the race of man of which he had become a part. The course of ever-increasing approximation to the life of Christ, enabled by the Spirit, is that which brings the human person, step by step and little by little, into a deeper relationship with the Father. In turn the Father, through this approximation, becomes ever more 'our' Father through filial adoption. The words that Christ taught his disciples to pray petition that *our* Father, who is in heaven, will accomplish *on earth* – that is, in the human race – the perfection of his divine will manifested 'in heaven', not only in the realm of the bodiless powers but also, as Irenaeus is keen to point out, in the obedient relationship of will expressed by the Son and Spirit towards the Father from eternity.[64] For humanity to be created not only in but *into* economy, that is, designed *to be economic*, is to find in man – as image of the Father's Son anointed by the Spirit – a vision of human reality expressed in the history of relation to God. To situate the person in the *metaxy*, the 'in between' of created substance growing in receptivity to divine grace, is to establish *economy* as a constitutive reality for human life, until that life reaches perfection in fully imaging its creator.

---

63   *Ref.* 5.36.3.
64   This tendency to comment on the 'Our Father' in immanently economic, anthropological terms is common. We shall see it again below in our chapters on Tertullian and Cyril; see pp. 89–91 and 155.

Economy and recapitulation

The economic vision of human existence, wrought by the interplay of protology and eschatology, is central to Irenaeus because it is at the heart of his understanding of Christ as salvific 'recapitulator'. Indeed, it is the anthropological basis through which his doctrine of recapitulation holds together. Once again, the full nature of his anthropology in its protological/eschatological scope can only be ascertained in the person of the incarnate Christ and his economy as Saviour. In this regard, Irenaeus presents what has become his most famous Christological statement:

> Being a master, therefore, he also possessed the age of a master, not despising or evading any condition of humanity, nor setting aside in himself that law which he had appointed for the human race, but sanctifying every age, by that period corresponding to it which belonged to himself. For he came to save all through means of himself – all, I say, who through him are born again to God – infants, and children, and boys, and youths, and old men. He therefore passed through every age, becoming an infant for infants, thus sanctifying infants; a child for children, thus sanctifying those who are of this age, being at the same time made to them an example of piety, righteousness, and submission; a youth for youths, becoming an example to youths, and thus sanctifying them for the Lord. So likewise he was an old man for old men, that he might be a perfect master for all, not merely as respects the setting forth of the truth, but also as regards age, sanctifying at the same time the aged also, and becoming an example to them likewise. Then, at last, he came even to death itself, that he might be 'the first-born from the dead, that in all things he might have the pre-eminence', the prince of life, existing before all, and going before all.[65]

This text has become the cardinal definition of a recapitulative soteriology. That which Christ comes to save, he saves by becoming. The maxim of Gregory the Theologian, that 'what is unassumed is unhealed', has a forebear in Irenaeus.[66] Christ's salvific action is primarily to become human, to exist as human, redeeming what is human by joining it to God. Irenaeus is literal here, insisting that this means Christ must have entered into old age so as to be 'an old man for old men [. . .] sanctifying the aged'. Jesus was nearly fifty when he was crucified, a tradition Irenaeus curiously claims was passed down from John.[67] The entering of the

---

65   *Ref.* 2.22.4.
66   Cf. Gregory of Nazianzus, *Ep.* 101 (*'To Cledonius'*).
67   Cf. *Ref.* 2.22.6; a puzzling statement inasmuch as we retain no textual evidence in support of its being part of the Johannine tradition. Yet Irenaeus inherits his sense of proximity to John through his relationship to Polycarp, received orally by 'sitting at his feet' (cf. our note above on Irenaeus' discipleship to Polycarp), and likely refers to this oral tradition.

Son into the *full realm* of human existence is guaranteed through Christ's great age, the requirement for the whole range of 'ages of life' further emphasizing Irenaeus' point that humanity is 'unable to have any participation in incorruptibility if it were not for his [the Word's] coming to us'.[68] He must come to humanity as it is, in every stage of its being.

The question that lies behind many a student's discomfort with this doctrine of recapitulation is 'how?' *How* does the Son's becoming man, specifically a historical man who exists on earth under Pontius Pilate at a precise moment in world history, have salvific bearing on the life of others in the race? A ransom theory of atonement, while presenting theological difficulties of its own, at least provides a straightforward answer to how Christ saves humanity: a ransom is paid (either to God the Father or the devil) and the shattered relationship of creator and created is thereby restored. Yet Irenaeus, while affirming the sacrificial character of Christ's offering on the cross, stringently dismisses the idea of ransom.[69] What, then, is the answer to 'how?' in his recapitulative understanding of Christ's salvific work?

The answer lies in the two principles at the root of his anthropological discussion. Humanity as image of the Son, the very creation of God the Father by the Son and Spirit, has from the first (and to the last) its antitype in Christ. Moreover, the conception of 'image' embraced by Irenaeus, which we have explored as grounded in the participatory imaging of the Son's relation to the Father and Spirit, makes Christ as 'antitype' more than a mere example or paradigm for human life. For humanity to be in the image of Christ means, above all, that Christ's life *is* man's life. The foundation of the creature's being is the life of the creator. Thus is man fashioned at the beginning as actively in the image of God, actively in participatory communion with the Son who is his Father's image, breathed to life by none other than the Spirit of this same Father. If it is the life of God through the image of the Son that is the defining characteristic of human being, then there is a unifying principle that runs right across the human race. Human persons may each be individuals, but *as human persons* are all, through the image in which they participate (whether or not the likeness is manifest) united as one through the common foundation of the Son. This idea stands behind Irenaeus' repeated statement that God forms, in Adam, 'one race' or 'one blood'.[70]

---

68   *Epid.* 31. Irenaeus' conception in this regard does, it should be noted, tend to promote a reading of Adam and Eve's 'infancy' as literal as that of his reading of the great age of Christ; cf. Steenberg, 'Children in Paradise'.

69   Most specifically of ransom paid to the devil; cf. the assembled notes to *Ref.* 3.18.7 in Steenberg and Unger, *Against Heresies* III (*ACW*, forthcoming 2009); cf. Wingren, *Man and the Incarnation* 129. We will have more to say on the sacrifice of the cross in what follows.

70   See for example, *Ref.* 3.12.9 – a comment on humanity as one blood and race that has direct bearing on Christ's recapitulative economy; for, as at 5.14.2, 'If the Lord became incarnate for the reason of any other economy, or took flesh of any other substance, then he has not summed up human nature in himself, nor indeed can he even be called "flesh"; for flesh has been truly made to consist in a transmission of that thing moulded originally from the dust'. It is the singularity of the human race that makes Christ's recapitulative life redemptive to all.

Humanity is multiple, complex and divided, but also intrinsically unitary, simple and whole. Adam was a particular human person, but as the first of the one race is also The Human Person – the prototypical manifestation of the 'one blood' shared by all humankind. Only here does it truly make sense to say, as does Paul, that 'in Adam all sinned' (Romans 5.12); or, as Irenaeus, that 'because all are implicated in the first-formation of Adam, we were bound to death through the disobedience'.[71] Irenaeus does not believe the guilt of Adam's transgression was imputed to his descendents, but he does believe that Adam's act *as transgressor* was of impact on future generations.[72] The one life of the one race (especially in Eden where that race is as yet confined to two persons who together transgress) becomes a life imbued with, and thus accustomed to, transgression. When the race is expanded, the lives born within it are members of that common life, now the harbour of sin. So does Irenaeus characterize the expansion: 'wickedness, spreading out for a long time, seized the entire race of men, until there was very little seed of righteousness in them'.[73] It is only because humanity is one race and one blood that the life of Adam can be of such universal impact on his descendents.

'One race' in Christ, by the Spirit

The notion of humanity as 'one race' founded after the image of Christ, the image of the Father, is the key principle in discerning not just humanity's interconnection, but also Christ's saving power as recapitulator. Irenaeus follows Paul in calling Jesus the 'new Adam', and even more dramatically, simply 'Adam', grounding his soteriological discussion in this terminology.[74] These are not mere poetic titles or aesthetic pairings. Irenaeus calls Christ 'Adam' because Christ *is* the image in which Adam was fashioned – he is 'in person' that which the whole race is as *eikon*. At length the image has become wholly visible in an economy that had grown ever less aware of it through the departure in likeness occasioned by sin. So explains Irenaeus:

> In times long past it was said that man was created after the image of God, but this image was not actually shown, for the Word was as yet invisible, after

---

71   *Epid.* 31.
72   On Irenaeus' belief that responsibility/guilt for disobedience cannot be imputed to another, see *Ref.* 4.27.2–3, 4.33.2, 5.15.2. Yet sin in one generation clearly effects those of subsequent eras; thus the whole scope of Irenaeus' treatment of Cham, Sem and Japheth in *Epid.* 20, 21, the latter two of whom are enlarged by a blessing of prosperity, while the descendents of Cham are marked by his transgression, 'whence it happened that every generation after him, being cursed, increased and multiplied in sin (cf. Gen 10.6–20). [. . .] They all fell under the curse, the curse extending for a long time over the ungodly' (*Epid.* 20).
73   *Epid.* 18; cf. *Ref.* 3.23.7. A similar comment is found in ps-Justin, *Sole Gov.* 1.
74   See *Epid.* 31.

whose image man was created [. . .]. When, however, the Word of God became flesh, he [. . .] showed forth the image truly, since he became himself that which bore his image; and he re-established the likeness after a sure manner, assimilating man to the invisible Father through means of the visible Word.[75]

Irenaeus speaks of the image becoming 'visible', that is, present before the eyes of humanity in the true reality of the likeness the latter has failed to approximate. The incarnate Son manifests to the world the authentic reality of that which it is called to be 'like'. This we might extrapolate somewhat, relating the concept back to Irenaeus' discussion at *Ref.* 2.22.4 on Jesus passing through every age of human life. In experiencing childhood, Christ shows forth the likeness to himself in the realm of human childhood. As an aged man, he reveals the likeness as it ought to be expressed at that stage of human existence.

But thus far Irenaeus' notion of Christ as recapitulator seems only a doctrine of manifestation. It might be suggested that Christ's salvific function is nothing other than to 'show' humankind what the realized image ought to look like, how it ought to be actualized, and what it implies for obedience and the human-divine relationship. A reading of *Ref.* 2.22.4 as solitary testimony to recapitulation might allow for such an interpretation, and too often does precisely as much. To understand why this cannot in fact be Irenaeus' meaning, however, we are obliged to read his comments in the *Refutation*, on Christ becoming the visible image, alongside a treatment of the same theme in the *Epideixis:*[76]

He united man with God and wrought a communion of God and man, we being unable to have any participation in incorruptibility if it were not for his coming to us, for incorruptibility, whilst being invisible, benefited us nothing: so he became visible, that we might, in all ways, obtain a participation in incorruptibility. And because all are implicated in the first-formation of Adam, we were bound to death through the disobedience, it was fitting, therefore, by means of the obedience of the one, who on our account became man, to be loosed from death. [. . .] And for this reason our Lord received that same

---

75   *Ref.* 5.16.2. See also 3.9.1.
76   The relationship of the two texts to each other, vis-à-vis date of composition, is highly contested. Composition of at least book 3 of the *Refutation* can be fixed to sometime within the episcopal reign of Eleutherus in Rome (c. 175–189); cf. *Ref.* 3.3.3. Whether the *Epideixis* was written before or after the longer text is at the heart of continuing scholarly debate. In a paper given in Oxford, S. L. Graham, 'Irenaeus and the Covenants: Immortal Diamond' (Oxford: 22 August 2003), argued against the traditional ascription of *Ref.* as the earlier text; J. Behr, in attendance at the communication, agreed with her assertions of an earlier date for the *Epid.*; see his comments to this end in *Way to Nicaea* 30 n. 34; cf. Behr, *Apostolic Preaching* 118 n. 229. For my support of a traditional later dating, and a summary of the situation, see Steenberg, *Irenaeus on Creation* 218–19.

embodiment as the first-formed, that he might fight for the fathers and vanquish in Adam that which had struck us in Adam.[77]

Once again, Irenaeus employs the conceptual framework of 'visible' versus 'invisible' image. The Word 'became visible' in the incarnational communion of the Son and humanity, wrought through the economy of the Virgin, making manifest that which humankind might never have beheld without that coming. But here Irenaeus makes a clarification: the Word comes visibly into the human economy, that the one race might *obtain participation* in the incorruptibility properly his as Son of God. Without the 'communion of God and man' the latter has no participation in the fullness of divine life thus beheld, for the iconic participation by which this life is realized in humanity has been held captive by the non-likeness of a fallen bondage to sin. When Christ binds together that which is after the image and the prototype of the image proper, he enables between them the union which is the eschatological hope of the kingdom. The economic attainment of the likeness is made a new possibility in visibly beholding the eternal Son-made-flesh.

An offering as and for the human race: the place of the cross in recapitulation

Christ accomplishes the 'communion of God and man' by, to use again Irenaeus' own words, 'vanquishing in Adam that which had struck us in Adam'. That which had struck is defined as the violent strength of sin, instigated through the devil's provocation but expanded into humanity's own will and action through the accustomization of time. Christ vanquishes this not from without, but by coming into the realm of human existence and experience, becoming 'Adam' as a full member of the one race of which he is himself the ultimate antitype. It is precisely because Irenaeus has centred his anthropological discussion so deeply on the reality of image, on the unity across the race that the divine image implies, that his soteriology can be defined so summarily as recapitulative. Christ enters into the race of humanity *as human*, as himself the personal reality of the whole race, since this reality has from its formation been defined as created in his image. What he accomplishes as human becomes universally recapitulative inasmuch as he accomplishes it in the person of the whole human family. When he becomes a child and exists as a child, he exists as the personal reality of all that human childhood is, since childhood is fundamentally his image in a particular age of economic expression. He sanctifies 'young-manhood', as Irenaeus calls it, not merely because he is 'a young man', but because he lives that age of life as the visible reality of all that constitutes human young-manhood. The living image of

---

77   *Epid.* 31.

that which it means to be a youth, himself exists in the economy *as youth itself*, restoring through that living the fundamental reality of human experience in this age. What the incarnate Christ is, he is for all humankind, as all humankind. So Irenaeus:

> For the Lord came to seek back the lost sheep, and it was man who was lost; and, therefore, he did not become any other formation, but being born from her who was of the race of Adam, he maintained the likeness of the formation.[78]

Irenaeus' discussion at *Ref.* 5.17 sets this conception squarely in the framework of the cross, the tool by which the incarnational recapitulation offered by Christ is fully accomplished. In the act of Christ's offering on the cross is epitomized, and indeed actualized, the full measure of the human story summed up in the incarnate Son. The unity of God and man inherent in the formation of the human creature, described by Irenaeus here and elsewhere as 'friendship', is broken on account of transgression; and since such union was the gift of God at creation, its loss can be considered and termed a 'debt':

> For this reason he has taught us to say in prayer, 'Forgive us our debts', since indeed he is our Father, whose debtors we were, having transgressed his commandments.[79]

It is through this framework of debt, not as proprietary claim requiring ransom or restitution, but as transgression fracturing union, that Irenaeus is able to see in the cross the manner in which recapitulation both demands and involves propitiation – a term he uses directly at *Ref.* 5.17.1. Such propitiation is understood as joined to the unifying act of healing and restoration: in offering himself in obedience, the incarnate Son 'cancels (*consolatus*) our disobedience with his obedience'. It is in this remitting of sins, of vanquishing what had struck humanity in Adam, that the full measure of his recapitulative healing is effected. The source of human disunion – the disobedience that since Adam has held the world captive – is reclaimed by Christ, re-fashioned into an obedience that, through the cross and resurrection, conquers death which is the ultimate force and power of sin. So in Irenaeus' chief passage on the sacrifice of the cross:

> Therefore David said beforehand, 'Blessed are they whose iniquities are forgiven, and whose sins are covered; blessed is the man to whom the Lord has not imputed sin' (Psalm 32.1, 2; cf. Romans 4.7, 8), pointing out thus that

---

78 *Epid.* 33.
79 *Ref.* 5.17.1.

remission of sins which would follow upon his advent, by which 'he destroyed the handwriting' of our debt, and 'fastened it to the cross' (Colossians 2.14); so that as by means of a tree we were made debtors to God, so also be means of a tree we may obtain the remission of our debt.[80]

It is in Christ seen on the cross that Irenaeus finds the full revelation of his incarnate being. The cross, and the obedience that leads to his offering and sacrifice thereon, shows the true, wholly incarnate reality of the Son-made-flesh. It is 'as man that he suffered for us' (5.17.3); but as this suffering is the divine offering of God for the remission of sin, the man making the offering must be acknowledged also as God, 'for if no one can forgive sins but God alone, then when the Lord remitted them and healed men, it became clear that he was himself the Word of God made the Son of man, receiving from the Father the power of remission of sins, since he was man and since he was God'. It is the act of remission, of healing the human person, that reveals completely who Christ is – 'by remitting sins he did heal man, while he also manifested who he himself was'. In knowing the Son humanly, the power of the offering of the cross is understood for the measure of obedience it requires; but conversely, it is in the offering on the cross that the meaning of Christ's humanity is disclosed as the sacrifice of love offered by the Father, through the Son, for the redemption of his creation. The cross, then, becomes the means of disclosing the hidden realities of the divine economy summed up in the human Son. In the latter portion of *Ref.* 5.17 Irenaeus takes up Elisha's prophecy of the axe with its iron head (representing the 'sure word of God') separated and lost in the water, found when the wooden handle (typifying the cross) is cast into the same, and the iron head floats to the surface (see 4 Kingdoms 6.5–7). To Irenaeus, this shows that it is the cross which discloses the deepest meaning of the will of God revealed throughout the whole of history, and provides the means to re-discover and re-obtain that which previously had been lost:

> This sure word, then, which had been hid from us, did the dispensation of the tree make manifest, as I have already remarked. For as we lost it by means of a tree, by means of a tree was it again made manifest to all, showing the height, the length, the breadth and the depth in itself. And, as a certain man among our predecessors has observed, this came about 'through the extension of the hands of a divine person, gathering the two peoples to one God'. For these were two hands, because there were two peoples scattered to the ends of the earth, but there was one head in the middle, as there is but one God, who is above all, and through all, and in us all.[81]

---

80 *Ref.* 5.17.2.
81 *Ref.* 5.17.4. The 'certain man among our predecessors' is presumably Papias.

What had been hid from the 'two peoples' scattered on the earth (this seems a veiled reference to the progeny of Japheth and Cham, whom Irenaeus reads as the progenitors of the various types of man[82]) was the reality that in the human Son, perfecting his Father's will through the Spirit, the union with the Father, imaged in humanity through iconic participation in the Son, is restored and perfected. Protological history and eschatological expectation are fully united in the moment of the Son's offering. The one who himself is the establishment of the race, becomes one of the race and the fulfilment of the race. His acts are redemptive inasmuch as he lives out, as man and as *a* man, the perfect relationship of Son to Father, sanctified by the Spirit, obedient unto death – a relationship that is the substance of the divine life of which all human existence is the created image, joining what is created to him who created it, perfecting humanity by the obedient offering of Christ's perfect divinity.

CHARACTERIZING IRENAEUS' ANTHROPOLOGY: TO SPEAK OF GOD AND MAN

Irenaeus' fundamental theological conviction, indeed his overarching Christian conviction, is that the crucified and exalted Jesus Christ is the personal revelation of God's truth in its fullness. He is so as the 'scriptural Christ', the one whom the law and prophets foretell. Moreover, he is the full truth by which these foretold what they did; and, as such, he is the means to understanding the full implication of their witness. When Irenaeus considers the mystery of humanity, he does so through this Christology of scripture as read from the perspective of the empty tomb. It is in the incarnate and resurrected Christ that the fabric of humanity, the nature of the human person and the economy of human existence all are to be understood.

The anthropology revealed by the incarnation is, for Irenaeus, the full story of the being fashioned from the dust. The human person is first and foremost the Father's unique creation, wrought of his two hands, formed through the immediate and personal action of his Son and Spirit. Scripture has God look upon this new creation and call it 'good', a proclamation that has meaning only when understood as grounded in the fact that the creation is, in the Son, an image of the goodness of his loving obedience to the Father – an *eikon* of the divine life, which the incarnation reveals to be one of relationship between the eternally co-relating Father, Son and Spirit. The human person is 'good' because it is wrought in the image of God who is good, and the God of the Christian confession is none other than 'the Father of our Lord Jesus Christ' who acts always with his Word and Wisdom, the Son and the Spirit.[83]

---

82 See Genesis 9.18–27, 11.10–32; cf. *Ref.* 3.5.3, 5.34.2; *Epid.* 20, 21, 42. Compare Justin, *Dial.* 139–40.
83 *Ref.* 1.22.1.

For the human person to be created in the image of this God is for it to be a material being fashioned of dust, joined to the divine life. 'Man is a living being composed of a soul and a body', Irenaeus writes, but this composition is genuinely alive only when the soul communicates to the body the life of the Holy Spirit.[84] The human person is thus a dynamic being in its ontological fabric, vivified through a communion with God that grows over time, until in the incarnation it is brought fully to the divine life. As such, the nature of human existence is one of development into the unfolding economy through which this communion is enabled and made real, both for the one race of humanity as a whole, and in the individual life of each human person.

Irenaeus' anthropology is thus fundamentally one of dynamic relationship between the created being and its creator. Human life is defined as much by 'being God' – that is, by receiving the life of the Father in the Son, through the Spirit – as it is by 'being dust'. To understand the person apart from God by means of an overt focus on the flesh, but even to define it by an improper emphasis on the soul as 'itself life', is to misunderstand the nature of the person. The human person is only rightly comprehended as a mystery of the material creation wrought into communion with the divine life of God, through the incarnational activity of the Son with the Spirit. Human nature is interwoven with the divine.

Irenaeus' anthropology is, moreover, dynamic at the level of economy. The human person is ever a changing being. Adam's 'state' at creation is not static: he is destined from the first for growth and development. All human history prior to the encounter with the incarnate Son was intended for growth into the reception of that experience. All human history since is intended for the accustomization of humanity to the life offered in the incarnate Christ – an accustomization that is the working in humanity of the Holy Spirit, who will bring to perfection at the eschaton that which man experiences in token even now. And, says Irenaeus, this dynamic of growth and maturation is not limited to the present historical economy: the perfection of the human being is to become an individual who grows perfectly, who matures always into the unapproachable splendour of the infinite God. As God shall always be transcendent, always immeasurable to the created order, so humanity's growth shall always be a real characteristic of its existence. Adam's development is eternal, for 'humanity will always have something to learn from God'.[85]

To read Christian anthropology from Irenaeus' framework is to explore humanity through an explicitly developmental, relational lens. The psalmist's pleading 'what is man?' is not a question that can be asked, certainly not answered, apart from the necessary correlate, 'what is God?' But for Irenaeus, this impersonal analysis centred on questions over 'what is?' risks separating the understanding of God from the experience of God. If the groups against which Irenaeus writes have

---

84   *Epid.* 2.
85   *Ref.* 2.28.3.

one theological deficiency from which he considers all their other problems arise, it is that they do not 'know the maker and creator of this universe, the only true God and the Lord of all things'.[86] To know man, one must know Christ; for it is Christ who, with the Spirit, reveals the Father, the creator of all. The Son in his humanity discloses his divinity, discloses the theological relationship of Son to Spirit, and these 'hands' to their Father. To be a human person, for all that this mystery means, one must be first of all in communion with the Son through the indwelling of the Spirit, whereby the material creation is made the living child of the Father. Irenaean anthropology is one of godly relationship, of the experience of he who is, in his living person, all that his creation is meant to become.

*   *   *

Apart from his specific means of articulating anthropological and theological realities, which are interesting and noteworthy in their own right, Irenaeus is of value for the general method of doctrinal articulation he embraces. As we have seen above, it is in his anthropological considerations of the human Jesus Christ that he is able to formulate doctrinal commentary on the nature of the divine Son this Jesus is, in relation to his Father and the Father's Spirit; as well as the scope of the humanity this incarnate Son is understood to embrace. His theology is anthropological, inasmuch as it is in the anthropology of Christ that the divinity of the Father and Spirit are known. Further, his anthropology is theological, inasmuch as his address of the human person, of human reality, is made always in reference to the divine reality of the incarnate Jesus Christ. This is nowhere clearer than in his address of humanity as 'in the image of God', which, as we have seen, is for Irenaeus an anthropological concept, surely, at the root of 'human nature' and economy; but which is also intrinsically theological, inasmuch as humankind's imaging of the divine is the avenue by which the divine is revealed and known. Not only does God reveal what is entailed in the human *imago*: the image realized in humanity is itself the book or framework from which one gleans understanding of the divine creator. That humanity 'in the image' is a corporeal body in receipt of the Father's life, made personal through accustomization by the Spirit to the Son's incarnate recapitulation of the one race, is a conception of 'image' that reveals something of God, even as it does of man – indeed, it is a conception that discloses the triadic reality of God in his relationship to man. Irenaeus' doctrine of God is articulated through and by his doctrine of humanity. His theology is conceived *through his anthropology*, precisely as an authentic incarnational confession demands – for the Word-made-flesh, the humanly incarnate Christ, declares directly: 'I am in the Father and the Father in me [. . .] he who has seen me has seen the Father' (cf. John 14.11, 9).

---

86   *Ref.* 3.25.7.

The substance of the anthropological vision revealed in Irenaeus is that of the Son's relationship to the Father and Spirit, imaged in the human person who, through her created soul, receives and communicates to the body the Spirit's life, which leads to union with the Father. The importance of the soul as the created, yet immaterial, means by which the life of the Father in relationship to his hands is realized in the corporeal reality of the human handiwork, is significant. 'Gnostic' dualism, favouring the soul over and above the body, is not met in Irenaeus with a converse favouring of the body over and above the soul, but with a redefinition of the soul as that which allows the body to participate in the life of God, even as the incarnate Christ is Son of the Father in the one reality of his human existence. To be 'in the image of God' is, for Irenaeus, to be both corporeal and ensoulled. It is in the body's receipt of the Spirit's life, through the soul, that the human creature in its totality images the incarnate Son's reception of the Father's Spirit, which establishes him as Saviour.

We have seen the manner in which this vision of anthropological substance is intentionally dynamic. Irenaeus' key words for defining the image are 'reception', 'transmission', 'accustomisation' and the like; and it is clear that such a dynamic conception is grounded in this relationship of soul to body. Irenaeus does not, however, explore in detail how the soul thus functions, or what its status as means of transmitting the divine life to the human frame suggests for a conception of the soul proper. For the exegesis of such questions, and the further light such exegesis may shed on the anthropological-theological exchange, we turn from Irenaeus to a near-contemporary, Tertullian, who more than any previous Christian author focuses on the theological anthropology of the soul.

Chapter 2

IMPATIENT HUMANITY: TERTULLIAN OF CARTHAGE

Tertullian's extensive treatment of the soul in his complex *De anima* indicates the centrality to his thought of a bi-partite conception of the human creature, with the soul 'housed' in the body as immaterial agent of the human person's life. In the present chapter we shall explore the manner in which Tertullian's definition of the soul as that which communicates the divine life of the Spirit to the mortal flesh, is connected to his notion of the *imago Dei* as a 'model' or archetype imaged in the creature. The soul bears the Spirit's presence into the human creature as an image of the Son's own receipt of the Spirit, in the perfection of his Father's glory. Linking his anthropology to a trinitarian articulation of Father, Son and Spirit as *una substantia*, Tertullian is able to speak of authentic human nature, and the departure from this authenticity, through a creative usage of his favoured term, 'patience'. Impatience of the Spirit becomes the context of human existence requiring redemption, which Tertullian understands as Christ restoring to humanity a receptivity to this Spirit. By again receiving growth into the Son's life, the model imaged in man might attain a real likeness, through the Spirit, to the Son's union with the Father.

* * *

For Irenaeus of Lyons, the protological and eschatological focus of Christian anthropology binds its vision of the human person to the course of history, of economy. The composition fashioned in the beginning as image of the communal life of God as Father with Son and Spirit, is enjoined to progress through the course of that God's progressive yet consistent interaction with the created order. In due course it meets perfection in the full image of its formation: Christ in whom the image is known. Human personhood, much less the concrete reality of the created individual, is not an object of stasis, but a reality whose constitutive elements – body and soul in receipt of the Holy Spirit – mark out its existence as necessarily historical. These elements define human reality as one of receipt, involving advancement and growth. The human person only ever *is* when this person is *becoming*; to be economically ensconced is part-and-parcel of authentic human existence. As we saw in our previous chapter, there is an eternal dimension to this basic component of Irenaeus' anthropology. The dynamic of growth into the Father will be made perfect (*teleiotes*) at 'the end', in the eschaton, as Irenaeus makes especially clear in book four of the *Refutation*; but even here this 'perfection' is into an intimate receipt of God's glory, which always transcends the created order. The handiwork of God will always, even in the eternity of the kingdom when 'always' and 'ever' no longer apply in the sense that they do in the economy, be actively in receipt of its creator's eternally greater glory.

A near contemporary of Irenaeus, who at first reading seems to resemble his thought in few respects, offers a glimpse of early Christian anthropological consideration that in fact reveals marked similarities of emphasis, focus and methodological approach, while making advances in articulation in the realms we saw as insufficiently addressed in Irenaeus. Tertullian of Carthage (c. 160–225), a man much maligned by the annals of history – due at least in part to a characterization by Jerome[1] – as the zealot-*comme*-schismatic who exemplified the 'Montanist' infiltration of the Church, is not most often read as an anthropological writer, though recent studies have focused on this aspect of his thought in some detail.[2] We most often encounter portraits of Tertullian the proto-Trinitarian theologian, Tertullian the charismatic, Tertullian the exclusivist, Tertullian the rigorist, Tertullian the 'founding father' of Latin theology.[3] He is, we might note, all these things and more, be the categories suitably qualified and de-sensationalized. Yet there lies buried in the folds of all that makes Tertullian 'different', a continuity with much of the theological – and more importantly to us, anthropological – reflection current in the early Christian theological community.

There can be little question of the anthropocentric character of Tertullian's writings, from the earliest tracts right through to the larger tomes of his later years. He is, in common with all Christian writers of the period, fascinated with the human and its stature before God. But Tertullian seems (and at this stage that qualifier is important) primarily to speak of such concerns in the context of the Christian community's corporate existence in relation to the righteousness of the just God. What is important is not the person *qua* person, but the person as he or she stands before God the righteous, in relation to the community of adopted heirs joined to God's righteousness. 'Tertullian's aim was not morality but holiness' wrote G. Bray in a seminal study, with whose findings we shall engage in the

---

1 See *De Ill.*, 53.

2 See J. Leal, *La Antropología de Tertuliano – Estudio de los trtados polémicos de los años 207–212 d.c.* (Rome: Institutum Patristicum Augustinianum, 2001); J. Alexandre, *Une chair pour la gloire – L'anthropologie réaliste et mystique de Tertullien* (Paris: Beauchesne, 2001). Nasrallah's recent work focusses on the anthropology of the soul at length, though with few references to the body; see L. Nasrallah, *'An Ecstasy of Folly': Prophecy and Authority in Early Christianity* (Harvard Theological Studies, 52; Cambridge, Mass.: Harvard University Press, 2003) 95–127.

3 See for example, C. B. Daley, *Tertullian the Puritan and his Influence: An Essay in Historical Theology* (Dublin: Four Courts Press, 1993) 81.

present chapter.[4] It is the irreproachability of the creator that is paramount, for his righteousness will save the corrupt world from its self-inflicted torment. All of Christian life and practice is, Tertullian argues, to be centred in gaining and maintaining a relationship with God's bestowed righteousness, such that sin may be overcome. The corporate body of Christianity, the Church, is understood as the haven of this righteousness in the midst of a depraved world. It was such considerations that led Tertullian to his famous, perhaps infamous, reflections on the relationship of Church and purity: those who have fallen from purity, from righteousness, are to be expelled from the Church's body, excluded from its fellowship.[5] Those who commit grave sins are to be cast out, not only temporarily but permanently.[6] If it is better to tear out one's eye than have the whole body cast into hell on its account (cf. Matthew 5.29), there can be little excuse for the ecclesial body if it clings to, rather than thrusts away in abhorrence, its own sinful members. Tertullian was, in the words of Daley, 'led by his insatiable desire to outlaw sin from the Church, to banish it from the lives of Christians'.[7] It was, after all, Adam and Eve's acceptance of the serpent's unrighteousness that caused the sin of Eden to spread throughout the world. There can be no repeat of their hospitality to sin in the restored community of the Church.

This manner of reflection, which is admittedly troubling (though hardly unheard of in the early Christian world), has often led to broad classifications of Tertullian as a 'rigorist' who saw the world, as also the human person, in static terms of righteous and unrighteous, sinner and saved, evil and good – in short, an early 'black-and-white' theologian in a tradition that ought properly concern itself with the reality of shades of grey. Indeed, if we read Tertullian in this way, taking on board also his muted and often misunderstood speculation that sins committed after baptism could not be forgiven, the contrast with a theologian like Irenaeus seems stark.[8]

A contrast between the dynamic Irenaeus on the one hand, with his gradations of sin and restorative authority of Christ, and the black-and-white Tertullian on the other, with his conviction that unrighteousness is not to be toyed with, not even for correction, but expelled for purity's sake, is, however, built on an unbalanced reading of 'Tertullian the puritan'. Too often the ways and words of the zealot are cast in a negative light by those who abhor the excesses of the zealotry; but one does not generally become a zealot simply to adopt hard-line positions for

---

4   Bray, *Holiness and the Will of God* 66.

5   See *Apol.* 2.18; 39.4; cf. *De Paen.* 5.1; 7.1–3. Cf. Osborn, *First Theologian* 179.

6   See *Pud.* 19; but cf. *De Paen.* 7.10, 11 for Tertullian's own qualification of this idea. On the question overall, see Dunn, *Tertullian* 55–56.

7   Daley, *Tertullian the Puritan* 11.

8   For a fair assessment of the subtleties involved in the question of sin and forgiveness in Tertullian, despite rather dichotomous language elsewhere, see ibid. 5. A fuller treatment is found in Trevett, *Montanism* 114–16.

the sake of their severity. Zealots are inspired by a deep-felt conviction that the truth to which they subscribe demands a full-scale transformation of life – more precisely, transformation to a degree beyond that of the average members of their community. The line of demarcation between zealousness (lauded as a virtue by most) and zealotry (which tends towards exclusivism, which risks schism) is, however, difficult to define, and this is borne out in the example of Tertullian's own life. Most would agree that the Tertullian of the early third century, the elder man of the *De anima*, *Adversus Marcionem* and *Adversus Praxean* has crossed that line, whatever it may be; but at what point did the move from zealous convert to zealot schismatic actually occur, if it occurred concretely at all? This proves an almost impossible question, and there are those who argue that it never occurred in even a nominal sense, with characterizations of 'Tertullian the schismatic' simply the flawed condemnations of a later age.[9] This type of careful argument, put forward most convincingly by Barnes, Rankin and Dunn, notwithstanding, his zeal clearly grows.[10] However – and here a cardinal point for our study – the anthropological convictions of Tertullian's later works in fact bear little categorical difference to those of his earliest writings. Humanity as it is encountered in the *De anima* or even the *Ad Scapulam*, probably Tertullian's last work in the extant corpus (c. 212), is more thoroughly treated than in his early tracts, and with respect to the *De anima* in particular he has had the time to construct his treatment with extended recourse to Soranus' volume by the same title; but the essential components have not changed from the confessions of the *De spectaculis*, *De idololatria* or *De tesimonio animae*, which are among his earliest.[11] His convictions become

---

9   The traditional characterization is summed up in the 'formal breach with the church' mentioned in the introduction to the *Adv. Marc.* by E. Evans, *Tertullian, Adversus Marcionem*, 2 vols. (i, books i–iii; Oxford: Oxford University Press, 1972) xviii. For a re-assessment, see Bray, *Holiness and the Will of God* 56, and more broadly 56–63. Bray's treatment of Tertullian's draw towards the 'Montanist' movement is among the best in print. His thought is reflected in the more recent little study of C. Munier, *Petite vie de Tertullien* (Paris: Desclée de Brouwer, 1996) 17–21, who writes that Tertullian saw the thought-world of the New Prophecy movement 'comme un courant extrêmement exigeant et rigoureux, mais qui demeurait parfaitement orthodoxe'. Munier does not maintain Bray's cautionary tone throughout, however, and still proffers that Tertullian made a formal and decisive split with 'l'église orthodoxe' around the year 213, based on 'Montanist' vocabulary and phrasing in that text (*Petite vie* 19–21). This late dating is doubtful in any case. Cf. Nasrallah, *Ecstasy of Folly* 100–01 for a good summation of a less dualistic approach, 'based on the ideas of struggle and negotiation of identity and authority in early Christianity'.

10   See T. D. Barnes, *Tertullian, A Historical and Literary Study* (Oxford: Clarendon Press, 1971/1985) 30–56, 131–36, who speaks of Tertullian 'working out the consequences of his acceptance of the New Prophecy' (p. 132); D. I. Rankin, 'Was Tertullian a Schismatic?' *Prudentia* 19 (1986), 73–79; D. I. Rankin, *Tertullian and the Church* (Cambridge: Cambridge University Press, 1994) 27–38; Dunn, *Tertullian* 6–7. The best treatment to date is in Trevett, *Montanism* 66–69.

11   On the dating of these tracts in particular, see Barnes, *Tertullian* 55. Nasrallah would date the *De anima* between 210 and 213 (Nasrallah, *Ecstasy of Folly* 111). For the difficulties of dating, see our n. 13. Tertullian's engagement with Soranus throughout the *De anima* is still best treated by Waszink, *De Anima* 22*–38*.

more pronounced and points of emphasis change, especially as he engages with the cosmological and anthropological thought of Hermogenes,[12] but Tertullian presents what is in the end a markedly uniform reading of the human person – a point rendered particularly clear if one investigates the corpus chronologically.[13]

CONTROVERSY IN INTERPRETATION

'Tertullien déconcerte'. So did J.-C. Fredouille begin his important study of Tertullian and his role in ancient society, and so did he tie his characterization into a long heritage of Tertullianic unease.[14] While it may be true that Irenaeus deserved better of history than scholarship has till recently given him, Tertullian has deserved more from it.[15] The convenient stick of a so-called 'Montanism' has been used to beat him since his own lifetime, and while we would not wish to discount his involvement with the New Prophecy phenomenon of the second and third centuries (which careful scholars have argued is in fact authentically Montanist, if not necessarily sharply schismatic[16]), nor the problematic ecclesiological and theological doctrines to which it would give rise, it is nonetheless true that the stigma of his prophetic inclinations has branded him harshly and often unfairly in the memory of history. 'Since the Enlightenment, no ancient Christian writer has attracted more hostility' wrote E. Osborn, and this remains true even today.[17] It continues to be suggested that there is something peculiarly schismatic

---

12   The same Hermogenes against whom Theophilus wrote in Antioch, before the former moved to Carthage, under Waszink's speculations to take up the career of painter (see Waszink, *De Anima* 7*–8*; cf. *Eus. HE* 4.24.1). There is an interesting line of continuity provided in this figure, for a response to Hermogenes' cosmology grounded the developmental anthropology of Theophilus, whose writings seem to have been known to Irenaeus; and later prompted the sustained treatment of the same matters in Tertullian's *Adv. Herm.*, *De Cens.*, and *DA*.

13   On the difficulties of dating the Tertullianic corpus, see Munier, *Petite vie* 8, 24 It was A. von Harnack, 'Zur Chronologie der Schriften Tertullians', *ZK* 2 (1878) who first noted that these problems prevent a reflection on chronology sustaining a critical assessment of Tertullian's thought (see esp. p. 572) – in other words, that the dating of the texts cannot be ascertained with enough certainty to ground the kind of text-to-theme developmental linkage that was current in Tertullian studies prior to Harnack's clarification. His point of caution remains relevant; we do not wish here to make a strict chronological assessment of Tertullian's works, only to note that foundational themes remain consistent across the timeframe of his literary output. Cf. Dunn, *Tertullian* 7–9 for the valid importance on dating, 'even if it is complex and open to much disagreement', especially with reference to an author whose works span decades of increasing zeal and rigour.

14   J. -C. Fredouille, *Tertullien et la conversion de la culture antique* (Paris: Etudes Augustiniennes, 1972) 15.

15   See H. B. Swete's foreword to F. R. Hitchcock, *Irenaeus of Lugdunum: A Study of His Teaching* (Cambridge: University Press, 1914); for reference to which, with further assessment, see Behr, *Apostolic Preaching* 1.

16   See Trevett, *Montanism* 68.

17   Osborn, *First Theologian* xv.

in his personality, redolent in his theology, despite the work of such scholars as Monceaux, who over a century ago showed its predictable concord with general ecclesiastical sentiment in early Christian Africa.[18] Christianity in Africa was 'different', to take up Trevett's characterization of Frend,[19] and Tertullian's zeal is hardly more 'schismatic' or exclusivist in orientation than that of his environs, which would not long later produce the Donatists, which had already entertained the Manichaeans. As such, we have also seen the inverse side of Tertullianic studies; for where there is harshest condemnation, there often arises fiercest support. In the twentieth century there were those who painted an entirely golden portrait of the man, such as that found in the posthumously collected works of Princeton Seminary professor Benjamin Breckinridge Warfield – hardly a balanced scholar, but one who had his influence, and whose characterizations demonstrate the variety of assessments available:

> Ardent in temperament, endowed with an intelligence as subtle and original as it was aggressive and audacious, he added to his natural gifts a profound erudition, which far from impeding only gave weight to the movements of his alert and robust mind.[20]

Assessments of Tertullian seem to oscillate between positive and negative, and for every Warfield there is at least one Knox, who labels Tertullian an outright propagandist,[21] while others, desiring to lump him in with the 'Montanist heretics', are happy to characterize him as would Epiphanius that movement's eponymous founder: a 'horrid little man'.[22]

However one reads Tertullian's zeal, unexceptional though it may be, it is certainly a real aspect of his personality. But in the midst of an increasing zealotry and polarizing exclusivism was expressed a vision of the human person that itself has never been directly challenged by subsequent charges of heresy or schism, but which has at the same time never received ample investigation in its own right, largely on account of these same allegations. His anthropology, when seriously considered at all, is usually explored as a kind of excursus of the *De anima*, itself presented as a 'Montanist' tract of questionable orthodoxy. Yet despite such modern trends, patristic sources writing in the era of harshest criticism of Tertullian would take pains to note that it was not his theology that was disputed, but what

---

18   See P. Monceaux, *Histoire littéraire de l'Afrique chrétienne* (1901).

19   So Trevett, *Montanism* 70, in reference to W. H. C. Frend, 'Heresy and Schism as Social and National Movements', in D. Baker (ed.), *Schism, Heresy and Religious Protest* (Cambridge: Cambridge University Press, 1972) 39.

20   B. B. Warfield, *Studies in Tertullian and Augustine* (Oxford: Oxford University Press, 1930) 3. The text carries on in this manner for some length.

21   R. A. Knox, *Enthusiasm: A Chapter in the History of Religion* (London: Collins, 1950/1987) 25 .

22   Epiphanius, *Pan.* 48.11.9; cf. Trevett, *Montanism* 1.

was perceived as an exclusivist ecclesiology[23] – a reminder that has never fully sunk in, and modern studies must still repeat it.[24] While today's scholarship is enamoured of Irenaeus, it still looks to Tertullian primarily for other reasons, some of which we have already mentioned: his use of the term *trinitas* and fledgling conception of the trinity, his witness to the entire 'Montanist' phenomenon, his Latinization of theological discourse, etc. Perhaps for this reason, he still represents an under-explored resource for understanding early patristic anthropology in relation to doctrinal theology.

A vision of humanity in both its compositional and economic realities is the heart of Tertullian's theological attention. 'Who is man', that he becomes the centrepiece of the cosmic economy? Who is the one that Christ saves, whom the Spirit now fills, inspires and guides? Who is the one on whom the sacramental grace of Christian worship – baptism, confession, prayer, Eucharist – acts, and how does it so act? Such questions consume Tertullian's theological output, convinced as he is from his youth that humanity's lot in the cosmos must be of concern, down to the most minute activities, such as attendance at public spectacles or the dress of women and soldiers. The acts of the person effect the life of the person, which in turn effects his relation to God; for, as becomes clear in Tertullian's later reflections, human 'life' itself is nothing less than communication and participation in divine life. Humanity's life is that breathed by God into the womb, divine as sprouting from a divine source (cf. *De anima* 41). *How* the human person lives is therefore of concern, for one lives the life of God in the economy of God, either preserving and perfecting the gift of that life, or disfiguring it to the end of personal death. It is, then, the 'how', the economic process of being a living person in the cosmos, situated before God, that drives Tertullian's anthropological reflections.

Viewed in this light, the extremist stance to which Tertullian eventually comes is propelled by concerns similar to those we have seen ground Irenaeus' discussion. The constitutive elements of the human creature are of value as insights into the manner of the creature's life, but ultimately Christian anthropology is driven not so much by the 'what' as the 'how' of economic reality. Human life is seen by Tertullian, as much as Irenaeus, as defined both by the creature's ontological and economic relationship to God. Humanity's lot, its position in the cosmos, is shaped by the manner in which these relationships are realized and actualized. Here, however, their paradigms differ. For Irenaeus, the actualization of this relational being is analogized to the developing life of a human child, growing from infancy to adulthood and maturing in receptivity to divine glory. Disfigurement comes – both to the being of the child and the history of her growth – through the departure from God's intended economy, onto a path of stagnancy or, worse, regression.

---

23   See, for example, Augustine, *De haer.* 86.
24   So see Bray, *Holiness and the Will of God* 11.

For Tertullian, the paradigm is one not entirely his own in origin, but which he makes uniquely his in utilization: patience.[25] The human formation is that which is, from the first, grounded in God's presence, a relational reality manifested in its composition. Moreover, the creature constituted of this union of God and his creation is fashioned to wait patiently on the God who strengthens, develops and calls forth to full fruition the object of his creative activity. To be human is to wait patiently on the God of human life. To be impatient, therefore, becomes the paradigm for human corruption: it represents everything involved in the movement away from the divine reality intrinsic to human life – a reality actualized in phases and ages – to anything other than the creator's authentic presence.

While being equally as convinced as Irenaeus that the economic, progressive dimension of human existence in relation to God is key to understanding human life, and in turn becomes a source of our awareness of the God imaged in this human formation, Tertullian addresses this concept in more compositional terms. As we saw in the preceding chapter, Irenaeus' exploration of man as 'in the image of God' is articulated through some consideration of humanity's constitutive elements *per se* (thus there is a physical body and an immaterial, yet nonetheless corporeal, soul), but more extensively by theological considerations of how such elements image the life of the Son in relation to the Father and Spirit. Tertullian in a sense works along an opposite approach: the precision of how the composition images the divine lays behind, rather than at the forefront, of a more extensive compositional anthropology, considered in its various aspects and elements – especially with reference to the soul. A knowledge of what comprises the *persona* is key both to understanding the human, and the God who fashions it. Tertullian's understanding of human composition leads, in turn, to his notion of human economy, or the actual living-out of the life this composition engenders. It is in this economic aspect that Tertullian's paradigm of patience is discovered most directly, first through an analysis of its perversion – the impatience that is human sinfulness – and then through the vision of its reparation: the return to patience, enabled by Christ, that leads to renewed development in the Holy Spirit, fostering communion with the Father. As such, it is in the economic vision of man that the interconnection of the image with the God who is imaged is exposed most directly.

The basic paradigm employed by Tertullian for understanding humanity 'in the image and likeness of God' is that of a model or archetype represented in an image that bears its resemblance. His small quip in the *De praescriptione haereticorum*, that 'in all things, the reality precedes the image',[26] not only sets the standard for his interpretation, but forges a real connection between that which images

---

25   The most significant study of patience in Tertullian is that of Fredouille, which focuses extensively on the cultural and philosophical background to the theme in precedent writers: *Tertullien* 59–65, 363–410.
26   *Praes.* 29.5.

and that which is imaged. Where for Irenaeus, the basic analogy of image might be that of the *typos*, or seal impressed in wax which, to take up Minns' explanation, bears the contours of the metal that depresses it (as such, humanity as image bears the contours of the hands of the Father who fashion it, as we explored in the preceding chapter),[27] for Tertullian the basic analogy is that of a model realized in those handicrafts that image, or reflect, it. In its anthropological context, humanity images the model which is, as per Genesis 1.26, God, but which Tertullian clarifies (at *Adv. Prax.* 12.1–4) is Christ in particular. What is meant by this 'imaging of a model' will be explored as the present chapter unfolds, but at this juncture it is necessary to set the framework of his articulation as one in which the thing 'in the image' directly correlates to that whose image it is. Less abstractly, definition of man correlates to definition of Christ, Son of the Father, who is the model on which man is based. So Tertullian:

> The scripture [. . .] distinguishes between the persons [of the trinity]: *And God made man, in the image of God he made him* (Genesis 1.27). Why not 'his own image', if the maker was one and there was none in whose image he was making him? But there was one in whose image he was making him: namely, the Son's, who, because he was to be the surer and truer man, caused that man to be called his image who at that time had to be formed of clay, as the image and similitude of the true. (cf. Hebrews 9.24)[28]

We have here a concrete example of image-anthropology grounding articulation of divine reality in that of the human. Since man is fashioned after the 'model' of Christ, Son of the Father and sender of the Spirit, understanding the reality of man becomes a path to understanding the one who is his model, who is imaged in the human creature. Tertullian's intricate exploration of the compositional attributes of the human person, which we shall explore in the next section, is important precisely here: God is imaged in the complex fabric and formation of the human, and as such, a detailed awareness of that formation reveals the nature of the God who has created it – the one who stands behind and before Adam as the 'surer and truer man'; the one who is the model of Adam and the fulfilment of Adam.

The present chapter shall proceed along the following lines. We shall explore first, and in some detail, Tertullian's understanding of humanity as composite being – namely, of material body and immaterial soul, with substantial detail given to each. The importance of this discussion lies in his conviction that the soul is the primary force in human life, and is so as the means by which its development correlates to a maturing reception of the Holy Spirit. Having painted what is in some sense Tertullian's ideal picture of human nature, we will then explore his

---

27 See Minns, *Irenaeus* 86.
28 *Adv. Prax.* 12.3–4.

unique sense of its distortion as grounded in impatience; more precisely, an impatience of this development in receipt of the Spirit. It is in this context that Tertullian links his anthropological discussion to the trinitarian: impatient humanity requires salvation in the form of a renewal of union with God, wrought in the soul, which Tertullian understands as the work of the eternal Son through his entrance into the human condition. The latter half of the chapter will address the manner in which Tertullian's anthropological and economic understandings of sin are articulated in reference to a distinctly trinitarian – and heavily pneumatological – doctrine of God.

COMPOSITIONAL ELEMENTS IN THE HUMAN CREATURE

Fundamental to Tertullian's anthropology is the compositional assertion that the human person is a bi-partite reality of body and soul. Where it is more difficult to apply 'bi-partite' or 'tri-partite' terminology to the articulation of Irenaeus, with his alternating language of body/soul and body/soul/spirit, it is a direct matter to assign Tertullian the bi-partite label. From his earliest tracts this anthropological standpoint is clear. 'Man himself, guilty as he is of every iniquity', he writes in the *De spectaculis*, 'is not only a work of God – he is his image; yet both in soul and body he has severed himself from his maker'.[29] The basic biblical assertion, that in humanity is found both the material and immaterial, is cast by Tertullian into language gleaned from scripture, though substantially expanded. The conjunction of body and soul comprises the 'human', realizes the 'person', and their disjunction dissolves this human reality. This second point, central to Tertullian's later discussions, is present already in his early tract *On the testimony of the soul*:

> We maintain that after life has passed away you still remain in existence, and look forward to a day of judgement, and according to your desserts are assigned to misery or bliss, in either way of it forever. Moreover, that to be capable of this, your former substance must return to you, the matter and the memory of the same human being: for neither good nor evil could you feel if you were not again endowed with that sensitive bodily organisation; and there would be no grounds for judgement without the presentation of the very person to whom the sufferings of judgement were due.[30]

Tertullian defines 'human being' (*eiusdemque hominis*) as 'matter and memory', the latter term frequently a synonym in his corpus for the soul.[31] With an eye

---

29 *Spec.* 2.
30 *De Test.* 4.
31 Technically, Tertullian sees memory as a faculty of the soul (cf. *DA* 12.1; Dunn, *Tertullian* 37); but to prevent misunderstanding this faculty as distinct from or higher than the soul, Tertullian regularly uses the terms synonymously. See Nasrallah, *Ecstasy of Folly* 117–22 .

towards the final judgement, the just judgement of the *person*, the concrete individual under review at the final tribunal, could not be authentically *of that person*, unless she or he were fully present. Such a full presence requires the restored integration of body as well as soul.[32]

The full reality of the person is only encountered in the integration of humanity's material and immaterial elements. 'As death is defined as nothing else than the separation of body and soul', he writes elsewhere, 'life, which is the opposite of death, is susceptible of no other definition than the conjunction of body and soul'.[33] Already in his earlier treatise, Tertullian began to expound on the distinction of natural properties between these elements. His assertion that 'after life has passed away you still remain in existence' gives indication of what will be developed later as his conviction of the soul's inherent immortality; whilst his articulation of the person as 'matter and memory' in some sense foretells his lengthier descriptions of the manner in which the soul and body interact in the human formation. Body and soul may equally be parts of the human composition, but they are not equal parts as respects their lot and function. So will he write in the *De anima*:

> For the flesh is no doubt the house of the soul, and the soul is the temporary inhabitant of the flesh. The desire, then, of the lodger will arise from the temporary cause and special necessity which his designation suggests – with a view to benefit and improve the place of his temporary abode, while sojourning in it; not with the view, certainly, of being himself the foundation of the house, or himself its walls, or himself its support and roof, but simply and solely with the view of being accommodated and housed, since he could not receive such accommodation except in a sound and well-built house.[34]

This is a later reflection on body and soul than that we saw above – the *De anima* represents Tertullian's fullest reflection on the soul and, by consequence, the body in which its expresses its life – but the point of emphasis is unchanged. Just as the human being is persistently 'matter and memory', but not an amalgamation of these, so can the soul more specifically be described as 'dwelling in' the 'house' of the flesh, the two retaining in this arrangement their distinct and abiding properties. There is beneficial modification of the one (the flesh) by the other (the soul) for the sake of its improvement; but never does the soul/body combination become ontologically singular in its union. The person is always soul *and* body – distinct realities brought together in creation to a single life. This is essentially the same point made by Irenaeus: that while both body and soul are 'parts' of a man, neither

---

32 So for Waszink, *persona* for Tertullian is 'nec ita caro homo tanquam alia vis animae et alia' (with reference to *DA* 40.3 in particular); see his *Index verborum et locutionem quae Tertulliani De Anima libro continentur congessit* (Petri Hanstein, 1935) 164.

33 *DA* 27.

34 *DA* 38.

is man in exclusion. The 'man', the person, is what these are together. Tertullian offers a more verbose explanation of the idea, precisely because, as shall be seen later, it is in this persistent distinction that the component 'parts' of the human person find their iconic significance in imaging the divine life.

For reasons of their being persistently distinct, the soul and body may also be rent apart, and it is possible to consider the one without the other, beyond the realm of their union. Two arenas of discussion therefore present themselves: the 'before' of somatic and pneumatic existence, and the 'after' of the soul and body following their dissolution. It is the latter that draws Tertullian's attention first, treated both in his *On the testimony of the soul* and *Apologeticum*, occasioned by discussions on metempsychosis or the transmigration of souls encountered in contemporary philosophical discourse (he mentions the circulating views of Pythagoras and Laberius by name[35]). It is in the longer *Apologeticum* that his view is clearest:

> If there is any ground for the moving to and fro of human souls into different bodies, why may they not return into the very substance they have left, seeing this is to be restored, to be that which had been? [. . .] But [. . .] a man will come back from a man – any given person from any given person, still retaining his humanity; so that the soul, with its qualities unchanged, may be restored to the same condition, though not to the same outward framework. Assuredly, as the reason why restoration takes place at all is the appointed judgement, every man must needs come forth the very same who had once existed, that he may receive at God's hands a judgement, whether of good dessert or the opposite. And therefore the body too will appear; for the soul is not capable of suffering without the solid substance [the flesh]; [and for this reason also,] that it is not right that souls should have all the wrath of God to bear: they did not sin without the body, within which all was done by them.[36]

The soul, after the dissolution from the body that Tertullian has described as death (cf. *DA* 27), retains its existence 'with qualities unchanged', awaiting restoration to its 'solid substance' in which the immaterial is made material and the human person complete, ready for judgement and reward.

The implications of what Tertullian says here are important. The soul persists after bodily death, and persists unchanged; yet this soul is itself not 'a man', not a person (*persona*). This we have seen before. The person is – and this is the brunt of Tertullian's refutation of re-incarnation – only that soul in union with its body. Here the emphasis on *its* body is critical: the soul is not made human simply in conjunction with a vague or amorphous material element, or even with a generic

---

35   Pythagoras is mentioned in *Apol.* 11; and together with Laberius in *Apol.* 48.
36   *Apol.* 48.

human 'house' or frame. There is one body to which the soul belongs, which it perfects, in which it too grows. Once rent from this body at death, the soul only again comes to exist as fully human person when restored to union with *this* body, and no other. So while the soul may persist after death, and while the body may dissolve into the earth, the confession that human *persons* will be brought to judgement in the eschaton requires both that the soul again receive material embodiment (for it is 'not capable of suffering without its bodily element'); and also that the restored body must be the same that had previously died and dissolved – else the resulting formation would not be 'a given man from a man; a human person from a human person'.[37] In other words, belief in a final judgement requires not only a confession of the eternal reality of souls, but of particular, physical resurrection. When Tertullian comes to defend this claim – that specific bodies might be resurrected and restored to life, which his rhetorical opponents claim is less credible than a notion of re-incarnation that transmutes a soul into another bodily frame – he does so through a line of reasoning close to that of Irenaeus, in the latter's refutation of Valentinian objections to bodily resurrection. Tertullian writes:

> But how, you say, can a substance which has been dissolved be made to reappear again? Consider thyself, O man, and thou wilt believe in it! Reflect on what you were before you came into existence: nothing. For if you had been anything, you would have remembered it. You, then, who were nothing before you existed, reduced to nothing also when you cease to be, why may you not come into being again out of nothing, at the will of the same creator whose will created you out of nothing at the first? Will it be anything new in your case? You who were not, *were* made; when you cease to be again, you *shall* be made. Explain, if you can, your original creation, and then demand to know how you shall be re-created. Indeed, it will be still easier surely to make you what you were once, when the very same creative power made you without difficulty what you never were before.[38]

The body and soul are, for Tertullian, always unique and personal realities. There is no generic soul just as there is no generic body. Tertullian is ready to admit that this predication demands a leap of faith: if both it and the final judgement are true, there is mandated a belief that the bodies commonly seen to decompose in the earth will be resurrected and restored. Yet if God as creator could fashion them at the first 'from nothing' (Tertullian's employment of creation *ex nihilo* as evidence of God's power in this regard is another trait he shares in common with Irenaeus), is it any more incredible to believe he could re-create them after their

---

37 Though the body is not exactly identical; cf. his comment on 'not the same outer frameworks'. Perhaps Tertullian here alludes to the contents of 1 Corinthians 15.42–49, esp. v. 44.

38 *DA* 48; cf. Irenaeus, *Ref.* 5.3.2, 3.

dissolution?[39] Such discussion creates for Tertullian a context in which both soul and body have implicit value and, by extrapolation, the need for growth.

The question of beginnings

That which awaits the person at the eschaton is for Tertullian abundantly clear: the one fleshly body of the individual person is restored to its one soul, and the re-fashioned person stands before God and his judgement. But what of the beginnings? If the persistent distinction of soul and body implies the possibility of their separation at death, cannot they also be envisaged to exist before their union? The question is perhaps simple with regard to humanity as fashioned at the first: Genesis states that the physical frame existed prior to its union with the soul ('and the Lord God formed man of the dust of the ground, and breathed into his nostrils the breath of life; and man became a living being'). But with regard to the situation *writ large*, Tertullian takes a firm line: while the soul may be immaterial, even immortal, it is still a thing created, just as the body, and is created simultaneous to the body.[40] If there is any temporal distinction noted in the scriptural account of Adam's formation, this is absent in subsequent generation through procreation.

> Now we allow that life begins with conception, because we contend that the soul also begins from conception; life taking its commencement at the same moment and place that the soul does. Thus, then, the processes which act together to produce separation by death, also combine in a simultaneous action to produce life. If we assign priority to [the formation of] one of the natures, and a subsequent time to the other, we shall have further to determine the precise times of the semination, according to the condition and rank of each. And that being so, what time shall we give to the seed of the body, and what to the seed of the soul?[41]

Body and soul are not only both creations, but simultaneously fashioned creations – a point that reinforces his belief that the whole of a soul's 'life' is experienced in and manifested through its body. Even without his lost *De censu animae*, which forged the link between Tertullian's *Adverus Hermogenem* and the *De anima* by addressing the origin of the soul in presumably great detail, his point

---

39 It is worth noting that in the above passage, Tertullian's fond equation of 'soul' with 'memory' serves him argumentatively: a soul that previously existed in another body would, as memory objectified, 'remember' such an existence.
40 Though Alexandre takes a rather firmer line than I on the simultaneity of the creation of body and soul in Adam according to Tertullian, his conclusions here remain compelling; see Alexandre, *Une chair pour la gloire* 291–300, esp. 293.
41 *DA* 27; cf. 25.

is clear.[42] There is not a single moment in which the soul lives and grows without its corporeal 'house', which would be precisely the case if it pre-existed the body in formation. Rather, the two come into existence together, subsist and develop together; and while the soul may persist after the body's dissolution, Tertullian nowhere suggests that its development continues after bodily death. His claim that the soul 'with its qualities unchanged' will meet the body at the resurrection, cements this point. Pneumatic existence may continue after death, but complete personhood does not. This awaits its promised restoration in the kingdom, when body and soul are again joined unto life and united with God.

The significance of this conception on Tertullian's larger trinitarian anthropology of man as 'image of God' requires some extrapolation. By allowing for distinct existences of soul and body after death, while insisting that these do not exist separately before birth, and that they must be particularly reunited prior to final judgement, Tertullian provides concrete terminology to explain that it is neither body nor soul that constitute the person as 'in the image', but the conjunction of these. It is for this very reason that questions of anthropological composition hold such importance for him. It is in the conjunction and interrelation of distinct, compositionally unique elements, that God is imaged in the human person – not in any single element or attribute linked to the divine, but in the interrelation in man of those elements that make him what he is as human person. If the nature of the imaging is to be apprehended, clear knowledge of the characteristics of each of these elements is necessary, so that *how* they interrelate may be comprehended in relation to God who is imaged in their conjunction. The key element in this conjunction is for Tertullian the soul. This he explores more fully in the context of the full compositional reality, leading him in due course to his reflections on the life of the Spirit, Father and Son, joined to the life of the human person.

The developing life of the soul

Tertullian's comments on the divine creation of the soul (it is God who creates it, as much as it is God who creates all[43]) set the groundwork for exploring what the soul is understood to be. First, since the soul as part of the human person was created *ex nihilo*, not formed by an arrangement of substance, 'it may be seen that the soul is rather the offspring of God than of matter'.[44] There is a divine origin to

---

42 For speculation on the character and content of the *De censu animae*, see Waszink, *De Anima* 7*–14*. Whatever the specific contents of that tract may have been, it is clear from the references in the *De anima* explored by Waszink, as well as from the character of that tract proper, that Tertullian's address of the soul represents a continuation of his discourse on the creation of the world. See J. Daniélou, *The Origins of Latin Christianity*, tr. J. A. Baker and D. Smith (The Development of Christian Doctrine Before the Council of Nicaea, 3; London: Darton, Longman & Todd, 1977) 371.
43 See *De Test.* 2; cf. *DA* 3.4 – presumably the internal reference is to the *De Cens.* (so Waszink, *De Anima* 5*; Nasrallah, *Ecstasy of Folly* 115).
44 *DA* 22.

the soul, and this stands behind much of what Tertullian wishes to say; but one must not read this statement too dramatically. By the logic that asserts it, the body is also of divine origin, since it is equally created by God. Nonetheless, as the soul is the immaterial 'breath' of human life, whereas the body is of a material essence common with the cosmos, the soul bears a more direct connection to its maker. Daniélou's claim, that Tertullian is concerned above all to show that the soul has a different origin and *census* from the body, is borne out here.[45] It is even to be called 'divine', for reason of its sharing in the immaterial and eternal attributes of God's nature. So can Tertullian suggest:

> We, however [against Tertullian's reading of Plato], who allow no appendage to God (in the sense of equality), by this fact reckon the soul as very far below God: for we suppose it to be born, and thereby to possess something of a diluted divinity and an attenuated felicity, as the breath [of God], though not his Spirit; and although immortal – as this is an attribute of divinity – yet for all that passible, since this is an incident of a born condition, and consequently from the first capable of deviation from perfection and the right, and by consequence susceptible of a failure in memory.[46]

This dense text condenses Tertullian's view of the soul as connecting the theological and anthropological realms. The soul is not to be equated with God *qua* God; it is not an 'appendage' or emanation of the divine nature. An emerging Platonic anthropology in the early third century, as in some sense a reformation in the popular mind of a loose Stoic model popular in the second, is a phenomenon Tertullian rejects with vigour.[47] As regards God's nature as divine being, the soul is not only slightly 'diluted' in its divinity, but 'very far below God'. It is, after all, a thing created – in human procreative terms generated, born – and 'that which has received its constitution by being made or by being born is by nature capable of being changed'.[48] But, second, the thing born is so of God's breath, thus possessing attributes of the divine, just as human breath possesses characteristics gleaned from its source (warmth from the lungs, moisture from the mouth, etc.). Still, while this breath comes directly from God, the breath and God's Spirit (the Holy Spirit) are not one and the same. Tertullian, like Irenaeus, sees the divine breath of Genesis 2.7 as spiritual but not the Spirit proper – though as coming from God the Father, Father of the Spirit, it is not disconnected from him. Third, and significantly, the soul, which is thus a created and generated reality born of the Father's breath, is by virtue of that birth passible, even as it is eternal. It shares in the divine attribute of immortality, yet creation nonetheless implies transforma-

---

45   See Daniélou, *Origins of Latin Christianity* 375.
46   *DA* 24.
47   On this cultural shift, see Munier, *Petite vie* 53–55.
48   *DA* 21.

tion. A thing made is a thing capable of change, a change that may be to the better or the worse. This is a note of interpretation we have already seen in Irenaeus, where it was key in understanding his articulation of human reality as necessarily *in history*. It is here reiterated in Tertullian, and it will similarly reappear in every author we examine. The finitude and mutability of the created, held alongside confession of the eternity and immutability of the creator, is a basic building block of Christian anthropological discussion.

These various assertions combine to form a picture of the human soul that is itself profoundly dynamic, even before it is examined in light of its necessary union with the body – a fact that causes Tertullian to see the soul as primary means of understanding how the trinitarian life of Father, Son and Spirit is imaged in the human person. The soul is a thing divine, receptive of God's divinity, through which divine attributes are made the proper characteristics of the human. A revealing passage in the *Testimony of the Soul* has Tertullian query the reality of divine prophecy and revelation, ultimately to exclaim that such prophetic insights come as 'outbursts of the soul', as teachings 'of a nature congenital [to it] and the secret deposit of inborn knowledge'.[49] The divine property of God's foreknowledge becomes a human property, because the soul is the partaker of divine attributes. Nonetheless, it partakes always as created, generated entity. While the body may be more impatient than the soul (cf. *On patience* 13), still both are finite realities. With this background in mind, Tertullian can make his bold claim that the soul in fact grows and develops, just as the body grows and develops. It is not a generic 'divine principle' any more than the body is a generic material element. Rather, just as the body remains ever body, yet grows over time and through the phases of life, so the soul possesses always its same created nature, yet develops in its existence over time and through the same phases of life as does the body. The two are precisely co-ordinated. An important passage from the *De anima* refines this discussion:

> Here, therefore, we draw our conclusion, that all the natural properties of the soul are inherent in it as parts of its substance, and that they grow and develop along with it, from the very moment of its own origin at birth. Just as Seneca says, whom we so often find on our side: 'There are implanted within us the seeds of all the arts and periods of life; and God, our Master, secretly produces our mental dispositions'[50] – that is, from the germs that are implanted and hidden in us by means of infancy, and these are the intellect: for from these our natural dispositions are evolved. Now, even the seeds of plants have one form in each kind, but their development varies: some open and expand in a healthy and perfect state, while others either improve or degenerate, owing to the conditions of weather and soil, and from the appliance of labour and care

---

49 *De Test.* 5.
50 See Seneca, *Epist.* 66, 67.

[. . .], in like manner, the soul may well be uniform in its seminal origin, although multiform by the process of nativity.[51]

Tertullian is the first Christian author to assert in so direct a manner this developmental characteristic of the soul. It is nowhere as clear in Irenaeus, though one might argue it is implied in his developmental discussion overall. For its uniqueness, Daniélou characterized it as part of Tertullian's 'profoundly original' expansion on earlier thought, specifically that of Irenaeus; namely, that for Tertullian there is a process by which not only the body, but the soul itself, advances and becomes spiritual.[52] The soul changes and grows over time, and while all souls should be considered uniform in nature in that they are created equally *as souls* by God, the necessarily individual course of development of each (begun in 'the process of nativity') means that souls *as found* in realized, individual human persons will express infinite variation. Tertullian draws the parallel of flowers from seeds: every poppy is born of a poppy-seed, each of which is equally 'poppy' in nature and each of which will produce the same species of flower. Yet each poppy is unique, for each encounters different accidents of development – soil quality, water, sunlight, etc. This can be exactly co-ordinated to the developmental progress of the soul:

> How much more, in fact, will those accidental circumstances have to be noticed, which, in addition to the state of one's body or one's health, tend to sharpen or to dull the intellect! It is sharpened by learned pursuits, by the sciences, the arts, by experimental knowledge, business habits and studies; it is blunted by ignorance, idle habits, inactivity, lust, inexperience, listlessness and vicious pursuits. [. . .] It is evident how great must be the influences which so variously affect the one nature of the soul, since they are commonly regarded as separate 'natures'. Still, they are not different species, but casual incidents of one nature and substance – even of that which God conferred on Adam, and made the mould of all. Casual incidents they will always remain, but never will they become specific [i.e. natural] differences.[53]

The developmental maturation of the physical body is read by Tertullian – given his insistence on the unified character of soul and body as 'person' – as exactly paralleled in this developmental quality of the soul. Nowhere is this clearer than at *De anima* 37:

> We have already demonstrated the conjunction of the body and the soul, from the concretion of their very seminations to the complete formation of the foetus. We now maintain their conjunction likewise from the birth onwards;

---

51   *DA* 20.
52   So Daniélou, *Origins of Latin Christianity* 377–82.
53   *DA* 20.

in the first place, because they both grow together, only each in a different manner suited to the diversity of their nature – the flesh in magnitude, the soul in intelligence; the flesh in material condition, the soul in sensibility.

Carefully qualified later in the passage to make clear that the soul never increases 'in substance' – that is, it never becomes 'larger' or more substantively soul than it is at its creation[54] – Tertullian here spells out a distinctly developmental conception of economic personhood. It is not merely the bodily substance of the person that grows and develops in the progression of history, but the immaterial soul as well. Tertullian has articulated in more detail than Irenaeus the manner in which humanity's development relates to its participation in God's glory. Irenaeus had argued that humanity 'could not have received' God's full glory at its initial creation, nor, if such glory had been received, could humanity have retained it (cf. *Refutation* 4.38, 39); but the defence he gives for this statement is entirely physical in orientation. Just as a human child cannot eat solid foods in infancy, and so a mother gives instead milk, so God revealed his glory to primal man in a lesser degree than he might otherwise have done. What remains unanswered, at least in a technical sense in the writings of Irenaeus, is precisely how the physical analogy of infantile bodies and solid food relates to the transcendent reality of God's glory revealed in the immaterial soul, which Irenaeus sees as its means of communication to the body. With Tertullian this is explained precisely through his articulation of the soul's development, too, from nativity to its adulthood. This development is primarily moral and intellectual, but also a development of function, of receptive capability. Its capacities increase as its natural properties are 'drawn forth' in the process of development, a process that is intimately connected to the developmental maturation of the body – so much so that Tertullian can speak of the 'puberty of the soul, which coincides with that of the body, that they attain both together to this full growth at about the fourteenth year'. More generally, the stages of development of the soul 'advance by a gradual growth through the stages of life and develop themselves in different ways'.[55]

The body and soul in relation: actively imaging in the Spirit

That which is divine in attribute, then, grows and advances in actualization. However, while the soul grows just as the body, the two are, as we have already

---

54   See the remainder of *DA* 20. This line of argumentation grounds a rather humorous discussion earlier, at *DA* 32, where Tertullian suggests – apparently as a 'reasonable' merit for rejecting metempsychosis – that a human soul could never grow to such a size as to fill the frame of an elephant; nor could the soul, accustomed to bodily life in a dry (i.e. airy) climate, reasonably exist in the watery surroundings of an eel, etc. Humorous imagery aside, Tertullian, like Irenaeus, argues that the soul does indeed have a specific shape, similar to that of its material body.

55   Both quotations from *DA* 38.

seen, never technically one. To the contrary, the development of the soul is to be
seen as the maturation of that element in the human person which allows the
developing body to become a thing joined to God. The growing soul corrects and
perfects the growing body. As such, while both are requirements for complete
personhood, the soul takes a place of anthropological precedence as that which
glorifies the body and raises it beyond the level of mere corporeality. It is this
conviction that grounds Tertullian's theology of martyrdom: were body and soul
of absolute equality, the martyr's lot would be the defeat of the former as well as
the latter. But the soul bears and transforms the body's weakness, communicating
to the flesh the divine attributes (e.g. immortality) it has received as the breath
of God.[56] So Tertullian can quote Christ in his exhortation to the martyrs:

> From the saying of our Lord we know that the flesh is weak, the spirit willing.
> Let us not, withal, take delusive comfort from the Lord's acknowledgment
> of the weakness of the flesh. For precisely on this account he first declared the
> spirit willing, that he might show which of the two ought to be subject to
> the other – that the flesh might yield obedience to the spirit, the weaker to the
> stronger, the former thus getting strength from the latter. Let the spirit
> converse with the flesh about their common salvation, thinking no longer of
> the troubles of the prison, but of the wrestle and conflict for which they are the
> preparation.[57]

'The spirit is willing but the flesh is weak' summarizes Tertullian's belief, more
scientifically expressed, in the anthropological precedence of the soul. Both it
and the body are created elements in developmental progression from birth to resurrection, but the soul grants to the body the divine qualities that make the whole
of the human person godlike.

If it is the case, then, that body and soul develop in harmony and exist as the singular being that is the human person, it is Tertullian's logical conclusion that the
developmental progress of each is of effect on the other. As the soul progresses in
its immaterial development, its divine attributes are communicated to the body.
So, too, with the body's growth: affairs seeming to pertain solely to corporeal
existence (e.g. the eating of only vegetables in Eden, as Tertullian, like Irenaeus,
reads the primal diet) are in fact 'in the interest of the soul also', for only in the
body does the soul have its progressive existence.[58] Similarly, development
need not always be positive, and just as the body can become sick or suffer injury
which effects the person's state of soul, so too can the soul become infirm, which

---

56 Including its proper existence as *body*, rather than simply matter. So Alexandre: 'La chaire
n'existe pas sans l'âme puisque, précisément, elle tient du rôle fondamental de l'âme, principe de vie,
de ne pas être un amas inerte de matières diverses, mais de vivre'; *Une chair pour la gloire* 293.
57 *Ad Mart.* 4.
58 See *DA* 38.

infirmity is passed to the body (so *On prayer* 29). Tertullian affirms this principle explicitly:

> The soul certainly sympathises with the body and shares in its pain, whenever it is injured by bruises, wounds and sores. The body, too, suffers with the soul and is united with it (whenever it is afflicted with anxiety, distress, or love) in the loss of vigour which its companion sustains, whose shame and fear it testifies by its own blushes and paleness.[59]

Tertullian is clearly suggesting some manner of non-material corporeality to the soul. While it is evident to him that the soul is immaterial, it is nonetheless impossible to think that a bruise inflicted on the material body could in any way wound the soul unless there were a certain corporeality to the latter. This is in line with his argument at *De anima* 38 on the 'shape' of souls vis-à-vis bodies, and is a point of parallel with Irenaeus, who not only insists that souls have a corporeal shape that persists after death and is equal in form to the body previously inhabited, but who also claims that the body's 'slower velocity' hampers the soul in its activities.[60] So too with Tertullian. Waszink has argued that this question of the corporeality of the soul is in fact the central thesis of the *De anima* in its entirety, a sentiment echoed by Barnes with reference specifically to *DA* 5.6.[61] The idea is not a mere flourish (though we might also add, against Waszink, that it is not necessarily sign either of the influence of pagan physicians), but part of an inherited tradition of Christian anthropological discussion we have seen already in Irenaeus, and will see again in later writers. But it is precisely that: part of this discussion, not the whole, and Nasrallah is right to question too emphatic a claim of its centrality to the *De anima*.[62] Tertullian's assertion of an immaterial corporeality to the soul serves to tie together his declarations of both the persistent distinction of body and soul on the one hand, and their intimate relation on the other.

It is pertinent to reflect further on the fact that we have now seen this concept of the soul's 'corporeality' – which Alexandre described as at first seeming 'une pensée plus naïve qu'incompréhensible'[63] – present in both of the major authors thus far addressed. This is not an accident of circumstance, nor evidence for a widespread adherence to the anthropological vision of any specific philosophical school, for there is none that uniformly unites these sources. We might take issue with Dunn's claim that Tertullian is simply following the Stoics, though agree

59 *De Test.* 5.
60 Irenaeus, *Ref.* 2.33.4; see above, p. 38.
61 See Waszink, *Index verborum* 48; Barnes, *Tertullian* 207.
62 Nasrallah, *Ecstasy of Folly* 116.
63 Alexandre, *Une chair pour la gloire* 241.

with Alexandre that he does borrow from them.[64] It is, however, evidence of
the importance the early Church laid upon showing the intimate connection
of soul to body, each as *actual entities* that comprise the human person. While
Tertullian may at times loosely define the soul as the 'immaterial element' in
man, in a wider reading it is clear that the soul is not a principle or concept. It is a
quid, a 'thing' that is part of the person, and which as corporeal (yet immaterial)
possesses the 'genre particulier de corporéité': specific mannerisms and finite
limitations.[65] To single out Tertullian, as many have, as a 'materialist' in this regard
is to ignore the common thread in his predecessors. The soul's corporeality, its
'shape' that persists after separation from the body, is paramountly a means of
showing its connection to that body. Surely there is in this little more than implicit
reflection on the Gospels, wherein the 'rich man' in Hades 'recognises' Lazarus
the poor beggar, now in the bosom of Abraham – soul recognizing soul after
departure from the body (cf. Luke 16.19–31).

With regard to his larger anthropology, Tertullian's qualifications on what is
involved in the body and soul that together make up the human person all point
towards a key principle that connects the human in the image to the God who is
imaged. As we have seen, the soul is in receipt of divine attributes as the breath
of God, but is not itself God, nor the Spirit of God. Yet it is through the human
soul that the reality of God's power is revealed and manifested in the corporeal
person. How does this come about? Tertullian's response is already intimated in
his address of the divine 'breath' as that which transmits divine properties (e.g.
immortality; see again *De anima* 24). In its transmission of attributes from God
to man, the soul, while not itself the Spirit of God, nonetheless is that which
brings the Spirit to the handiwork.

It is true that the ruling mind [i.e. the soul] easily communicates the gifts of
the Spirit with its bodily habitation.[66]

It is worth quoting again a passage from Irenaeus, to show the similarity of
approach these authors share in this regard:

As the body animated by the soul is certainly not itself the soul, but has
fellowship with the soul as long as God desires, so also the soul herself is
not life, but partakes in the life bestowed on her by God. [. . .] Thus the soul
and the life which it possesses must be understood as separate existences.[67]

---

64   Dunn, *Tertullian* 37. Alexandre, *Une chair pour la gloire* 241–50, discusses the Stoic influences
on Tertullian's conception of the corporeality of the soul, principally via Zenon and Soranus, as
also Chryssipus.

65   Alexandre, *Une chair pour la gloire* 253.

66   *De Pat.* 13.

67   Irenaeus, *Ref.* 2.34.4. Waszink draws the connection also to *Ref.* 5.12.2; see Waszink, *De
Anima* 13*.

For Tertullian, as for Irenaeus, the soul's vivifying and divinizing role lies not in its own immortality or immateriality, but in its function as the created means by which the uncreated properties of the divine are brought into the realm of the human – by which the Father's life is, through the Holy Spirit, wrought within the human frame. Tertullian grounds this notion firmly in his conception of the compositional structure of man: the soul that conveys divine life is spiritual, formed of God's breath (*afflatus*), yet precisely as being breath *of spirit*, is not spirit itself. What Waszink characterized as Tertullian's inheritance of Soranus' keen interest in etymology, comes into play here. Tertullian's famous criticism of Hermogenes' attempted re-writing of Genesis 2.7 from what Tertullian considers the original πνοή ('breath') to πνεῦμα ('spirit'), confusing *afflatus* and *spiritus* in a manner he finds incredible in the context of a genuine image-anthropology.[68] The human soul as *afflatus* is iconic of spirit, in a participatory sense of image, as Tertullian states in his tract against Marcion:

> *Afflatus*, observe then, is less than spirit, although it comes from spirit; it is the spirit's gentle breeze, but it is not the spirit. Now a breeze is rarer than the wind, and although it proceeds from the wind, yet a breeze is not the wind. One may call a breeze the image of the spirit. In the same manner, man is the image of God, that is, of spirit, for God is spirit. *Afflatus* is therefore the image of the spirit; and the image is not in any case equal to the thing itself.[69]

Here Tertullian places primacy on the spiritual in assessing humanity as 'in the image', on the twofold grounds that 'God is spirit', and that which is imaged is always lesser than that which it images. The end result of this consideration is a definition of the human soul, as *afflatus*, connected as image to the Spirit of the Father. Just as a breeze conveys a measure of the wind, so the human soul conveys to the body a measure of the divine Spirit. As such, Tertullian's compositional anthropology culminates with a thrust into the economic receipt of the divine: the 'what' of the human composition provides the basis and context for articulating the 'how' by which that composition comes into and maintains its receipt of divine life. The Spirit of the Father is, as Nasrallah characterizes it, 'accidental to [the soul's] nature'; yet as the latter is formed of God's breath, it is intrinsically bound to receive the Spirit – to 'breathe' (*spirat*) that which is, by definition, something 'other'.[70]

Not only does such an anthropology lack the static characteristics so often assumed of it, in a sense Tertullian has gone even further than Irenaeus – so often

---

68 See ibid. 13*, 27*. Cf. Leal, *La Antropología* 36–40, who, following Braun, argues that *spiritus* equates for Tertullian to the *substantia* of God; so R. Braun, *Deus Christianorum. Recherches sur le vocabulaire doctrinal de Tertullien* (Paris, 1962) 285.

69 *Adv. Marc.* 2.9.2, 3.

70 Cf. *DA* 11.1; Nasrallah, *Ecstasy of Folly* 132. Her comments in this section (pp. 131–34) are among the best available on the matter to hand.

thought the ultimate early 'dynamist' – in asserting that not only is the composite *person* developmental, but so too are each of its constituent elements. As these elements mature in their natural processes of growth, so does the realized person they engender grow in its receipt of the Spirit, unifying both the composite elements and the integral whole more fully with the Father. Further, Tertullian's discussion on the effects one element's development may have on the other, suggests that the 'what' and the 'how' of a Christian anthropology are related in both directions. Not only does the composition of the human creature influence how it is to live and engage in the economy, so also does the economic development of the individual influence his or her compositional qualities. An injured body defines, to some degree, the manner in which the person may live out his life (composition effecting economy), but so also a tortured or abused life may effect the soul or body themselves (economy effecting composition). As such, there is for Tertullian no real manner in which a Christian anthropology can address the constitutive elements of the human person, without simultaneously addressing the economic questions of human life. It is primarily for this reason, and not on account of some spontaneous rigour, that he is so concerned throughout his life – indeed ever more so as he aged – with the practical affairs of dress and speech, relationships and protocol. What we do does not simply relate to who we are; for Tertullian, what we do *is* who we are in a very direct sense, as the two become one in the progression of economy.

*   *   *

Tertullian's elaborate address of the compositional elements in humanity, which has warranted so lengthy a treatment, is important for a number of reasons. First, it gives an extensive grounding to the 'how' of human relation to the divine, inasmuch as it defines human nature in terms of composite elements designed to function in harmony as the means of receipt of divine life. The body exists as 'house' of the soul, which itself exists as the immaterial organ of receipt of the Spirit. As created, both body and soul are mutable, in flux, developing in stages that equate not only to their own maturation as created realities, but to the maturation of the composite person, with particular respect to the interaction with God they enable. Humanity's relationship to God is as developmental as each of its constitutive elements.

Second, Tertullian's elaborations on the nature of the soul in particular, demonstrate the degree to which compositional anthropology is articulated in relation to a vision of God the Father as actively present with and through his Spirit. It is the 'things *of the Holy Spirit*' that the soul transmits to its body. Man, as 'in the image of God', is articulated as in receipt of the Spirit of the Father, not as in some vague sense reflecting a 'God' generically or generally defined. God, which for Tertullian as much as for Irenaeus is the title proper to the Father, is imaged in man precisely inasmuch as he partakes of this Father's Spirit. And so, humanity's imaging of its divine 'model', conveys the reality of God the Father in relation to his Spirit – a theological doctrine given shape by anthropological discussion.

It is notable that Tertullian has thus far elaborated his key anthropological points without substantial reference to Christ – a characteristic that would seem to set him apart from Irenaeus. Here there is evidence of a difference of approach that will become more pronounced when Tertullian comes to consider economy and patience, the subject of our next section. Where Irenaeus' confession of Christ was centred in the Recapitulator as 'Adam' and thus the central reality and grounding of the image, Tertullian's confession of Christ is centred in the reality of the Son as Restorer. The Christ, the Messiah, is the one who saves, the one who restores humankind to righteousness before the Father. It is in this light that his address of Christ's relationship to anthropological matters focuses on the role of restoration – the one who renews, and newly enables, human receipt of the Spirit of the Father. Tertullian's reading of the particular place and function of the Son and Spirit in an anthropological vision is thus different from that of Irenaeus, occasioned by concentration on different aspects of Christ's incarnate mission; yet in both, anthropological discussion is directly tied in to a trinitarian articulation of God. This 'Trinity' – and Tertullian is the first to employ the title as such – is the reality imaged in the human; the articulation of each is and must be intertwined with the other. This becomes obvious when Tertullian turns from questions of composition to those of economy, of how that composition lives and exists in the cosmos in temporal history. In this context, Tertullian's confession of Jesus Christ chiefly as obedient redeemer, inspires a reading of sin and the human condition that unites his redemptive person to the fundamental concerns of anthropology – the nature of the *anthropos* he saves – and demonstrates the connection of trinitarian redemption to a trinitarian anthropology.

GROWING IMPATIENT: THE ECONOMIC DISFIGUREMENT OF THE ONE RACE[71]

The economy in which the creature lives out the life granted by God in its composition, is none other than the historical context of life initiated in Eden. Adam's story is not, for Tertullian, an historical myth of genesis, but the protological account of the economy still realized in the cosmos. It is here that the history of progress and development, which is intertwined for Tertullian with the substance of human composition, begins. It is this same story that continues in the present historical human experience.

---

71   This section, and following portions of this chapter, incorporate materials I have published previously in M. C. Steenberg, 'Impatience and Humanity's Sinful State in Tertullian of Carthage', *VigChr* 62 (2008), 107–32. I am grateful to Brill for kind permission to include re-worked portions of that article in the present volume.

Tertullian, like Irenaeus, is convinced that the concept of continuity between Adam and present-day humanity cannot be simply aesthetic. The common history of the human race is not common merely because one is able, in some exegetical sense, to see oneself as part of Adam's heritage. The reality is concrete. The common history of the human race is grounded in the fact that human persons are genuinely one in natural lineage – 'one race', despite unbridled individuality. As Tertullian frames it, in a passage to which we have already referred in part:

> It is evident how great must be the influences which so variously affect the one nature of the soul, since they are commonly regarded as separate 'natures'. Still they are not different species, but casual incidents of one nature and substance (*quando non species sint, sed sortes naturae et substantiae unius*) – even of that which God conferred on Adam, and made the mould of all.[72]

The 'one nature' conferred on Adam is the common nature possessed by all human beings. We have seen how Tertullian uses the analogy of seeds and flowers to account for the diversity that may arise from a common nature: so different and distinct may the independent realities be that they seem like – and may in everyday language be called – 'different natures', but this is to use the term loosely. Tertullian can at times speak of a 'second nature', which Nasrallah describes as 'almost original to the first', but this is precisely to show its economic, rather than ontological, character.[73] All humans are of one nature, since all have their nature inherited from Adam. If one were to impute individual characteristics to nature rather than the circumstances of development, one would arrive, Tertullian argues, at the impossible conclusion that in Adam were present all variations of human character – from piety and peace to murderous rage. 'For all these discordances ought to have existed in him as the fountainhead, and thence to have descended to us in an unimpaired variety, if such variety had been due to nature'.[74]

The variations of human individuality are not, therefore, to be attributed to the foundation of nature, which is common across the race. Whatever attribute of human existence one might investigate, Tertullian's logic argues that its individuating marks must be understood as springing from economy, rather than natural particularity. This is true even of the calling as Christian, as opposed to Pagan, for 'we are of your [Pagan] stock and nature: men are made, not born, Christians'.[75] It is this notion that leads Tertullian to state:

> Every soul, then, by reason of its birth, has its nature in Adam until it is born again in Christ; moreover, it is unclean (*immunda*) all the while that it remains

---

72   *DA* 20, quoted more extensively above, p. 72. See Waszink, *De Anima* 281–82.
73   See Nasrallah, *Ecstasy of Folly* 124.
74   *DA* 20.
75   *Apol.* 18.

without this regeneration; and because unclean, it is actively sinful (*peccatrix autem, quia immunda*), and suffuses even the flesh – by reason of their conjunction – with its own shame. Now although the flesh is sinful and we are forbidden to walk in accordance with it, and its works are condemned as lusting against the spirit, and men on its account are censured as carnal, yet the flesh has not such ignominy on its own account. For it is not of itself that it thinks anything or feels anything for the purpose of advising or commanding sin.[76]

All are of one stock, all the inheritors of the nature of Adam. As such, there can be no grounds for a racial heritage to Christian profession, nor indeed any other individuating feature in the diversity of humankind. All are human, commonly human, until redeemed in Christ. Yet Tertullian has, in this passage, introduced a notion of inherited *sinfulness* into his anthropological framework. All are not merely 'in Adam', but thereby 'unclean' and therefore 'actively sinful'. How is it that deviations from the nature created by God, which we have seen Tertullian address as always the result of economic development and not difference of nature, are described by him as part of the stock inherited from Adam? Tertullian's comments in *De anima* 40 raise the question of how one can understand sin, which is an active (and thus economic) reality of a person in developmental history, as effecting the nature in which all persons exist.

Tertullian's analysis can only be understood in light of the interrelation of composition and economy that is the central point of his anthropology. It is not only that nature effects economy, but that economy effects the nature realized within it. This is so in an understandable sense in the perspective of a given human individual, but Tertullian goes beyond this in advancing the anthropological vision of 'one race' to the same end as Irenaeus had done only a few decades earlier: that the nature realized in the human individual is the nature of the race *in toto*. One is neither divided nor divisible from the nature that lies within her, and this the nature that lies within all. The acts of the one are significant not only for the one, but for the many who draw their existence from the same foundation or nature. So can the martyr sanctify the whole community; so can the faithful wife hallow the disbelieving husband (cf. 1 Corinthians 7.14); so can the New Adam save the old. The 'one race' of the human family is one by blood, by genuine relational connection at the ontological level, implying the reality of the whole in the particularity of the individual.

It is in this light that Tertullian sees as straightforward the influence of Adam's sin on the individual realities of future generations. It is impossible for him to accept that the nature itself is distorted ('for that which is derived from God is

---

76 *DA* 40; cf. Waszink, *De Anima* 448–53 for a discussion that notes a distinction between 'original sin' and 'the sinfulness caused by evil spirits'. Waszink connects *DA* 40 directly to the classifications at the end of 39.

rather obscured than extinguished'[77]), but the economy in which the one human nature is actualized, in which it develops, is altered. This alteration of economy, in turn, effects the beings that develop in it. Specifically, the manner of coming-into-being of future possessors of human nature is distorted across the board. Tertullian explicitly connects this to the procreative act: the very means by which the generation of new persons is enabled, itself falls to the passion of lust. As such, the economy of life is from conception an economy of fallen life.[78] The effects of the first transgression are passed on to future generations in the persistence of the economic mire into which the nature is thrust from the first moment of conception. Yet it is inauthentic to claim that the inherited aspects of that sin are only of effect and not of substance. This may be true at an analytical level, but Tertullian's grasp of the interrelation of economy and composition makes clear that an inherited effect brings about a mis-developed nature. The nature itself is not transformed, but the changes in the context of history yield its deficient development.

The significance of this perception of sin, and the preponderance of sin in the world, to Tertullian's interrelation of anthropology and a doctrine of the nature of God, cannot be overestimated. The manner in which he understands sin and its effects in primarily economic, rather than ontological terms – as history effecting a nature's realization, rather than altering the nature itself – is the grounding for his exploration of the conquest of sin in terms of a newly ennobled economy of human relationship to God. It is not *what* humanity is that is altered by sin, but the *how* of the human-divine relationship, and the manner in which that disfigured relation alters its mode of growth. Tertullian's insight, in keeping economy and ontology distinct whilst nonetheless integrating their effects on one another, gives his perception of humanity, sin and redemption a particular weight. He does not view sin as a contortion of nature, with the problems of ontological alteration and challenges of redemption that such a view poses; nor does he see sin and its consequences as 'purely economic' – choices and their consequences alone – with the difficulties posed by that view of sin's universal preponderance.

It is worth fleshing out this distinction more carefully, for Tertullian is often considered to be an early exemplar of the doctrine of 'original sin' as later put forward by Augustine, if not in fact a direct precursor to Augustine's thought. Otherwise balanced studies regularly claim a source in Tertullian for this emerging doctrine, crediting him with 'laying the foundation' for later Augustinian teaching,[79] or 'making the first moves towards a doctrine of original sin'.[80] It is a dangerous game to read prolepsis and foundation-laying by earlier sources into the thought of later writers, especially one so prolific as Augustine, whose understanding of

---

77   *DA* 41.
78   See his rather graphic discussion to this effect at *De Carn.* 4; cf. Psalm 50.5: 'Behold, I was brought forth in iniquity and in sin did my mother conceive me'.
79   See Bray, *Holiness and the Will of God* 81.
80   Osborn, *First Theologian* 163.

'original sin' is itself not well-understood; yet such crediting persists. Tertullian's main point remains, however, that the sinful qualities in man 'must be supposed to arise from the mutability of its accidental circumstances, and not from the appointment of nature'.[81] As we have already pointed out, Nasrallah helpfully clarifies Tertullian's language of a sinful 'second nature' as not being ontological at its root. This seems to be Osborn's oversight in assessing 'second nature' language, for he treats it as a nature like in essence to the first – a new ontological reality initiated by sin.[82] Yet for Tertullian, the natural reality of human life can only be obscured but not extinguished, precisely because it comes from God. And here the brunt of his distinction: to obscure is a verb, an act, an aspect of economy. Tertullian nowhere suggests that the economic act of 'obscuring' ontologizes the fallen or broken disfigurement that results; but just as a disfigured gramophone will inaccurately render the music contained on any good record placed upon it, so a distorted economy will yield a disfiguration of every human nature realized within it. This remains true, despite the fact that those natures retain always their proper, natural character. So while nature may remain unthwarted (and as such there can never be authentic talk of a 'fallen nature' in Tertullian), one can still speak of a guilt passed on from one generation to the next – not because children are held accountable for their parents' crimes, but because in the distorted economy the children realize the fundamental crimes of their ancestors. So Tertullian suggests rather boldly:

> Albeit Israel washed daily all his limbs over, yet is he never clean. His hands, at all events, are ever unclean, eternally dyed with the blood of the prophets, and of the Lord himself; and on that account, as being hereditary culprits from privity to their fathers' crimes, they do not dare even to raise them unto the Lord, for fear some Isaias should cry out, for fear Christ should utterly shudder.[83]

So, too, can he speak of proper guilt and pardon in terms Irenaeus would not have used, precisely because he is able to attribute a universal disfiguration of nature to a cause of economy.[84] The nature of every person is disfigured, and every human individual guilty of sin, because of an inheritance *of economy* that causes an ever-pure and ever-godly nature to be realized personally after the sin common from Adam. This is Tertullian at his most insightful. It is inasmuch as he distinguishes between the ontological and the economic in the human person – and not, as some have claimed, because he maintains a materialism that cannot distinguish

---

81 *DA* 41. A clear treatment of the problems at stake in this debate is found in Leal, *La Antropología* 119–25.
82 See Osborn, *First Theologian* 165–66.
83 *De Or.* 14.
84 See, for example, his discussion at *De Or.* 7 on the Lord as 'only guiltless one' and honest humans as those who admit their inbuilt guilt and beg for pardon.

between spirit and matter[85] – that Tertullian is able to see sin as universal to the human condition whilst nonetheless external to human nature. Here one locates the full force behind one of his most famous comments:

> Thus some men are very bad and some very good; yet the souls of all form but one genus (*unum omnes animae genus*). Even in the worst there is something good, and in the best something bad.[86]

All are sinful and all genuinely guilty of the sin of their ancestors, not by imputation, but by an economic making-real of the ancestral sin in the pleroma of human individuality. Here Tertullian's assessment of the *imago Dei* as a fashioned reproduction, imaging its model, further serves his anthropological paradigm.[87] It is God himself, and more precisely (as we have seen) the Son of the Father, who is the 'model', the reality imaged in man. No act of human depravity can alter this divine model at the core of human nature, only disfigure its realization.[88]

The question then becomes how the one race comes to actualize, economically, not the purity of its created nature but a disfigurement of it. It is here that Tertullian spells out his paradigm of 'impatience' as descriptive of the human condition. Antecedently, the primal condition of the human economy is described as one of patience (*patientia*), for 'patience is set over the things of God, that one can obey no precept nor fulfil any good work if estranged from it'.[89] This has been re-stated most potently in the modern era by Fredouille: 'sans la vertu de patience, l'homme se trouve dans l'impossibilité d'être agréable a Dieu. La patience est, pour Tertullien, une vertu éminente et privilégié'.[90] It is, as such, an attribute of economy established by God at the beginning of creation, the context within which its intended form is to be realized. Tertullian is making more than a poetic characterization of the human-divine relationship, as if patience equated simply to the creature's trust in its maker. Building on his compositional anthropology, with its core belief in the necessarily developmental maturation of body and soul, Tertullian has established a conception of human life that mandates a temporal aspect. Growth requires time (here Tertullian makes a point parallel to that of Irenaeus' developmental discussion in *Refutation* 4), but he also spells out that the time required for growth must be *applied to the project of growing*. Maturation may require temporality, but temporality does not necessarily engender maturation. Temporal advance may occasion disfiguration, injury, may even enmesh ever more firmly a maturational stagnancy. It is for this reason that the ontological mandate that human beings, as creatures, exist in time, gives rise in turn to the

---

85 See Osborn, *First Theologian* 165–67.
86 *DA* 41.
87 See *Praes.* 29; *Adv. Prax.* 12.1–4.
88 Cf. Alexandre, *Une chair pour la gloire* 161–64.
89 *De Pat.* 1.
90 Fredouille, *Tertullien* 370.

moral imperative that this sequence of time be applied to their proper and healthy growth. Stated in another way, the compositional elements of the human creature define the responsibilities necessary in its economic realization. If human persons must exist in history, then they are charged to use this history to foster their growth.

Tertullian has, in a sense, given a natural mandate to the ethics of Christian living. The 'moral code' of the human economy is not a subjective measure imposed on that economy by any being or societal body. It is humanity's created nature, which as created must develop and grow, that necessitates an approach to growth which moves forward and not backward in developmental progression. For Tertullian, this approach, or right attitude towards the development engendered by nature, is patience: waiting upon God to ensure and guide the process of maturation, for it is inconceivable that God's guidance of his handiwork would result in anything other than the latter's perfection. Again, a reading of 'image' as bespeaking 'model' aids this point. Since the model is Christ the eternal Son, this model (i.e. the reality which is imaged) is constant. It is, as Alexandre argued, the substantive definition of the 'real' of human nature. The lot of man is thus to wait upon that which consistently under-girds his reality – to advance in likeness to Christ, the model that stands at his core. To reach such perfection, the human person has only, Tertullian suggests, to wait patiently upon the Lord. To do anything else is to deviate from an economy of growth into an economy of death. Tertullian speaks of this bluntly: 'Every sin is ascribable to impatience, for evil is but the impatience of good'.[91] There is naught but impatience at the root of humanity's corruption.[92]

---

91   *De Pat.* 5.

92   In assessing the advent of impatience in an economy initiated by Christ, Tertullian, like Irenaeus, sees the devil as primary agent; see esp. *DA* 39, elsewhere in which Tertullian addresses the question of childbirth and its engendering of the disfigured economy, once more drawing on the procreative act as grounds for the transmission of economic disfigurement. Tertullian expounds such notions at *De Pat.* 5, which ties the devil's acts directly to impatience ('Therefore I detect the nativity of impatience in the devil himself, at that very time when he impatiently bore that the Lord God subjected the universal works which he had made to his own image, that is, to man', etc.). It is when the devil looks upon Edenic creation and sees the Lord grant to Adam sovereignty over all the created realm (cf. Genesis 1.28) that Tertullian sees him become infected with an impatience of the good that God will work from such an arrangement. The devil ought rather have 'patiently borne' that which God intended, for – and Tertullian sees a clear chain of cause-and-effect – if he had patiently borne God's intention he would not have become grieved as to God's goodness; and had he not thus become grieved he would not have become envious of Adam, whom he believed was unjustly in receipt of a goodness unfairly bestowed; and had he not thus become envious he would not have deceived Adam and Eve in an attempt to ease his grief, and the disfiguration of the economy would never have taken place. It is thus the devil's impatience that is the root cause of the Edenic tragedy. His envy (which earlier writers were wont to stress as motivating force) is an ancillary vice, explainable by this more fundamental characteristic.

Here Tertullian has made a certain advance in interpretation. Whereas Irenaeus would go on to see the devil's primary tool in the advancement of his envy as deception and the art of the lie, Tertullian sees Satan's impatience itself as the means by which he advances his purposes. The devil lies to Eve in their encounter in Eden (Genesis 3.1–7), but his lie is effective inasmuch as it engenders in Eve the very impatience that possesses him.

Once again, Tertullian does not leave his concepts to apply in general terms. Impatience is a causal phenomenon, a spur which goads on all deficient actions in the human economy:

> Whatever compels a man, it is not possible that without impatience of itself it can be perfected in deed. Who ever committed adultery without impatience of lust? Moreover, if in females the sale of their modesty is forced by the price, of course it is by impatience of contemning gain that this sale is regulated. These I mention as the principal delinquencies in the sight of the Lord, for, to speak compendiously, every sin is ascribable to impatience.[93]

Impatience is the cardinal sin because it is at the root of all sin. All transgression is act, but impatience as a *disposition of act*. As Tertullian understands it, impatience sets up a context in which the motions of transgression seem, and indeed become, normative. The right context of economic existence is skewed in an impatient life, for those acts which are harmonious to an advance of growth are spurned, while those ultimately leading to death become the objects of desire. Nonetheless, despite this context of the increasing normalization of sin, 'this must never be accounted as a natural disposition; it was rather produced by the instigation of the serpent [. . .], being incidental to [humanity's] nature'.[94]

The primary effect of impatience on the human creature is an alteration of the disposition of its economic development. Human nature, as a soul bearing the life of God in a material body, is by its design meant for harmonious and dynamic relationship with God. The impatient person becomes, to the contrary, one who wars against God in the depths of her being, acting against the image of the stability of the Son.[95] The course of authentic development is, for Tertullian, always that devised and realized by the creator, who has established both the person and the economy of the person's existence as a progression in likeness towards the one imaged in its formation. To battle against God and the unfolding of the economy as God wills it to be realized, is to battle against one's own salvation – here clearly seen in developmental terms, reflecting Tertullian's anthropological groundwork. This is a clear line in his thought from his earliest writings:

> God has enjoined us to deal calmly, gently, quietly and peacefully with the Holy Spirit, because these things are alone in keeping with the goodness of his nature, with his tenderness and sensitiveness; and not to vex him with rage,

---

93   *De Pat.* 5.
94   *DA* 21.
95   Cf. Tertullian's comments to Scapula as acting proconsul: 'We [. . .] are not seeking to frighten you, but we would save all men, if possible, by warning them not to fight with God' (*Ad Scap.* 4).

ill-nature, anger, or grief. Well, how shall this be made to accord with the shows?[96]

Tertullian's attentiveness to the ethics of day-to-day living, by which he is so often characterized, are here connected to anthropological considerations. A proper interior disposition of quietude and calm, engendering receptivity to the Holy Spirit, lies behind his insistence in this passage that public games are unsuitable to Christian audiences. Such acts engender the opposite interior qualities. An individual taking in this kind of spectacle willingly turns from God, an act of the same general quality as that fostered in Eden by the serpent. The devil's function is internalized, and humanity fosters impatience in itself without need for the external agent so influential in the garden.

Patience and growth in the Spirit – a trinitarian foundation

Tertullian's comments in the above passage from the *De spectaculis* reveal the trinitarian dimension to his concepts both of patience and its inverse. To 'deal peacefully with the Holy Spirit' is not a flourish in the text, it is an essential ingredient – though perhaps at the time of its writing Tertullian had not yet come to appreciate its importance. By the time he writes *De patientia* (only a few years later[97]) its significance has become clear. In chapter five of this latter tract, from which we have already quoted extensively, Tertullian concludes his argument with a listing of Old Testament instances where impatience barred Israel from receiving the 'good things of God', which the Lord would otherwise have offered freely. In chapter thirteen, it becomes clear that what is lost through impatience is not only the receipt of particular economic or substantive goods from God, but more particularly the full receipt of the Holy Spirit's presence in the human frame. The life of the Spirit, which the soul is created to convey to the body, is rejected in the impatience of one who will not wait on God.

> Thus far, finally, we have spoken of patience simple and uniform, and as it exists merely in the mind [and thus soul]: though in many forms likewise

---

96   *Spec.* 15. Daniélou, *Origins of Latin Christianity* 154, noted the influence of *Hermas* on this section of the *De spec.* (cf. Mandate 5.33.3: 'The Holy Spirit, who is delicate [. . .] seeks to live in gentleness and peace'), despite Tertullian's harsh attitude towards the document elsewhere. Frédouille had earlier noted the centrality of this passage to Tertullian's later *De pat.* 15; see Fredouille, *Tertullien* 63–65, 356. This calling upon *Hermas* is a common attribute of Tertullian and Irenaeus; see M. C. Steenberg, 'Scripture, *graphe*, and the Status of *Hermas* in Irenaeus', *SVTQ* (2008).

97   Fredouille sees *De Pat.* as part of a collection of texts Tertullian produced between 198 and 206, all dealing with discipline and morals; see *Tertullien* 363.

I labour after it in body, for the purpose of 'winning the Lord', inasmuch as it is a quality which has been exhibited by the Lord himself in bodily virtue as well; if it is true that the soul easily communicates the gifts of the Spirit with its bodily habitation (*animus facile communicat spiritus inuecta cum habitaculo suo*).[98]

When the person is impatient of soul, he becomes, too, impatient of body. In such a situation, both elements involved in the receipt of the divine life into the human – that is, the soul which receives the Spirit and the body into which the Spirit's life is manifest – are corrupted. Rather than receive the Spirit, they come to war against it actively, becoming stagnant in a willing lack of receipt of God's presence. This yields not only a human creature devoid of communion with God (or at least hindered in that communion), but further, a person not fully or authentically human. Tertullian's anthropological vision sees as 'human' that which is in receipt of God's divine life; without this latter, part of that reality is missing. Impatience ultimately breeds subhuman existence.

   This is the observation that sets the preceding anthropological discussion into a context of relation to a trinitarian vision of God the Father with his Son and Spirit. Humanity's compositional elements – body and soul – are developmental, and thus economic. With the advent of sin, the actual economy of their existence became one that disfigured their growth and function. It is critical for Tertullian that this disfiguration itself be defined in economic terms, as we have examined above, as this sets the stage for a reading of the redemption offered in Christ. The constitutive elements of man are the *means of receiving the Father's life through the Spirit*, providing the context for conceiving human fallenness as interruption of this reception and participation. It is a right articulation of humanity's constitutive elements that enables, for Tertullian, authentic exegesis of the 'fallen' human condition and the redemption experienced in Christ, and so right anthropology points directly towards right theology. Christ's work as saviour, then, will both illumine, and be illumined by, the anthropological conception of the human reality he redeems, for he is the 'model' imaged in the creation of his fashioning. In turn, it is in the redemption effected by this Christ, Son of the Father, that Tertullian sees the human person, in receipt of the Father's Spirit, at length fully defined.

THE SALVATION OF IMPATIENT HUMANITY: ANTHROPOLOGY GROUNDING SOTERIOLOGY

The state of humanity, infected with an impatience that divides it from the Father's Spirit, rendering it not even an authentic human individual, is for Tertullian the

---

98   *De Pat.* 13.

inheritance of ancestral sin made real in every subsequent phase of human history. It is a hopeless situation, for as we have already seen, there is no possibility but that a disfigured economy will produce disfigured individuals. Every soul is born 'in Adam', each economically rendered unclean, actively sinful, 'with its own shame'. From this disfigured economy there is no escape, save for one cardinal reality: God's power to transform is stronger than the human ability to distort.[99] That which God wills, Tertullian notes, he has authority to effect. The will of God for his handiwork, in the face of its impatience and sin, is evidenced from the beginning: God responds to impatience with patience. So while humanity waged war against God in Eden, and God could rightly have responded in full indignation, Tertullian reads scripture as revealing a more measured reaction:

> Whence the first indignation came upon God, thence came also his first patience. For God, content at that time with malediction only, refrained in the devil's case from the instant infliction of punishment. Else what crime, before this guilt of impatience, is imputed to man? Innocent he was, and in intimate friendship with God, and the husbandman of paradise.[100]

So the impatience of humanity is to be met not with fire and wrath, which might rightly be called upon as its corrective agents. It is met more forcefully with the antithesis of impatience: the patience of God himself in his economic dealings with creation. This is evident, Tertullian makes clear, from the first instance of sin, and so the salvific work of the economy is begun already in Eden. It becomes most full, however, in the life of the incarnate Christ.

To culminate in reflections on Christology is the natural destiny of a Christian anthropology; though one culminates here only because one began here – with the theological witness of the incarnate, resurrected Christ to the stature of man and the cosmos. In Irenaeus this was clear, inasmuch as Christ, the new Adam and true Adam, is seen as both beginning and end of the human economy. The empty tomb, with the God-made-man confessed as rising from it, encompasses the whole of history and defines every aspect of anthropological measure. This is no less true for Tertullian, and no less important to a full understanding of his vision of the human. The advancing economy is primarily to be understood as the unfolding of God's will, the will expressed in the Father's Son, who is the personal reality of this will and the model for the image present in man. It is the will of this Son, and thus the will of the Father, that the desire and intention of the Father as creator be realized in the economy in which his creation struggles. The Father wills, in the Son and through the Son, that the human handiwork become that which exists according to his intention in the chorus of creation, a chorus which refrained again and again 'it is good'. This is, in some sense, the primal declaration of God's

---

99   So *DA* 21.
100   *De Pat.* 5.

desire for the created order. So the will of the Father in Christ is that the economy
reflect and give life to that which is authentically human nature, truly imaging
its model. This idea is made clear in an important passage from Tertullian's *De
oratione*, dealing specifically with Christ's example of prayer to his disciples. It
is a lengthy text, but one which must be examined in full:

> According to this model, we subjoin, 'Thy will be done in the heavens and on
> the earth' – not that there is some power withstanding to prevent God's will
> being done, and we pray for him the successful achievement of his will; but
> we pray for his will to be done in all. For, by figurative interpretation of flesh
> and spirit, it is we who are 'heaven' and 'earth', albeit, even if it is to be under-
> stood simply, still the sense of the petition is the same: that in us God's will
> be done on earth, to make it possible, namely, for it to be done also in the
> heavens. What, moreover, does God's will mean, but that we should walk
> according to his discipline? We make petition, then, that he supply us with the
> substance of his will (*substantiam voluntatis suae*), and the capacity to do it,
> that we may be saved both in the heavens and on earth; because the sum of his
> will is the salvation of them whom he has adopted. There is, too, that will of
> God which the Lord accomplished in preaching, in working, in enduring: for
> if he himself proclaimed that he did not his own but the Father's will, without
> doubt those things which he used to do were the Father's will; unto which
> things, as unto exemplars, we are now provoked – to preach, to work, to
> endure even unto death. And we need the will of God, that we may be able to
> fulfil these duties. Again, in saying, 'Thy will be done' we are even wishing
> well to ourselves, in-so-far that there is nothing of evil in the will of God; even
> if, proportionally to each one's deserts, somewhat other is imposed on us. So
> by this expression we admonish our own selves unto patience. The Lord also,
> when he had wished to demonstrate to us, even in his own flesh, the flesh's
> infirmity by the reality of suffering, said, 'Father, remove this thy cup', and
> remembering himself, added, 'save that not my will, but thine be done'. He
> himself was the will and the power of the Father; and yet, for the demonstra-
> tion of the patience that was due, he gave himself up to the Father's will.[101]

Tertullian has allegorized the prayer taught by Christ, to speak directly of the flesh
and soul of the human individual.[102] As the Son petitions the Father that the heavenly and earthly realms might exist in harmony with the divine will, so Tertullian
sees him instructing that the soul (the 'heavenly' element in humanity) and the
body (the 'earthly') come into harmony with the will of the Father expressed in
himself. Here this is specifically indicated as a will of patience, and the manner of

101   *De Or.* 4.
102   Cf. our comments on the 'Our Father' in the previous chapter on Irenaeus (p. 43), and below on
Cyril (p. 155).

living that patience inspires: endurance, suffering, martyric witness, authentic teaching, etc. The cosmic scope of the prayer, which calls the whole of earth and heaven to come into divine concordance, becomes for Tertullian intimately personal, exhorting all the elements of the person to be united to, and expressive of, the creator's will and design.

It is interesting to observe that, in this passage, Tertullian sees the incarnate Christ's role as chiefly paradigmatic. He shows through the example of his own life, patience and suffering endurance, the path that all should follow. It is in living human life the way the Son lived human life, that the subhuman reality of a fallen economy is overcome. Christ is the example of a new and better way. With respect to individual characteristics of human living, Tertullian makes, in *De patientia* 4, the same point that Irenaeus had previously made in *Refutation* 2.22.4 with respect to the ages of human life ('and so Christ passed through every age, becoming a child for children, being an example . . .'). The didactic value of Christ the recapitulator in Irenaeus is mirrored in strong terms. Yet just as Irenaeus insisted that the instructive role of Christ as exemplar only has redemptive value if it is conjoined to a genuine anthropological renewal, overcoming that burden of sin which prevents any pure example from being followed fully, so too does Tertullian link the paradigmatic function of Christ to an ontological framework. This is made clear already later in his same tract on prayer, when Tertullian gives his commentary on the phrase 'give us this day our daily bread'. First, he notes, Christ gives in personal example an instruction on the value of petitioning God for earthly necessities. If in want of bread, one should ask God that it be provided. But the implication of the petition does not end in the material realm:

> For the Lord had issued his edict, 'Seek ye first the kingdom, and then even these shall be added' (Matthew 6.33), that we may rather understand, 'Give us this day our daily bread' spiritually. For Christ is our bread, because Christ is life and bread is life. 'I am', he says, 'the bread of life', and a little earlier, 'The bread is the Word of the living God, who came down from the heavens'. Then we find, too, that his body is reckoned in bread: 'this is my body'. And so, in petitioning for 'daily bread', we ask for perpetuity in Christ, and indivisibility from his body (*itaque petendo panem quotidianem perpetuitatem postulamus in Christo et indiuiduitatem a corpore eius*).[103]

In what is clearly a eucharistic text, Tertullian has linked the paradigmatic role of Christ as teacher of authentic economy, to a redemption at the level of ontology or nature. Humanity seeks, in Christ, to become one with the body of Christ, attained in Christian life through the eucharistic mystery. That which humanity is, is transformed in the life and offering of Christ. The disunion that a misused economy has

---

103 *De Or.* 6.

rendered universal is transformed into a new reality that is 'in Christ' perpetually, indivisible from his body.

How Tertullian understands this bringing together of Christ and the full scope of humanity is not relegated solely, or even primarily, to Christ's act of forgiving the human race its transgression and offering a renewed moral relationship to the Father. It is, above all, discovered in the incarnational reality of divine union with the human. The Son of the Father interjects himself into the human economy, not as an outside force or messenger (as might be the case with angelic pronouncement or prophetic inspiration), but in the most fundamental manner possible: by taking to himself the nature by which the economy is made real. The Son becomes human, effecting human history by becoming that which gives rise to history, and which that history effects correspondingly. It is only in seeing Christ's function incarnationally, as the coming-together of the human and the divine, that Tertullian's Christology and broader anthropology find their inherent correlates. He is willing, therefore, to insist on this principal feature of an incarnational soteriology even in locations that would seem unlikely candidates for such discussion. This is the case, for example, in his long *Apologeticum*, where he is surprisingly at his most articulate on the matter. Speaking in the twenty-first chapter in profoundly trinitarian terms, articulating the Son's union with the Father as substantive (i.e. according to *substantia*), as a ray from a source of light, he goes on to note:

> This ray of God, then, as it was always foretold in ancient times, descending into a certain virgin and made flesh in her womb, is in his birth God and man united. The flesh formed by the Spirit is nourished, grows up to manhood, speaks, teaches, works and is the Christ.[104]

It is as God-and-man-united that the 'flesh' of Christ (and here Tertullian refers to the whole incarnate reality of the Son, not merely the body) is, through the nourishing presence of the Spirit, made redemptive to humanity. It is as incarnate that the Son is 'the Christ', the redeemer. This is not an instance of Tertullian attempting a kind of chronology to the existence of the Son, from pre- to currently-incarnational 'phases', but his means of articulating how the encountered Jesus, the one who 'is the Christ', is at once also 'the ray of God foretold in ancient times'; that is, 'God and man united'. The passage is Tertullian's way of accomplishing that which the evangelist articulates at John 1.1: 'The Word became flesh and dwelt among us' – not a record of the 'history' of the eternal Son, but a confession of the incarnational reality of Jesus confessed as Son of God. The virginal birth of this Son, by which he took to himself the human flesh in which he is encountered and known (he was 'made flesh in her womb'), is the surety of his redemptive power.

---

104   *Apol.* 21.

Tertullian's implication could not be clearer: it is *as human* that the Son is known as Christ, that Jesus effects his work as Saviour. The outcome of such an incarnational union in Christ is disclosed later in the same chapter: it is as human that the Son 'aims to enlighten men already civilised', and that he is enabled to make this 'enlightenment' full and complete. This is precisely because the human life he lives is the human life of the divine Son, and not merely another personal reality bound to the enslaving disfiguration of the economy. 'Search then', writes Tertullian, 'and see if that divinity of Christ be true. If it be of such a nature that the acceptance of it transforms a man, and makes him truly good, there is implied in that the duty of renouncing what is opposed to it as false.' It is precisely the incarnate divinity confessed of Jesus Christ that allows him to 'transform' humanity, to make it a thing 'truly good'. The divine power of the Father, which is the Son's from all eternity as a ray from a fire, is that which makes the personal reality of 'God and man united' redemptively capable.

The ransom of the cross

This redemption is effected through the cross. The incarnational reality of the Son is made fully salvific for humanity here, and in the resurrection of the one who was crucified on the cross, completing the redemptive recapitulation of human existence by embracing and defeating death. As Osborn reminds, Tertullian follows Paul's confession to 'know only Christ and him crucified',[105] embracing the paradoxical dishonour as that which stands at the heart of Christ's salvific act. It is this that is the heart of Christianity, a thing 'to be believed because it is absurd', to quote one of Tertullian's most famous apothegmata.[106] His point is not to embrace irrationality for its own sake, as the saying is too often taken to suggest, but to proclaim that the honour bestowed on humanity requires the 'indispensable dishonour of our faith', the true incarnation with true offering of the Son.[107] This stems from Tertullian's firm expression, witnessed throughout the present chapter, of the incarnational offering of re-creation that is the Son's human life in Galilee. It is this offering in which Christ takes to himself the full lot of the human condition, that having embraced it he may recapitulate and restore it from its beginnings:

> Now, to what god will most suitably belong all those things which relate to 'that good pleasure, which God has purposed in the mystery of his will, that in the dispensation of the fullness of times he might recapitulate' (if I may so say, according to the exact meaning of the Greek word) 'all things in Christ,

---

105 Cf. 1 Corinthians 2.2; *Pud.* 14; see Osborn, *First Theologian* 16.
106 See *De Carn.* 5.
107 Ibid.

both which are in heaven and which are on earth' (Ephesians 1.9, 10), but to
him whose are all things from their beginning, even the beginning itself; from
whom issue the times and the dispensation of the fullness of times, according
to which all things up to the very first are gathered up in Christ?[108]

The Son's incarnate life must be one that embraces the human condition from
its beginnings. More than this, it must involve the offering of death. The one who
is mediator (Tertullian follows Paul's mediatorial language at 1 Timothy 2.5 in
De res. 51) must conquer the full division occasioned by sin. If the lot of humanity
in sin is chiefly the loss of union with God, as we have explored above, then the
greatest obstacle to restoration is the deepest wound of such disunion: the death
which seems permanently to cement it. And here Tertullian identifies the limit of
human ability to restore. By joining himself to his human creature, the Son works
redemption by renewing the creature's authentic reality, repairing the damage of
sin through obedient recapitulation of proper relationship with the Spirit and the
Father. But at death is encountered the obstacle no human life can conquer, however well restored to obedient relation with God. This is the one effect of sin that
cannot be rebuffed by repentance or change – death stands as the strong fruit of
man's sin, of greater strength than the sinner. As such, humanity's redemption
requires something beyond incarnational union alone. Christ, then, sacrificially
offers his life for the defeat of death, paying the 'ransom' that man could not offer
for himself. Speaking to those who would flee persecution, Tertullian explains:

> That you should ransom with money a man whom Christ has ransomed
> with his blood, how unworthy is it of God and his ways of acting, who spared
> not his own Son for you, that he might be made a curse for us, because cursed
> is he that hangs on a tree! – him who was led as a sheep to be a sacrifice, and
> just as a lamb before its shearer, so opened he not his mouth [. . .] and, being
> numbered with the transgressors, was delivered up to death, nay, the death of
> the cross. All this took place that he might redeem us from our sins. [. . .] Hell
> re-transferred the right it had in us, and our covenant is now in heaven; the
> everlasting gates were lifted up, that the king of glory, the Lord of might,
> might enter in after having redeemed man from death (cf. Psalm 23.7), nay,
> from hell, that he might attain to heaven. [. . .] And the Lord indeed ransomed
> him from the angelic powers which rule the world – from the spirits of
> wickedness, from the darkness of this life, from eternal judgment, from ever-
> lasting death.[109]

There is a ransom paid in this death, but it is a ransom not to the rights of another,
but to the power that lingers as the effect of sin – both the sin of humanity's design

---

108   *Adv. Marc.* 5.17.1.
109   *Fug.* 12.

and that of the devil's provocation.[110] The ransom is of the power of death and hell. Tertullian takes the scriptural imagery of the Psalmist's 'king of glory entering in', in parallel to the incarnate Christ's rising from death, entering into life in defeat of death's power, taking with him the race united to him in the incarnation. Thus the ultimate effect of the sacrifice on the cross is reconciliation: the defeat of death, that man and God be at length renewed to communion. Tertullian quotes Colossians 1.20 ('Christ reconciles all things by himself, making peace by the blood of his cross') with an excursus on '*re*-conciliation', distinct from 'conciliation', indicating the paramount issue of *restoration* effected through the cross.[111] The final hurdle to such reconciliation is the defeat of death, witnessed in the dead Christ's rising from the tomb. So again Tertullian cites Psalm 23:

> Therefore it is of a war such as this that the Psalm may evidently have spoken, 'the Lord is strong, the Lord is mighty in battle' (Psalm 23.8); for with death, the final enemy, he fought, and through the trophy of the cross he triumphed.[112]

One could suggest that this idea of Christ transforming humanity into new union with the Father seems problematic in conjunction with Tertullian's assertion of the immutability of human nature. It is in fact here that Tertullian's anthropological convictions provide the grounding by which he understands the incarnate life of Christ as soteriologically potent. That which Christ effects in the human person is a restoration of the capacity for growth. This is a transformation wrought by the economy of the incarnation, granting to human nature renewed potential for maturation hindered since Eden by sin. Thus, while Tertullian can see that God has always been active in the economy, bestowing favour on the people of Israel throughout their history, the will of the Father has nonetheless always been for the fuller development of his creation that a union with himself, wrought through the Son, would bring. This Tertullian perceives as the clear witness of the scriptures:

> The sacred writers, in giving previous warning of these things, all with equal clearness ever declared that, in the last days of the world, God would, out of every nation, people and country choose for himself more faithful worshippers upon whom he would bestow his grace, and that indeed in ampler measure, in keeping with the enlarged capacities of a nobler dispensation (*ob disciplinae auctioris capacitatem*). Accordingly, he appeared among us,

---

110   Tertullian's argument in his tome against Marcion refutes thoroughly the idea of ransoming any other, and his mention of the 'angelic powers that rule the world' in this passage is meant to indicate influence, not juridical possession.

111   This in *Adv. Marc.* 5.19.5. Would for space we would present the entire passage, which is one of Tertullian's most potent images of the sacrificial redemption on the cross.

112   *Adv. Marc.* 4.20.5.

whose coming to renovate and illuminate man's nature (*ad reforandam
et illuminandam eam*) was pre-announced by God – I mean Christ, the Son of
God. And so the supreme head and master of this grace and discipline, the
enlightener and trainer of the human race, God's own Son, was announced
among us, born – but not so born as to make him ashamed of the name of
Son or of his paternal origin.[113]

Tertullian's perception of history is undeniably supercessionist. This is, in the
end, the only reading of history that could accord with his views on development
and maturation.[114] That which is realized in the incarnation is the 'enlarged capacity of a nobler dispensation' – and the terminology of capacity (*capacitatem*) is
significant. Tertullian describes Christ coming to 'renovate' and 'illuminate'
human nature, carefully wording his description to remain free from any trace of
fundamental change or mutation. Human nature is freed from its bonds, illumined
and refreshed in Christ, and by this renovation has its 'capacities' enlarged for
greater receipt of the divine. Put more succinctly, the soteriological work of
the incarnate Son is to enable a renewed development of human nature, freeing
it from the restrictive bonds of the disfigured economy by his divine power.
Tertullian looks backward through history, reads the scriptures from the perspective of this incarnate Son, to exegete a whole economy of preparation for this
human ennoblement and expansion.

An enlarged capacity for the Spirit

The language of 'enlarged capacity' employed in the *Apologeticum* is important,
not only because it shows Christ's redemptive work to be the fostering of humanity's growth into maturity, with the increased capabilities this maturity entails; but
also because it describes this work of redemption in relation to the Spirit. It is not
Christ's actions in exclusion that redeem the creature: humanity's 'capacities' are
increased by Christ – but capacities for what? The answer is grounded again in
Tertullian's anthropological framework, and harks back to his fundamental conviction that the function of the rightly developing soul is to communicate the
Spirit of the Father to the material frame. The function of the soul is to unite
the person to God. Authentic humanity is the union of body and soul, receiving

---

113 *Apol.* 21.
114 See Dunn, *Tertullian* 48–51, esp. 49–50, on this mode of supercession, rather than sheer novelty,
as explanation of the ferocity with which Tertullian attacked Marcion, as well as his demarcation of the
grounds on which Tertullian would retain a difficult relationship with Christianity's Jewish roots. For
an excellent treatment of Tertullian's approach to scriptural authority, see the same author's 'Tertullian's Scriptural Exegesis in *De praescriptione haereticorum*', *JECS* 14.2 (2006), 141–55, esp. 148.

the life of God in the Spirit. The 'capacity' enlarged through Christ's incarnation is precisely this capacity to receive the Spirit, and as such to be joined to the divine life. The advent of a new level of human union with the Spirit is the gift of the incarnate Christ, forging a communion deeper even than that known by Adam and Eve.[115] The redemptive work of Christ is thus connected directly to the work of the Spirit. This latter is both received into the human frame by an attitude of patience (which Christ exemplifies and, incarnationally, enables), and fosters the patience by which that receipt becomes ever more potent.[116] At the end of a poetic refrain on the 'sublime qualities' of patience personified ('her countenance is tranquil and peaceful, contracted by no wrinkle of sadness or anger . . .'), Tertullian has the following to say on the relationship of patience and the Spirit:

> Patience sits on the throne of that calmest and gentlest Spirit, who is not found in the roll of the whirlwind, nor in the leaden hue of the cloud, but is of soft serenity, open and simple, whom Elias saw at his third attempt (cf. 1 Kings 19.11–13). For where God is, there too is his foster-child, namely patience. When God's Spirit descends, patience accompanies him indivisibly. If we do not give admission to her together with the Spirit, will he [the Spirit] always tarry with us? Nay, I know not whether he would remain any longer. Without his companion and handmaid, he must of necessity be straitened in every place and at every time.[117]

Patience and the Spirit are not to be found in abiding perpetuity the one without the other. Where patience is dismissed, so too departs the full union with the Spirit who abides in the human person through the context of patient receptivity. Conversely, when the Father's Spirit is received into a human life, patience is expanded, for it is infused into the economy by the Spirit as much as it is required for the Spirit's continued presence. Thus, while freedom of action allows for a departure from patience, resulting in a disruption of communion with the Spirit, nonetheless the Spirit's work is the increase of patience that brings divine union. When the incarnate Christ increases, through the ransom of the cross, the human capacity to receive the Spirit, the Spirit in turn comes to foster new heights of patient receptivity in the human race, bringing it into closer union with its creator. So before Christ's incarnation there were prophets and kings, but after it there are martyrs who, filled with godly patience borne of the Spirit, endure all things for the Lord: for the Spirit fosters human endurance, 'that it may bear with all

---

115 See *Adv. Marc.* 5.10.7. Cf. Daniélou, *Origins of Latin Christianity* 376–77 on Tertullian's statements, earlier in life, that Adam had fully received the Spirit in Eden. Such infrequent comments (cf. *De Bapt.* 5.7) are made before Tertullian's dispute with Hermogenes, during and after which he consistently rejects this idea.

116 Cf. Fredouille, *Tertullien* 394, where patience is the guarantee of the Spirit's presence in man.

117 *De Pat.* 15.

constancy stripes, fire, cross, beasts, sword – all which the prophets and apostles, by enduring, conquered'.[118]

What is realized in the human person redeemed in Christ, is the perfection of the image in which she was fashioned: the created being in receipt of the Father's Spirit, 'modelled' on the Son who exists in union with this Spirit. This is made possible by the Son's incarnate offering, which re-establishes in the creature the authentic attributes of its model. Tertullian is, as we have already seen, emphatic that to be formed 'in' or 'after' (κατά) the image is to be less than that which is imaged. Humanity is inherently lesser than God, as an image is based on, but not identical to, its model. But in Christ the model is fully revealed, and in this Christ who 'is God and man', humanity who is *after* is joined to the one who *is* the image of the Father. The fact that it is the *incarnate* Christ who is, reveals, and perfects in others the full reality of this image, indicates to Tertullian that while the soul receiving the Spirit is central to humanity's *imago*, the integration of the bodily into any definition of 'image' remains essential. So in his *De res.*:

> The divine creator fashioned this very flesh with his own hands in the image of God; which he animated with his own breath (*afflatus*), after the likeness of his own vitality.[119]

The Father's will for man, to image the Son's union with himself in and through the Spirit, is enabled by the Son's restoration and perfection of human natural potential. It is this which the Spirit then advances and perfects through patient growth. The full human, soul together with body, participates, through the work of Christ, in the reality of God the Father's eternal communion with his Son and Spirit. The anthropology that underlies Tertullian's soteriology makes clear the fully trinitarian character of humanity's redemption.

WEDDED TO THE SPIRIT: A DYNAMIC ANTHROPOLOGY OF GROWTH

A reading of Tertullian that looks beyond the stereotyped title of 'rigorist' to the anthropological convictions that grounded his zeal, discovers a vision of the human person, and indeed of human history, that is far from the realm of static categories often assumed. Tertullian may indeed have come to believe that certain sins are beyond the Church's purview to correct – that expulsion is the only reasonable option – but he did so not out of a black-and-white conception of right and wrong that bears no qualifications, but because he believed that economy and

---

118   *De Pat.* 13.
119   *De Res.* 9

nature are inseparably interwoven. Act and ontology cannot be divided, even if they must always be distinguished. For this reason, act, and exposure to act, have a direct effect on the manner in which the human realizes its nature given by God. One's code of dress and conduct are important, for they may stunt or foster authentic growth. Moreover, one's exposure to others' codes of conduct is similarly important (hence his attention to Christian presence at public spectacles); for the fundamental context of act is an interior disposition, patience, which can be roused to its opposite by what one sees and hears as much as by what one says and does.

All this makes Tertullian's zealous ethics and ecclesiology intently dynamic in motivation. It is because human nature, both in its bodily and spiritual aspect, is dynamic and requires of growth, and not on account of over-simplified categories of right and wrong, that such zeal must be exhibited in the Christian person. Just as one tends to the body, that it may grow from infancy to adulthood without injury or impediment, so must one tend also to the development and growth of the soul. Unless this latter develops in harmony with the body, that which the human individual is as person becomes stunted. This occurs chiefly through becoming less receptive to the Holy Spirit, thus ever less in union with the Father, which is the intended lot of the creature that images the Son, who is eternally in union with his Father. The tragedy of sin is precisely that it distorts and disfigures the economy of human life that is meant to provide for development, causing it instead to cripple and deform the person who would be in union with the divine. Yet, as we have seen Tertullian state directly, God's power to transform is stronger than humanity's power to disfigure. The incarnation of the Son, which is the direct communion of the Father's will and power with human nature and economy, is the ultimate manifestation of this reality. God becomes man, that in so doing the Father's power might overcome the bonds of the fallen economy through the sacrificial offering of the Son. This offering propels the nature of the human race to new heights of development and growth, increasing its receptivity to his Spirit. The impatience that stands behind all economic distortion is met with the patience of the Father who sends his Son, enabling the Spirit's greater receipt, which in turn engenders a renewed human patience that is a freedom from sin and union with the divine. The whole human person can only be saved by the whole trinitarian reality of the Father with his Son and Spirit. As such, the human person finds in the Church – and Tertullian makes direct connection of the incarnational reality to the sacramental mysteries of the ecclesia – the means for progression and growth into new heights of iconic existence. So will Tertullian characterize the reality of Christian redemption in the full wording of a passage we have already excerpted in part above:

> As therefore light, when intercepted by an opaque body, still remains – although it is not apparent, by reason of the interposition of so dense a body – so likewise the good in the soul, being weighed down by the evil, is, owing to

the obscuring character thereof, either not seen at all, its light being wholly hidden, or else only a stray beam is there visible where it struggles through by an accidental outlet. Thus some men are very bad and some very good, yet the souls of all form but one genus. Even in the worst there is something good, and in the best there is something bad. For God alone is without sin; and the only man without sin is Christ, since Christ is also God. [. . .] Just as no soul is without sin, so neither is any soul without seeds of good. Therefore, when the soul embraces the faith, being renewed in its second birth by water and the power from above, then the veil of its former corruption being taken away and it beholds the light in all its brightness. It is also taken up by the Holy Spirit, just as in its first birth it is embraced by the unholy spirit. The flesh follows the soul now wedded to the Spirit, as a part of the bridal portion – no longer the servant of the soul, but of the Spirit. O happy marriage, if in it there is committed no violation of the nuptial vow![120]

Tertullian's anthropology cannot be understood except within the framework of his trinitarian articulation – that is, his increasingly nuanced and precise discussion of God the Father as ever active in relation to his Son and Spirit. Tertullian's steps into the language of *una substantia* to describe the relationship of the divinity of these three, his proffering of the title *trinitas*, 'Trinity', to express a sense of abiding unity even in their triadic multiplicity, are what enable him to speak clearly on the divine stature of each. They are what enable him to state unequivocally that 'Christ is also God'. They are what ground his proclamation that union with the Spirit is simultaneously union with the Father as an active imaging of the model, who is the Son.

   What is clear in Tertullian, then, is that this doctrinal precision on the nature of God is the substance of his anthropological investigation. Unless Father, Son and Spirit are articulated and confessed in this way, the whole of Tertullian's compositional anthropology breaks down. This is so because it is the forum of anthropology that has provided Tertullian with his insights into the divine, and so the two are fundamentally connected. To equate being 'in the image of God' to receiving corporeally the Spirit in the created soul, requires that the Spirit be understood as fully divine in stature, united to God the Father. To confess Christ's redemptive act as divinely enabling this receipt by uniting the human creation to the perfected will of the Father, himself the model imaged in this union, requires that Christ be known as the eternal Son and Will of the Father. Tertullian does not, and indeed cannot, conceive of human reality apart from such confessions.

   We have in Tertullian's person a link between the early period of Christianity's doctrinal articulation, in which the primary concern was the discernment of an authentic scriptural witness to Christ in a largely polemical and apologetic framework, to the phase that would rise out of the third century and consume the

---

120   *DA* 41.

fourth – in which refinement of this articulation would lead to internalizing disputes over the confession of the Son more carefully as the *Father's* Son, bestower of the Spirit. Matters 'trinitarian' do not spring forth spontaneously in the fourth century as a distinct arena of theological discussion, in succession to the 'apostolic', 'apologetic' and 'polemical ages'. The apostolic confession that 'you are the Christ, the Son of the living God' (Matthew 16.16), meant that from the first, Jesus as 'Son of the Father', 'Son of God', would require articulation and definition in Christian experience. There is an unbroken line of continuity between the apostles, the so-called apostolic fathers, the apologists, Irenaeus, Tertullian and a host of others in the earliest centuries, as respects the desire to articulate further this essential and basic confession of Christ in relation to his Father, and with him the Spirit sent at the Pentecost. Specific contextual concerns – apologetic necessity, polemical zeal – frame in the approach used in the advancement of this project, but do not themselves define it. The theological work of early Christianity is the exploration in increasingly doctrinal terms of the basic confession that it is God who has been made known humanly in Galilee, saving man who is fully known in his God.

In this chapter and the previous we have seen how, in two very different authors in independent historical and ecclesiastical contexts, the articulation of a 'doctrine of God' is from the first to the last intertwined with the articulation of a 'doctrine of man' – of the development of a Christian anthropology grounded in the concept of the divine image. The reality of this necessary correlation has been apparent in both our authors, despite the fact that they are in many ways quite different. Tertullian is something of a systematist, while Irenaeus is more spontaneous, though not disorganized. Irenaeus articulates his doctrinal discussion largely in reaction to a specific grouping of cosmologically speculative thought; Tertullian's voluminous tracts treat of everything from polemical strikes against perceived heretics, to Pagan apologetic, to matters of ecclesiastical ethics and expositions on the fabric of human composition in dedicated study. Yet at the heart of both authors' projects lies the common goal of further articulating the mystery of God's being, with reference to the human reality that this God has come to save. As this is articulated more carefully as an eternal and active relationship between Father, Son and Spirit, so the theology of 'image' comes to be seen itself in more dynamic, relational terms. This is true well before the age called 'trinitarian', before Christian writers had constructed the word 'trinity' or articulated God's being in the manner of later trinitarian currency. Already in Irenaeus, the human person as 'in the image of God' is explored and articulated as the image of the Father, the image who is Jesus Christ, who is first and foremost obedient Son. Irenaeus does not explore the ontological relationship of the Father to his Son, nor, when he speaks with such zeal of the Spirit as the one who brings humanity to the Son's obedient life, does he make any attempt to explain the divine stature of this same Spirit. The Father has 'two hands' ever present to himself and active both in fashioning and sustaining the created order. Yet what is central to Irenaeus is that God *must always be conceived* as this Father with his two hands. When the human person is defined as in the 'image of God', it is to this co-relating, co-active reality of Father, Son and Spirit that the person is iconically connected.

This is just as true in Tertullian, though in this latter we have a more refined articulation of the manner in which the Father, Son and Spirit are interrelated as the 'one God'. Tertullian's introduction of *'trinitas'* and *'una substantia'* provides a manner of conceptual reification of the unity-in-multiplicity that had been articulated in Irenaeus, as much as in others before him (notably Justin, through his application of earlier Logos-terminology to the task of explaining the Son's relationship to the Father – though most would agree that his discussion in this regard was limited and warranted its relatively short lifespan in Christian doctrinal language). It is with Tertullian that we first see the Christian community able to refer, singularly, to the multiplicity that is God as Father with his Son and Spirit. The notable side-effect of this new mode of articulation is that it further reifies the dynamic of relationship proper to God. Once we begin to speak of this relationship as 'trinity', we no longer have need always to specify – as did Irenaeus – that this God is relational as being Father together with Spirit and Son. To speak in more articulate trinitarian language is to define 'God' inherently *as* Father *with* Son *and* Spirit.

This nominal development in language has notable repercussions in the connected realm of anthropology, for explicit definition of 'God' as triadic reality further enforces the point made by Irenaeus, that the 'image of God' must be an image of the Father in relation to the Son and Spirit. Tertullian does not scientifically explore a direct connection of anthropological discourse to his advance in conceptual terminology, but the presence of such a connection is clear in its effects. His reflections on humanity's composition and modes of economic expression are more articulate in their manifestation of human relation to the relating God than are those of Irenaeus, who, as we have already noted, is famed in modern study precisely for his dynamic thought. God as triadic reality, as substantive unity (*una substantia*) of Father, Son and Spirit, provides Tertullian with the context for exploring the human *imago* in terms of relatedness to this relation, imaging the model of such a God. This leads, as we have seen, to a definition of the various elements of humanity's composition, namely body and soul, in terms of growth, change and transformation, precisely because they are elements in communion with the Father who draws them into the relation proper to his own relation to the Spirit and Son. The Spirit 'advances' the soul and body into communion with the Son, who renders them fit for the glory of the Father.

The distinct development of the second and third centuries, with respect to anthropological considerations in particular, is the refined linkage of the doctrine of the image to the increasingly articulate expression of what is, by this era's end, properly being called 'the trinity'. To speak of humanity as the 'image of God' is current from the very first, and is not a confession unique to Christianity. We have seen that Irenaeus reflects on it so directly for reason, at least in part, of its being part of the *lingua franca* of anthropological consideration across a wide spectrum of early- to mid-second-century reflection, including that of the groups against whom he inveighs so passionately. The concept of 'image' is not, however, left to the realm of generality, merely an indication that the human creature is good in formation because it in some sense resembles God who is good. This might have been enough, were the anti-Valentinian focus of Irenaeus' primary works the full extent to which he wished such a doctrine to apply. His employment of 'image' goes much further. The connection of this concept to the articulation of God as Father with Son and Spirit is taken up in even greater measure in Tertullian, who is able to offer additional refinements to this anthropological discussion precisely because he further refines the vocabulary of trinitarian thought. Whilst Christianity inherited its doctrine of humanity as 'image of the divine' from Judaism and shared these origins with other groups in its environs, in connecting the image so centrally to its formative reflections on the nature of a triadic God, the second and third centuries claim the *imago Dei* as something peculiarly Christian. From at least the time of Irenaeus, and clearly from the era of Tertullian, the human person as 'in the divine image' has no meaning apart from confession of Christ as the Son of the Father, bestower of the Holy Spirit.

It is impossible for us not to notice how, in all of this, the role of the Spirit in particular is emphasized so strongly. The central place held by developed views on the Spirit in relation to the Father and Son sets the stage for another curiosity of early Christianity: the apparent silence over the Spirit at Nicaea and the first half of the fourth century in general. By many standards of historical reading in current scholarship, speaking of a 'doctrine of the Spirit', or 'trinitarian thought', in the third and especially second centuries is, at least partially on these grounds, judged as anachronistic. The groundwork for genuine trinitarian articulation is perceived as laid at Nicaea, in particular through the Nicene *homoousion*, with the extension of this articulation from Father and Son to Father, Son and Spirit patently the project of later decades, most notably those leading to Constantinople in 381. Yet the whole substance of our study thus far makes clear that it is emphatically within a *pneumatologically central* confession of God as Father with Son *and Spirit*, that the significant anthropological advances of the second and third centuries are grounded. How, then, to read the pneumatological 'quiet' of Nicaea and its era? Here the study of early Christian anthropology provides an insight into understanding an era of theological dogmatics that are directly connected to our points of interest. The real curiosity is not that Nicaea is so silent about the Spirit, but that the Christian world of the early- to mid-fourth century is so silent about Nicaea; and a tracing of anthropological development helps to explain why. As we shall see in the next chapter, Nicaea is not left largely in the quiet for 25 years because it is too novel, too vague, too radical. Theological emphasis on Nicaea is slight because its dogmatic assertions are insufficient in certain regards, and are perceived as insufficient precisely from the framework of pneumatology that had been so dominant in the anthropological convictions of previous generations.

Chapter 3

A CHANGING PICTURE OF NICAEA

The present chapter explores the position and influence of the council of Nicaea at the beginning of the high conciliar age, and in particular the question of its continuity with previous centuries of Christian thought. The common tendency to treat Nicaea as a new beginning, rather than a moment within an ongoing dialogue of anthropological/theological articulation, lies behind the enigmas that surround its place in history, and contributes to the problematic compartmentalization of 'trinitarian theology' as a fourth-century, post-Nicene phenomenon.

*   *   *

When Tertullian died c. 225, the centrality of Africa to the coming century of theological discourse could not have been anticipated. The catechetical 'school' in Alexandria, whatever its precise constitution, would be the intellectual home of Clement and Origen in the decades immediately to follow, and the city would rise in prominence to one of the primary milieux for refining discussions on the being of God. While the linguistic divide between Roman north Africa, significantly Latinized and Latinizing, on the one hand, and Alexandria as the Hellenic capital of learning since at least the first century BC on the other, was already forging a division in theological approaches in Tertullian's day, the basic themes of address transcended linguistic lines. Tertullian's coining of *trinitas* to reify verbally the relationship of the Father to his Son and Spirit as 'trinity' may have been a notable first, but it was hardly original. The Greek *trias*, while less novel than its Latin counterpart, was used in a similar manner earlier in Theophilus of Antioch, and it is a developed theme in the writings of Origen. By the end of the third century, the question was not whether an articulation of God was to be triadic, trinitarian, in nature, but how.

Precisely one century after Tertullian's death, some 300 bishops assembled in the city of Nicaea to consider, among other things, the response to this question proffered by a fellow African, and one squarely on the Greek side of the emerging linguistic and intellectual divide: Arius of Alexandria. Were one to accept without qualification the portrait of the council painted by Athanasius some 30 years after its convening, it would seem a monumental shift in the life of the Christian Church and the definition of its theology, summarized in 'the council's zeal for the truth and the exactness of its sense' against those who 'stood out in their irreligion and attempted to fight against God'.[1] Or, to follow the characterization of Eusebius:

> The place [. . .] selected for the synod, the city of Nicaea in Bithynia – named from 'victory' – was appropriate to the occasion. As soon as the imperial injunction was generally made known, all [the bishops] hastened there with the utmost willingness, as though they might outdo one another in a race; for they were impelled by the anticipation of a happy result to the conference, by the hope of enjoying a present peace and the desire of beholding something new and strange in the person of so admirable an emperor. When they were all assembled, it appeared evident that the proceeding was the work of God, inasmuch as men who had been most severely separated, not merely in senti-ment but also personally and by difference of country, place, and nation, were here brought together and comprised within the walls of a single city, forming as it were a vast garland of priests, composed of a variety of the choicest flowers.[2]

Both Athanasius and Eusebius had specific goals they wished to advance through their reporting on the council. Even the most devoted reader will recognize a bias in these words, though clearly bias is not always negative, nor a thing to be shunned. Largely through the influence of these two men, at least in practical terms, Nicaea does become a figurehead council, and its creed a centre-point of doctrine, in the centuries to follow – 'the cotter pin of Christian doctrine and the necessary ground of the very possibility of Christian God-talk', as Alan Torrance has characterized it.[3] The whys and hows of this centralization we shall explore to a degree in the present chapter, though a thoroughgoing study of the history of Nicaea is hardly our proper aim.[4] What is, however, of bearing on the present study is the position of Nicaea at the beginning of 'the conciliar age', and the ques-tion of its continuity with past generations of theological discourse in the Church. However one reads the coming-to-centrality of the Nicene creed in the decades and centuries following the council, its eventual significance is undeniable; and this makes all the more pertinent the matter of its placement within the broader trajectories of early Christian theological articulation.

---

1 Athanasius, *De Decr.* 32; 3. The precise dating of the *De decretis* is difficult to determine, but should be placed somewhere c. 350–56. See T. D. Barnes, *Athanasius and Constantius: Theology and Politics in the Constantinian Empire* (Cambridge, MA: Harvard University Press, 1993) 110–12.

2 Eusebius, *Vita Const.* 3.6.

3 A. Torrance, 'Being of One Substance with the Father', in C. R. Seitz (ed.), *Nicene Christianity: The Future for a New Ecumenism* (Grand Rapids, MI: Brazos Press, 2001) 52.

4 Two recent (and almost simultaneously published) studies have engaged in such a project: L. Ayres, *Nicaea and its Legacy: An Approach to Fourth-Century Trinitarian Theology* (Oxford: Oxford University Press, 2004); and Behr, *Nicene Faith*.

Most directly for our current purposes, the seemingly non-anthropological character of the creed – which speaks explicitly to no anthropological themes at all, and mentions humanity only implicitly in stating that the Son 'became man' – stands out.[5] This is especially so when Nicaea is seen in succession to the great theological writings of the second and third centuries, which as our two examples have shown, are significantly anthropological, not simply in their desire to explore the human, but in the anthropological framing-in of their exploration of God.

Further, the creed lacks any substantive discourse on the Holy Spirit, which we have seen ground the whole address of Christian anthropology in the preceding centuries. Our observation of the centrality of the Holy Spirit to this earlier anthropological and soteriological discourse, demands some manner of explanation of the near absence of any pneumatological discussion in the Nicene symbol. Thomas Smail's comments on attention to the Spirit in the Constantinopolitan revision of Nicaea seem even more pertinent as to the Nicene original:

Attention is so concentrated on the binitarian question of the right relationship of the Father to the Son that the properly trinitarian question that deals with the relating of the Spirit to both the Father and the Son is dealt with in a way that lacks focus and specificity and that, on any reckoning, is quite inadequate to the rich biblical and especially New Testament material that deals with the pre- and post-Pentecostal activity of the Spirit among God's people.[6]

And this of the creed of 381, which contains a whole article on the Spirit. One wonders how Smail might characterize Nicaea's mere 'and in the Holy Spirit'. How does it come about that the creed that will become the bedrock of dogmatic definition for centuries following 325 (indeed, in some sense, ever after) seems to abandon so thoroughly the pneumatological focus of previous generations of Christian theology? Certainly much of the response is situational: Nicaea responds to specific concerns, which are essentially Christological; but this does not wholly eliminate the question.

In the present chapter, I suggest a somewhat revised, though not radically new, reading of the history of Nicaea and the content of its creed, drawn from the

5   For an interesting reading of the phrase 'for us [. . .] was made man' in the creed's later Constantinopolitan rendition, see R. W. Jenson, 'For Us . . . He Was Made Man', in C. R. Seitz (ed.), *Nicene Christianity: The Future for a New Ecumenism* (Grand Rapids, MI: Brazos Press, 2001) 78, where he describes it as 'simply a narrative explication' of the creed's starting point, of 'the fact of the incarnate Logos, of the man Jesus who is the Son'. Needless to say, given my treatment in the present text, I find Jenson's words in this article compelling. Later in the same contribution he writes, 'The soteriological and metaphysical – not chronological – outcome of this passage is "and was made man." There is one who is simultaneously one of us and *unus ex trinitate*. He is either only inasmuch as he is both; he does the things of his divine reality through his life as a man and does the things of his human reality through his life as one of the Trinity' (pp. 84–85). Cf. my comments in the introduction, pp. 2–7.
6   T. Smail, 'The Holy Spirit in the Holy Trinity', in C. R. Seitz, ibid. 149.

anthropological-theological focus of the first three centuries and set in the context, too, of later theologians such as Cyril of Jerusalem, whom I will examine in subsequent chapters for signs of continuity with those earlier writers. What the fathers at Nicaea were really doing, and what they were not doing, is a popular scholarly topic at the present moment, and I am convinced that a more authentic understanding of the anthropological focus of early patristic thought sheds light on what is an interesting and curious discussion. To see how Nicaea does in fact bear the marks of continuity with the anthropological-theological discourse of those earlier centuries, and to appreciate more authentically the character of its influence on the continuation of that discourse into the fourth, we must first of all attempt to read accurately the history and output of the council proper, still very much a mystery despite its centrality in so much modern study.

RE-READING NICAEA

The council of Nicaea is rightly treated in nearly every study to deal with the early Church, and an engagement with 'Nicene orthodoxy', in conflict with non- or anti-Nicene theologies, forms the context of most volumes that deal with Christian history from the fourth until at least the end of the fifth centuries. Nonetheless, the definitive tenor of many such studies, especially those that appeared in the nineteenth and twentieth centuries, conceals a reality that has come more pointedly under the gaze of historians already in the twenty-first: that the council at Nicaea is in fact one of the least-documented of all pivotal events in Christendom. While it is possible, through documentary exploration, to re-create in minute detail the proceedings of later councils, our knowledge of Nicaea comes almost exclusively through the writings of later authors whose primary interest was not in presenting its history, but in furthering (or disparaging) its theological aims as they were then perceived. Sourcing our history from such later dogmatics, pictures of Nicaea as a resolutely theological assembly, determined to combat 'Arianism' and establish securely the framework of a trinitarian theology, have long become commonplace. These images are difficult to dislodge, in large part because this is precisely how Nicaea was often considered by the later writers to whom one looks as sources. But it is a picture full of holes, and holes that come to throw into question much received commentary on the period when the council is examined on its own grounds, rooted in its continuity with the past rather than its projected stature as the foundation of things to come.

The common anachronistic tendency to understand Nicaea as the 'starting point' for the fourth- and fifth-century trinitarian disputes, rather than a progressive move forward in continuity with two preceding centuries of focus and articulation, is a case-in-point. Nicaea is regularly addressed, directly or implicitly, as primarily a doctrinal gathering focused on articulating a proper conception of the Son's relation to the Father, spurred on to one degree or another by perceptions of

Arius' thought. Here already a substantial distortion of even our scant evidence, however, for the Nicene council was, like the majority of local councils before it, primarily administrative in nature. While today we may most often read solely the 'creed' or symbol of Nicaea, the council's real character cannot be represented without at the first recognizing that some 90 per cent of its deliberations had no specifically doctrinal bearing. Of the various texts recorded of Nicaea, all 20 of its canons are (predictably, as canons) concerned with matters of ecclesiastical over-sight and administration; and a synodal letter to the church of Alexandria and the bishops in Egypt recounts the circumstances of the synod and its summons, together with a summary of its creedal statement and canons, encouragement in recovering from the schism surrounding Meletius, and a comment on the settle-ment of the Paschal debate.[7] This latter issue seems to have captured the attention of most who focused on the council in early records: it forms, for example, the main thrust of Eusebius' interests in his account of the council in the *Vita Constantini*. One document alone, that containing the brief confession of faith, contains directly doctrinal material.[8] Moreover, this confession, which is the council's sole doctrinal document, is primarily traditional; that is, it contains a refined version of much earlier statements of faith – such as the various forms of the 'canon of truth' found in Irenaeus, and theorized local baptismal creeds from Palestine – though presented in newly creedal format.[9] In addition, and impor-tantly, this minimal theological output is demonstrably case-specific in scope. It is clear that the creed of Nicaea is deliberately anti-Arian (by which we should read, levelled against the perceived teaching of Arius himself, not a distinct group or movement called 'Arianism'), and not intended as a stand-alone summation of Christian belief. This is the only means of accounting for the manner in which it is so heavily centred on the Son's relationship to the Father in precisely the cate-gories questioned by Arius, while simply repeating older proclamations of the Father as creator, and indeed substantially diminishing the attention paid to the Spirit in comparison with earlier confessions and *regula*. In all this, any notion of Nicaea as self-professedly unique in scope or character faces a challenge. A coun-cil called for primarily administrative means, with some confessional re-statement of the faith maintained in those administrative deliberations, aimed to counteract individuals in the environs who professed otherwise, is characteristic of every local council held prior to 325, as far back as the 'council of Jerusalem' recounted in Acts 15.

---

7   Letter preserved by Athanasius, appendix to *De Decr.*, ed. Optiz, *Athanasius Werke* 2.1, p. 35. (Berlin, 1935) /CCO 22. Cf. N. P. Tanner, *Decrees* vol. i., pp. 3, 16–19.

8   For the documents of Nicaea, see N. P. Tanner, *Decrees of the Ecumenical Councils, vol. i* (1; London: Sheed & Ward Limited, 1990) 5–19. The creed itself is found as 27 lines of Greek on p. 5.

9   Cf. Irenaeus, *Ref.* 1.10.1–2. See J. N. D. Kelly, *Early Christian Creeds* (3rd edn.; London: Longman, 1972) on the relationship of Nicaea's creed to earlier statements of faith. Kelly's work disproved the once-popular argument that the Nicene creed was simply a refinement of the baptismal creed of Caesarea.

The one situational element that sets Nicaea notably apart from precedent councils is the presence of a Christian emperor enthroned as its overseer. But the nature of Constantine's presence, too, needs qualification. Eusebius certainly exaggerates the emperor's role in the theological deliberations of the council, though there is little question that he took a keen interest in those deliberations and played an important role in the council overall.[10] While Eusebius presents him as essentially the guiding light of all its activities, the actual documents speak of Constantine primarily as imperial patron and overseer (he who 'called' the council, as per the letter to the bishops in Africa[11]). The confession of faith is recorded as the faith 'of the 318 fathers', by which are clearly meant the assembled bishops;[12] and of the other, administrative, deliberations of the meeting – such as regulations on the ordination of priests and bishops (canons 2, 4, 9, 10, etc.), the frequency of synods (5), regulations on kneeling on Sundays and the Pentecost season (20) – there can be no serious suggestion that Constantine would have played, or wished to play, any direct part. The emperor clearly took an interest in the council *writ large*, and with regard to its final determinations became an active proponent: letters from Constantine announced the outcome of Nicaea to the empire and emphasized its usefulness for promoting ecclesial unity.[13] But Constantine's role, while significant, must not be overstated. The presence of an enthroned Christian emperor at a council of bishops would certainly have influenced the sobriety of the assembly, and suggested implications for the body's relationship not only to the larger Church but to the newly Christianized state; but Constantine's presence at Nicaea should not be seen as itself establishing the council as profoundly different in character from its predecessors.

The other usual claim to uniqueness granted Nicaea is that of its universal scope, its ecumenical status. Here, too, qualifications must be made. The term 'ecumenical' is not applied in a technical sense until Chalcedon, and then not as a description of any peculiar characteristic of conciliar constitution, but as regards reception in the Church as a whole.[14] Conciliar ecumenicity is bound up in reception at least as much as intention. The impossibility of grounding Nicaea's ecumenicity in the idea that it was the Church's first global synod, or gathering of the

---

10   See, for example, Eusebius, *Ep. Caes.* 16. For a summation of the role likely played by Constantine, see Ayres, *Nicaea and its Legacy* 90–92; cf. M. J. Edwards, 'The Arian Heresy and the Oration to the Saints', *VigChr* 49 (1995), 379–87.

11   See Tanner, *Decrees of the Ecumenical Councils* 16.

12   Though the actual number of bishops present was more likely in the range of 200–250.

13   Preserved in Eusebius, *Vita Const.* (on the dating of Pascha) and *Soc. HE* (on the creed). Constantine's concern with unity provoked his interest in Nicaea from the beginning: Eusebius records a letter written from the emperor to Arius and Alexander before the council convened; see *Vita Const.* 2.63–72.

14   Cf. N. P. Tanner, *The Councils of the Church – A Short History* (New York: Crossroad Publishing/Herder & Herder, 1999) 21–33, esp. 29–31. See also H. Chadwick, 'The Origin of the title Oecumenical Council', *JTS* NS 23 (1972), 132–35.

whole Church throughout the world, is established by the evidence as much as by common sense. The large number of bishops in attendance, even if swollen to the traditional 300 or 318, is hardly the extent of the episcopal population, an observation justified at least in part by the fact that one of the surviving texts is a letter addressed to bishops not present. It is reasonable to suggest that the first council to be called under imperial patronage would have inspired greater attendance than those in decades past, that Nicaea was more ecumenically representative than the localized synods of the earlier decades (it was certainly the largest council the Christian world had yet seen); but it is not possible to maintain that there was any truly universal representation at Nicaea, any more than this would be true of other councils called ecumenical (most notably Ephesus in 431, given ecumenical status despite the fact that essentially only three cities were represented in its official deliberations).

What we are left with, if we treat of the historical evidence as it stands, is a somewhat different picture of Nicaea than that often proffered. The tradition of local, administrative councils prior to 325 is carried forward at Nicaea, though the Christianization of Constantine only a short time prior meant that for the first time a Christian emperor would be present in the assembly. This emperor had a vested interest in the potential unity to Church and state that such a council would provide, especially in light of the discord arising out of the dispute with Arius – though more significantly with regard to the dissension over dating Pascha.[15] A Christian emperor sits as patron of a Christian council that neither presents itself nor is presented by others as otherwise outside the norm of such administrative gatherings in the life of the Church.[16] And that is what Nicaea primarily is: administrative. Details of ecclesiastical governance and administration are addressed, as predictably they might be given the Church's new acceptability to the state, which had seen it begin to expand more openly and quickly than in preceding eras. Regulating diocesan administration takes on a co-ordinately new immediacy and urgency. In the midst of this overarching administrative scope, the particular question of discord in north Africa surrounding Arius' dispute with his bishop, Alexander, a dispute gaining impetus in other areas of the realm, was addressed as part of the administrative purview of the assembled hierarchs – but in no different a manner than the teaching of Sabellius had been countermanded by a synod in Rome over a century before. A traditional statement of faith is issued by the

---

15   Eusebius argues this line in strong terms; see *Vita Const.* 2.61–69, and esp. 2.70–71. Grounding for the validity of the idea comes from Constantine's attitude towards other divisive affairs in his Christian realm, for example, the Donatist schism in north Africa. Cf. R. A. Markus, 'The Problem of Self-Definition: From Sect to Church', in E. P. Sanders (ed.), *Jewish and Christian Self-Definition, vol. i: The Shaping of Christianity in the Second and Third Centuries* (London: SCM, 1980); and Ayres, *Nicaea and its Legacy* 87–88.

16   So Ayres, *Nicaea and its Legacy* 85: 'The idea that the creed would serve as a universal and precise marker of the Christian faith was unlikely to have occurred to anyone at Nicaea simply because the idea that *any* creed might so serve was as yet unheard of'.

council, with those portions relating to the concerns at hand (namely Arius' views on the Son's relation to the Father) expanded in such a manner as to give clarity to the assembly's rejection of his thought. To make the matter emphatic, an anathema is appended to the confession such that any individual – and Arius himself is clearly intended – professing contrary to these statements, which are themselves presented as the traditional teaching of the Church, is to be held apart from its body. The council then moves on to other, and by most contemporary accounts, more important, matters.

If this reading of the assembly of the fathers gathered at Nicaea seems discordant with more customary portraits (at least until the re-visiting of Nicaea in the scholarship of the past few years), and if it seems to minimize the emphasis on its theological output in particular, it is worth recalling that most presentations of Nicaea's theological centrality are made in reference to the importance it would hold in later eras, not its own. With relatively few exceptions until our present century, 'Nicaea' as presented in ecclesiastical study is in fact the memory of Nicaea promulgated decades later by an Athanasius who felt an ever more urgent need to combat the fact that the thought of Arius had not gone silent with its progenitor – an Athanasius who felt himself to be surrounded by, to use his own term, 'Ario-maniacs' ('Αρειομανῖται).[17] Though the situation of theological debate in the mid-fourth century is intricate and complex, Athanasius is certainly not wrong; but this intensification of focus on Nicaea after 350 still leaves questions about those immediately post-Nicene decades. There is little solid accounting in scholarship for the fact that Nicaea comes and goes in 325 with relatively little impact apart from its directly administrative concerns. This is evidenced for us in several notable facts of the immediately post-Nicene period that, despite often being mentioned, rarely figure into a revised reading of the historical situation. First is the simple fact that Nicaea is not mentioned by anyone except its immediate chronicler, Eusebius, for nearly 20 years after it takes place.[18] Bishop

---

17   See, for example, *De Syn.* 1.13; *C. Ar.* 3.27, 44. This language found its way into the common parlance to follow; cf. *Theod. HE* 1.7; Basil of Caesarea, *Ep.* 266.2; Marcellus of Ancyra ('Pseudo-Anthimus'), *On the Holy Church* 8–9 (in A. H. B. Logan, 'Marcellus of Ancyra (Pseudo-Anthimus), "On the Holy Church": Text, Translation and Commentary', *JTS* NS 51.1 (2000), 95); etc. Nonetheless, it is not the most biting term in ancient usage. Epiphanius calls the followers of Arius 'nuts' and even 'crackbrains', according to Williams' translation, *The Panarion of Epiphanius of Salamis – Books II and III* (Leiden: Brill, 1994) 325, 341. See also C. Haas, 'The Arians of Alexandria', *VigChr* 47 (1993), 234–45, who draws attention (p. 235 n. 4) to the fact that Athanasius' attempts to brand all 'Arians' as maniacal followers of Arius must be tempered with numerous disavowals of Arius by such parties; cf. R. P. C. Hanson, *The Search for the Christian Doctrine of God – The Arian Controversy 318–81* (Edinburgh: T&T Clark, 1988) 123–28.
18   For a survey of awareness of the council and creed in various parts of the Christian world in the decades following 325, see Ayres, *Nicaea and its Legacy* 87. Ayres, following Hess, draws attention to the confusion over particular details of the creed, especially in the west, with reference to the canons of Serdica (343) regularly being confused with those of Nicaea. Cf. J. Ulrich, *Die Anfänge der abendländischen Rezeption des Nizänums* (Berlin: De Gruyter, 1994).

Hilary of Poitiers summarizes this silent reception in a famous aside: 'Though long ago regenerate in baptism and for some time bishop, I never heard of the Nicene creed until I was going into exile'.[19] There is a 'Nicene silence' after Nicaea that remains something of a puzzle.

Second is the connected but singularly significant example of this quietude with reference to Athanasius himself, perhaps the greatest pro-Nicene, who almost single-handedly brought the creed of Nicaea to centrality in the mid-fourth century. This same Athanasius neither mentions the council or its creed, nor grounds his theological reflection in its mode of articulation, linguistically or conceptually, for some 20 years after the council had taken place – despite the fact that he was present there as a deacon, assistant to bishop Alexander.

Third is the fact that during the decades following the council, significant theological texts were formulated that not only were not based on its creed, but based on others. When Athanasius begins, in the 350s, to suggest the Nicene formulation as a universal foundation stone for further doctrinal articulation, not only is he not suggesting what is by then normative, he is in fact making a highly controversial proposal. Nearly two decades have passed since the fathers of Nicaea had assembled, decades in which the projects of theological and anthropological articulation have continued without reference to its confession or language. Proposals for a centralization of Nicaea were met with hesitation even by those who would eventually come to accept and defend it. Basil of Caesarea famously writes to the later-anathematized Apollinarius, asking whether the language of the creed ought to be used at all, whether it was not in fact a distortion of proper teaching.[20] The other Cappadocians, like Basil himself, had reservations about the creed's language; and indeed the main focus of the heated disputes of the 360s–380s is not so much about defeating 'neo-Arianism' as about deciding whether, and if so, how, to read and employ the confession of the Nicene council as dominant in Christian articulation.

Numerous questions rise out of these observations. Why this long silence over Nicaea? Why, in an era fond of precise, confessional statements (borne witness to by the preponderance of local synods and confessions of belief), was its creed not picked up and employed more widely across the Christian realm? Why, when it at length did come to be considered as a basis for broader doctrinal articulation, was such concern expressed over its language? Why, indeed, did the Constantinopolitan council of 381 that ratified the 'Nicene creed', feel it necessary to modify it so heavily before ratification? There are a number of factors that must go into answering these and connected questions, and most current scholarship on the period is

---

19 *De Synod.* 91.
20 See Basil, *Ep.* 361; cf. H. De Riedmatten, 'La correspondance entre Basile de Césarée et Apollinaire de Laodicée', *JTS* 7–8 (1956–1957), 199–210 and 53–70. So too G. L. Prestige, *St. Basil the Great and Apollinarius* (London: SPCK, 1956); and the more recent survey of Basil's early thought vis-à-vis his correspondence with Apollinarius, in Ayres, *Nicaea and its Legacy* 188–91.

focused on exploring them. Yet one factor that rarely receives attention, largely on account of perceived issues of anachronism, is the matter of emphasis on the Holy Spirit. As mentioned already, an emphasis on the Spirit is usually understood as a development situated between Nicaea and Constantinople, given possibility by the former and articulated by the latter. But there are good grounds for questioning whether this was really the case, and the dialogue of preceding centuries suggests otherwise. As questions of anthropology intertwined with doctrinal theology in the second and third centuries, the presence and activity of the Spirit in relation to the Son and Father was central to the vision of both. As we have seen with both Irenaeus and Tertullian, it is the Holy Spirit that provides the grounding for understanding God as the Father of the Son, who creates 'in his image' through the working of this same Spirit, together with this Son. It is impossible to conceive of either the human person or the salvation offered in Christ, without a central significance to the Spirit of the Father.

In this light, the confession of faith of the Nicene council is at least partially inadequate, in terms of its ability to give expression to the focus of theological discussion in precedent Christian thought. The dispute with Arius may have centred predominantly around the question of the Son's relationship to the Father, but the broader arena of doctrinal articulation as a whole certainly did not. This larger context was grounded, as we have seen, in a more complex and authentically triadic vision of God as the Father with his two hands – and the 'hand' that is the Spirit was key to unlocking the mystery of the human person as imaging the divine life of this God. To one such as Tertullian, if we might indulge in speculation for a moment, the creed of Nicaea would likely have seemed acceptable as far as respects its intention and limited anti-Arian scope, but hardly sufficient as a broader grounding for theological articulation, precisely because it gave only minimal service to the Holy Spirit. This was not simply a feature of Tertullian's theological reflection: we have seen it also in Irenaeus, and it is present yet earlier in Paul's epistles.[21]

Read from this perspective of doctrinal history leading *to* and *through* Nicaea, one begins to locate coherent justification for the lack of theological attention paid to the council in the decades immediately following it. As a response to Arius it was sufficient and effective; but beyond this, it was insufficient to the already well-developed articulation of the Spirit in relationship to Father and Son, and the centrality of this articulation to the larger themes of doctrinal discourse. It is notable that among the most pointed of Basil of Caesarea's contributions, after being persuaded to accept the creed of Nicaea, is not an excursus on the meaning of *homoousios*, but his lengthy *De Spiritu sanctu* – an immense treatise on the Holy Spirit.

That the creed of Nicaea does not sufficiently address the pneumatological focus of earlier Christian reflection is one of the key observations to be gained

---

21   For example, Galatians 5.16–25; Ephesians 1.8–14.

from a study of that reflection in its anthropological scope. It is here that a developed articulation of the Spirit plays such a large part. One is provided at the same time with a means for redressing the relationship of Constantinople to Nicaea, a relationship often used as the framework for claiming as anachronistic the idea that a developed pneumatology or 'trinitarianism' is earlier than a fourth-century phenomenon. The council of 381 is too often seen as 'advancing' the trinitarian insights of Nicaea in 325, as if the nascent implications of the *homoousion* for the relationship of not only the Son to the Father, but also the Spirit to the Father and the Son, were only at length developed at that second ecumenical council into what could properly be called 'trinitarian' theology. This is, however, to read the relationship of Nicaea and Constantinople without sufficient reference to the thought of the preceding centuries. It is improper to say that Constantinople advances the nascent implications of Nicaea; rather, it seems deliberately to correct the pneumatological insufficiencies of the earlier creed, while also addressing other concerns. Before the confession of Nicaea is accepted and made universal, it is modified on exactly this point: clarification is offered of the clause on the Spirit, not to reflect a novel vision of trinitarian theology that had arisen or been newly developed since 325, but to present, in *the manner of language employed by Nicaea*, pneumatological articulations long precedent to that council, which its own confession had failed to convey sufficiently. Constantinople is a correction and refinement of, and not a conceptual advance upon, Nicaea.

This kind of reading helps makes sense of some of the puzzles bound up in the post-Nicene quiet: the articulation of doctrine between 325 and 360 in non-Nicene language; the reticence of even the most orthodox of bishops and theologians to embrace Nicaea between 360 and 380; the pneumatological focus of the texts written amidst that reticence; etc. It also provides a more authentic context for understanding the post-Nicene era in terms congruous with the thought of earlier decades and centuries. Nicaea is not a turning point in the history of doctrinal articulation in the early Church; it is a milestone along the way, and in later redaction will come to be seen as a significant watershed. Nonetheless, there is a continuity of focus and articulation between the second and third centuries on the one hand, and the fourth and subsequent on the other – a continuity minimized by the manner in which Nicaea is often read. We will move in the subsequent chapters to the anthropological thought of two post-Nicenes, Cyril of Jerusalem and Athanasius of Alexandria, the continuity of whose thought with that of previous generations is clearer when the nature and significance of Nicaea is properly understood. For one, his articulation of the human and the divine will take place as if Nicaea had never existed. For the other, both will come to be intimately connected to the framework of the Nicene confession, though only as that confession is understood as a terminological clarification of far earlier scriptural thought.

NICAEA'S THEOLOGICAL CONTRIBUTION

In light of the historical picture painted above, the immediate significance of Nicaea to the developing theological and anthropological articulation of the era appears, as it was, relatively minimal. It is primarily in its late-fourth-century reception that Nicaea and its creed gain status in doctrinal discussion. As we have stated, this is primarily on grounds not of deficiency but of insufficiency: Nicaea fails to give substantial expression to the pneumatological issues of such centrality to past – and, as we shall see in the next chapter, future – generations. A question then remains: what *did* the assembly at Nicaea regard as the theological contribution of the profession of faith it offered in response to Arius? While its aim may not have been pointedly dogmatic, Nicaea does offer an expression of the faith that bears its own unique contours, even as much as it can be seen to inherit modes of past expression. Our interest must lie in the degree to which the creedal statement of the council is a reflection of precedent articulation, and, in turn, what connection it authentically forges with the generations to follow.

Nicaea's genuine theological contribution is best explored by looking first at the broader theological continuum of which it is a part. The project of tracing trends in doctrinal discussion from various purifying movements in north Africa, through Sabellius, Origen and Arius, helps situate the concerns of the council accurately into their historical context. In particular, we will be concerned in the present section to demonstrate that the seemingly metaphysical concerns of individuals such as Origen and Arius have a discrete anthropological basis, not wholly distinct from the interests of Irenaeus and Tertullian, which also grounds Nicaea's considerations of the same. This is true especially as regards its establishment of *ousia*-based terminology for the description of older concepts of unified divinity. What is novel at Nicaea is not so much what is said, but how it is said. This reading places the council and its creed into the larger process of refining doctrinal discussion – a process in which it is more rightly seen as but a part, rather than a centrepiece.

The theological continuum

Nicaea's place on the timeline of doctrinal discussion locates it in direct succession to the moves towards more detailed confessional systems we have already witnessed in second- and third-century writers. Tertullian, at around the turn of the second century, was engaged in a project of refining the scientific language by which notions of God's multiplicity-in-unity were to be confessed. In his parlance, this took the form of a notion of 'one substance', identified generally with a coherent principle of divinity. There is one divine *substantia* common to the Father, together with his Son and Spirit, articulating a basic reification of the relationship of the Father with his hands.[22] In the century that followed, such refinements, or attempts at the same, flourished both in the form of formal theological reflection, and the larger scope of religious movements in the Christian realms. The Manichaean phenomenon of northern Africa, which later would so consume the attention of Augustine, took its grounding in the same moralizing questions over evil that had driven the second-century 'Gnostics'; but, as was the case with those earlier groups, these questions were raised in the context of dualistic cosmologies that brought understandings of divine reality into dialogue with questions of cosmological and anthropological nature. Combating this dualism would inspire Augustine's *De Trinitate* as much as it inspired his *De Genesi ad litteram* and other deliberately anti-Manichaean works. In other words, cosmological and anthropological questions inspired his trinitarian considerations, as well as (and often in direction connection to) his writings directly on those subjects. Similarly, while the renewed persecutions of the mid-third century promoted the kind of puritanical mentality in the region that would portend the Donatist schism – a schism that seems grounded in fairly little 'trinitarian' discourse – the same spirit of ecclesiastical purification and charismatic, divine leadership lay behind the retained popularity of so-called 'Montanism', with which Tertullian had sympathized, as later would Cyprian in Carthage. In groups connected with the 'New Prophecy', questions over the nature of God were central to considerations of human life and ecclesiastical vibrancy. The discourse we have already explored in Tertullian discloses the manner in which an increased precision of language in theological regard, grounded the anthropological and ecclesial principles with which he was concerned.

This ongoing project of establishing a more precise articulation of long-confessed realities presented new questions. If one is to decree that there is, with regard to the divine, one *substantia*, or confess that principle even if the language is not shared, the burden is to articulate what precisely the *substantia* is, and how it relates to the 'individuals' of Father, Son and Spirit. Declaration that there is a principle or concept of unity common to the three establishes the type of unity Tertullian believed was the common confession from the earliest Church; but its introduction presented him, and those engaged in similar modes of approach, with new conceptual challenges.

Sabellius is perhaps the most notable early figure to consider these challenges, and is certainly the individual most energetically attacked prior to Arius. In confessing one substance constitutive of 'God', he understood that the various perceived 'persons' of the Father, Son and Spirit were, in actuality, this single reality appearing or manifesting itself in distinct modalistic expressions.[23]

---

22   See, for example, *Adv. Prax.* 2; though the 'one substance' of unity is the Father's substance: see sections 4, and esp. 9. Cf. J. Moingt, 'Theologie trinitaire de Tertullien', *RSR* 54.3 (1966), 337–69; and C. Stead, 'Divine Substance in Tertullian', *JTS* NS 14 (1963), 46–66.

23   Cf. 'Hippolytus', *Refutation of all Heresies*, 9.12.16; Epiphanius, *Pan.* 62. But on the difficulties surrounding the matter of Sabellius and Sabellianism, see W. A. Beinert, 'Sabellius und Sabellianismus als

Rejecting what became known as 'Sabellian modalism' as passionately as they did, the early fathers indicated that while they had still to develop a language by which to articulate an inherited confession, that confession nonetheless was understood as demanding not only the common substance of unity, but the persistent reality of triadic individuality. Egged on by the challenge posed by Sabellius, there came a staunch denial that this individuality could be conceived in modalist terms, individuating solely in the area of manifestation.

The challenge of then explaining how one is to articulate both persistent individuality and commonality of nature or divine essence, came most carefully under the pen of another Alexandrian, predecessor to the great Athanasius, namely Origen. Origen offered what was to his day the most careful assessment of how one could posit both divine unity and persistent individuality, and he did so by what is usually characterized as an 'emanationist trinitarianism'. The clearest description of this concept is Origen's own, provided in the analogy of light, and 'light from light', as Origen addressed it (an analogy also employed by Tertullian, which seems to be drawn from the writings of John[24]). When a flame burns it produces light, and the light produced is distinct from the flame itself. An individual feeling the rays of light caused by a candle on the opposite side of a room, or sensing these rays in the eyes, would not suggest that he has touched the flame; its fire is present distinctly, on its own, elsewhere. At the same time, one would not claim that the light encountered was wholly distinct from the flame, for it is the light from the flame which *is* light – 'light from light'. Such an analogy, which Origen uses among several others, is meant to show that in an articulation of the relationship of Father, Son and Spirit as each commonly divine yet distinct, it is possible to have two, and by extrapolation three, entities that are genuinely individual and cannot be conflated, yet which have existence through a single essential source.[25] In this, Origen's analysis is, taken in its own right, markedly effective. The nature of 'the one God' is singular. There is but one divine reality, shared or communicated between three fully distinct realities, in the way that light from a source is itself light, yet from and of light. In this individuality one can only (and must always) say that there is but 'one God' – the Father who is the source and substance of the divinity common to the Son and Spirit – while at the same time maintaining that the realities of the Father, Son and Spirit are not modes of the one, but truly concurrent, eternally existing realities.[26]

---

historisches Problem', in H. Brennecke, E. Grasmück and C. Markschies (eds.), *Logos: Festschrift für Luise Abramowski zum 8 Juli 1993* (Berlin: De Gruyter, 1993) 124–39; and Behr, *Nicene Faith* 151–53, especially vis-à-vis the difficulties with Hippolytus's testimony.

24   Tertullian, *Apol.* 21; cf. John 1.6–13.

25   See Origen, *Comm. Jn.* 14.6, and also 9.4; cf. H. Crouzel, *Origen* (Edinburgh: T&T Clark, 1989) 186–87; J. Daniélou, *Origène* (Paris: La Table Ronde, 1948) 258–59; J. W. Trigg, *Origen* (London: Routledge, 1998) 97–99. Scriptural grounding comes from various places: Wisdom 7.25, 26; Colossians 1.15; Hebrews 1.13, etc.

26   See Trigg, 96–98.

Origen has applied a kind of scientific framework to the ideas put forward by Irenaeus, Tertullian and others in earlier generations; namely, that the 'one God' is confessed as the Father, the creator of all, yet this Father cannot be conceived of apart from his two 'hands', the Son and Spirit. On account of this immediate and inextricable connection, both Irenaeus and Tertullian can also at times call the Son and Spirit 'God', though for both this is rare. In terms of the relationship of these three, for Irenaeus the precisions are left undefined, though the significance of the relationship is central. In Tertullian there is some effort at refined articulation through language of *trinitas* and a definition of the unity of Father, Son and Spirit residing in *una substantia*, but this is far from a comprehensive articulation of divine relationality. It is such a comprehensive vision that Origen attempts, and to some success. The conceptual framework behind his refinement of the 'light from light' analogy is the Church's first approach to expressing synthetically the various points contributed by earlier writers. Modalism is prevented in the notion of the three hypostatic (i.e. subsistent) realities existing eternally;[27] and tritheistic tendencies are countered with the unitive reality of the one divine nature: the nature of God the Father (a consistency in use of this title between Origen and his predecessors). In this singular divine nature the Son and Spirit participate, and so it is, through this participation, able to be called also the nature proper to each. The Son, like the Spirit, *is God* in the way light from a source *is light*: not an appearance of light, but light proper – the source truly encountered in the ray shone forth from it.

Certain logical problems, however, present themselves in this approach. First are the notions of temporality and dependency. The ideas of emanation or communication necessarily raise, in normal speech and logic, the issue of time. When one switches on a light, first the light itself is illumined, then its ray shines across the room. The one is dependant on the other, not only causally, but temporally. Even in Origen's day, there was concern as to whether his language suggested that the Son, and by extrapolation the Spirit, have their existence in a temporal dependence upon the Father. For his part, Irenaeus had long ago asserted a co-eternity of the Father with his two hands ('the Father *has always with him* his two hands, the Son and Spirit . . .'[28]), and Origen echoes this belief, adamant in denying temporal dependency.[29] Analogy has its limitations, and 'light from light' risks precisely this kind of temporal, dependent aspect. To meet this shortfall, Origen gives us the language that will later become standard, of 'eternal generation'. The Son is generated from the Father as light from light; but where light comes temporally, finitely from a source, the Son's generation from the Father is mysteriously eternal. Though the phrasing, in a different context of application, will have a long and effective life in Christian discussion, usage of 'eternal generation' in

27   See Origen, *Comm. Jn.* 1, 2; cf. Trigg, ibid. 99–101.
28   Irenaeus, *Ref.* 4.20.1; emphasis added.
29   Cf. Origen, *Comm. Jn.* 2.2.18; 13.34.219; cf. Crouzel, *Origen* 187.

Origen is disappointing at a logical level. It serves as a loose escape clause for an important point of weakness in an otherwise effective analogy.[30] But this weakness is critical, and the mere ascription of eternity to the process of participatory generation does not rescue it.

While it is hardly possible to do justice here to Origen's fuller discussion of trinitarian matters, their relevance on a more general level comes by means of Arius' later objections to the preaching of Alexander. Calling Origen a 'pre-Arian Arian' has long been a useful stick with which to thrash him yet more severely than would be done centuries later at second Constantinople, asserting that his declaration of an ontological dependency of the Son upon the Father is a foretelling of Arius' conviction that the Son has no eternal stature, and possesses a divinity incongruous with that of the Father. Such arguments are still popular, despite the clear evidence that Origen says no such thing, and in fact insists on the opposite.[31] Nonetheless, it is true that both Origen and Arius seem to be motivated by the same kind of logical argumentation: in order to posit divinity to the Son (which we at times must remind ourselves Arius does in fact do[32]), his status must be maintained as being-in-reception. That is, the Son's divinity must be understood as received from the Father – else we are presented, both would agree, with a doctrine of two gods. For Origen this led to the conception of receipt by eternal emanation and participation, which effectively solved the problem of potentially confessing bitheism, but only at the cost of forcing an eternal dimension on that which, by the substance of his own analogies, is otherwise a temporally dependent act of reception and participation.[33]

Arius took a different approach to the same problem. Spurred on by what he considered the ample evidence of scripture,[34] his insistence on the Son's divine

---

30   On this see Crouzel, ibid.; Trigg, *Origen* 96–97.

31   See Crouzel, *Origen* 174–75, 268; cf. *Comm. Jn.* 20.22(20).182

32   So his *Confession to Alexander*: 'We say that the Son is not unbegotten, nor a part of the unbegotten in any way [. . .] but that he was constituted ("hypostatised") by God's will and counsel, before times and before ages, full of grace and truth, divine, unique, unchangeable'. O'Collins, perhaps a little too emphatically, calls this text 'an incoherent statement, ridiculed by Athanasius'; see G. O'Collins, *Christology – A Biblical, Historical, and Systematic Study of Jesus* (Oxford: Oxford University Press, 1995) 177.

33   I take a slightly different focus of criticism here than does C. Gunton, 'And in One Lord, Jesus Christ . . . Begotten, Not Made', in C. R. Seitz (ed.), *Nicene Christianity: The Future for a New Ecumenism* (Grand Rapids, MI: Brazos Press, 2001) 37–39, who sees Origen's main shortcoming, vis-à-vis emanationist concepts, as an overt focus on 'an a priori appeal to divine immutability, almost always a bad form of argument' (p. 37). I am not wholly convinced by this line of criticism. Gunton makes a more interesting, and more viable, criticism later in his contribution, characterizing Origen's emanationist schema by 'its lack of appeal to Jesus, in whom he is not really very interested' (pp. 40–41). Gunton is clearly influenced in this reading by D. Farrow, 'St Irenaeus of Lyons : The Church and the World', *PE* 4 (1995), 333–55, esp. 337, as per his comments in n. 9.

34   See, for example, Proverbs 8.22; Acts 2.36; 1 Corinthians 15.24–28; Hebrews 1.4, 3.1.

stature-by-receipt took the form of demanding his creaturely nature. The logical problem of Origen's eternal temporality is avoided: Alexander's proclamation that there is 'always Father, always Son', seemed to Arius to identify this difficulty, and he responded in logical riposte. The Father begets the Son and begets him once, for begetting is a process that, once carried out, is complete.[35] It is to be analogized, and held as equivalent to, creation – and Arius felt no sense of novelty in asserting that the Son was creaturely, given that the scriptures said as much. He did not go so far as to suggest directly that the Son was something made (a *poiema*), which would have suggested he amounted to a work or handicraft of the Father; but that his nature could be distinguished from the Father's in terms of its substance as *ktisma*, which the Father's was not. This assertion that the Son is a creature, together with what Arius considered the logical correlates to this confession – that he was therefore created/begotten (terms he uses synonymously in his epistle to Eusebius of Nicomedia[36]), and prior to this begetting 'was not' – was not an attempt to diminish the Son's divinity, but precisely to establish it. In order to be the one through whom God creates all things, without blasphemously declaring that there are two gods, Arius is convinced (just as had been Origen) that the Son's divinity must be understood as *received* divinity, and that this reception is constituted by the manner of the Son's 'generation, or creation' by the Father.[37] It is in this framework, Arius is convinced, that the Son can be confessed as truly divine, truly creator, truly saviour, without transforming Christianity into a bitheistic religion. It is a conviction that has had a long life, becoming, in the words of Gunton, 'perhaps the twentieth century's favorite heresy, and [. . .] among the most appealing of them all'.[38]

It is significant to our purposes that the motivation for both Origen and Arius is the assertion of a real divinity to the Son. To take up Gunton's words, specifically with regard to Origen:

> The purpose of developing a notion of the eternal Son of God is that it enables us to speak of one who is God in a different way from God the Father.[39]

Arius does not talk of the Son as eternal in the sense of which Gunton speaks – the sense in which Origen does – but his aim is the same. Both wish to insist that

---

35   This approach to generation as a process to be described in parallel to human generative terms was one of the issues attacked later by the Cappadocians; cf. Gregory of Nyssa, *Contra Eunomium* 2.

36   *Letter to Eusebius* 5, quoted below.

37   Cf. Torrance, 'Being of One Substance with the Father', 53. Torrance is critical of the circular logic of Arius' system: 'The Son was a creature, albeit the "first creature" (*proton ktisma*). Created first, he was the one through whom everything *else* was created, but emphatically *not* the one through whom *all* things were created. The effect of Arius' own argument was to deprive himself of any warrant for making even the claims he made' (italics in original).

38   C. Gunton, 'And in One Lord, Jesus Christ . . . Begotten, Not Made', 35.

in order for Christ, as Son incarnate, to be confessed as creator and saviour, he cannot be a mere man as are all men, but must be divine in order that his work be creative and salvific. Thus for Arius he is 'a creature, but not one of the creatures' – a comment usually read as diminishing the Son as less than divine, but by which Arius intends to show precisely that, while generation demands creatureliness, the Son is nonetheless unlike all others. He is divine, but not in a matter equivalent or congruous to the Father. In this sense of demanding some manner of divinity to the Son as essential to a view of economy and salvation, Origen and Arius are quite in line with Irenaeus and Tertullian. The creation in which humanity dwells, of which it is a part, is the working of the Son, who therefore must be understood as divine, in order that the salvation wrought upon this handiwork be authentic and effective.

The concerns are soteriological inasmuch as they are anthropological. Direct assertions of soteriological/anthropological motivations for Arius are difficult to establish, at least in part because we possess so little of his actual writings;[40] but it is clear in Origen, whose chief speculative articulations of the trinity come in the same text (the *De principiis*) as his chief speculative articulations of the human person in the economy of salvation. The two realms form a single, coherent body of address. The fact that both writers' approaches would be rejected as insufficient on various grounds (which we will address below), only goes further to show that the context of exploring, in a detailed and refined way, matters theological as related to matters anthropological, was widely in the air and perceived as critical to Christian life and thought.

All this points to the fact that Nicaea's deliberations over the relationship of the Son to the Father, spurred on by the effects of Arius' dispute with Alexander, are far from discordant with the conversation of previous generations, on which Arius himself grounded his objections. The insufficiency of the council for future theological discussion lies not in its intention or confession, but in its almost exclusive attention to the Son and Father, with no real connection to the Spirit. The technicalities of its articulation *per se*, which Athanasius would later ensure became the standard for conciliar discourse, were not the whole root of the problem. The challenges posed by the language and concepts used at Nicaea to explain the Son's relationship to the Father (difficult primarily for the novelty and ambiguity of language), were coupled with the fact that the creed did not apply this expression to the whole confession of God as Father with his Son and Spirit.

---

39   Ibid. 45.

40   Though see R. C. Gregg and D. E. Groh, *Early Arianism: A View of Salvation* (Philadelphia: Fortress Press, 1981). While their thesis on the contours of Arius' soteriology have been largely rejected, they have nonetheless played an important part in raising awareness of a soteriological aspect to Arius' concerns.

The theology of Nicaea

That its mode of expression is not discredited (though it is challenged), but its scope deemed insufficient, provides the groundwork for better understanding Nicaea's contribution to the Church's advancing theological discussion. It is the *mode of articulation of Nicaea* that endures, that is therefore important for understanding its place in the heritage of Christian theology.

In response to Arius, the assembled bishops chose famously (to some, infamously) to ally themselves to the language and concept of *ousia*. Most often translated as nature or essence, the 'Nicene confession' of the Father, Son and Spirit as 'one *ousia*' is regularly taken to mean that while all three are distinct in their existential reality, they are 'one divine nature', singular among the three. There are myriad problems, however, with this general definition. First, the creed nowhere states that the Father, Son and Spirit are 'one *ousia*'; all that is claimed is that the Son is '*homoousios* with the Father', as of the Father's *ousia*. That which is commonly seen as the 'Nicene definition' of the trinity is in fact the fruit of later reflection, not directly of the synod. For its part, Nicaea locates the unity of God not in the *ousia*, but, in common tradition with precedent voices, in the Father:

> We believe in one God the Father almighty, . . .
> πιστεύομεν εἰς ἕνα Θεὸν πατέρα παντοκράτορα, . . .

Creative attempts at hypothesis over punctuating the creed have attempted to make it sound more 'trinitarian', as trinitarian definition would later be perceived, by suggesting the separation of the reference to 'God' from those of the three persons:

> We believe in one God: the Father almighty [. . .] and the one Son [. . .] and the Holy Spirit [. . .].

As attractive as such readings may by some standards seem, the language of the creed clearly does not allow them. The repetition of belief 'in' (εἰς) stands before 'one God the Father', again before 'and in one Son' and 'in the Holy Spirit'. It is in the Father that the unity of God is found, as we have seen was the case a century and a half earlier in Irenaeus and more recently in Tertullian.

Second, a generalizing understanding of Nicene trinitarianism, which misappropriates the centre of unity from the Father to the *ousia*, also misappropriates the larger place of that term and concept in the creedal statement. *Ousia* is never discussed as a distinct element in the creed; it is used only as a means of explaining the relationship of the Son to the Father. The creed's most famous single term, '*homoousios*', is in fact a gloss in explanation of the terms that immediately precede it: *gennethenta ou poiethenta*, 'begotten not made'.[41] The most frequently repeated sentiment on the Nicene *homoousion* is that it was articulated as the great death blow to Arius, that charge from which he could not recover. Perhaps in effect this was so. But within the coherent structure of the confession itself, the *homoousion* is not the chief anti-Arian declaration. We have no record of Arius himself claiming the Son to be of a distinct *ousia* from the Father; and while perhaps this is a valid extrapolation for later writers to have drawn (as the logical conclusion, in a post-Nicene terminological context, to what Arius wished to say in his own), such commentaries would not emerge yet for some decades. But while Nicaea did not have a specifically Arian claim of 'hetero-substantiality' to combat, it did have Arius' direct assertion that the Son was created, and that this 'creation' was equivalent to the 'generation' proclaimed by such sources as John (cf. John 1.14, 18; 3.16, etc.). Arius' letter to Eusebius of Nicomedia preserves his important statement:

> Before [the Son] was begotten or created or defined or established, he was not.[42]

What is of particular interest here is not the claim that the Son 'was not' prior to his generation, but Arius' casual presentation of 'begotten' and 'created/made' as synonyms. To him it mattered not whether one called the Son begotten or created; the point of importance was that the immutable Father, in begetting/creating the Son, brought into being one other than himself, which had its being, its nature, defined by this coming-into-being. To suggest otherwise not only challenged the obvious everyday witness of both begetting and creation (since one neither begets nor creates something that already exists), but also the ancient confession of God's immutability. Only when creating something other, something new, is God's creative activity external, and not equivalent to an internal mutation.

It is in this light that the whole-hearted anti-Arian thrust of Nicaea's 'begotten not made' has its grounding. Nicaea sets in opposition concepts Arius defines explicitly as synonymous: 'begotten *not* made' is the creed's most direct attack on Arius' 'begotten *or* made'. Any assertion that the *homoousion* is, in its own right, the central rebuff of Arius suffers this observation, for, as stated before, there exists no evidence that Arius used terminology that he would have seen as directly challenged by it. Indeed, the decades of heated argument over *ousia*-related language that would follow Nicaea are strong evidence that, analysed on its own, the language of *homoousia* had little clear definition to anyone at all.[43]

---

41   See Torrance's comments on the centrality of this phrase to the creed in Torrance, 'Being of One Substance with the Father', 49.

42   *Letter to Eusebius of Nicomedia*, 5; Rusch p. 30.

43   Here see Behr, *Nicene Faith* in its entirety, which is a good treatment of the confusion and trajectories of interpretation in the post-Nicene era. So also Ayres, *Nicaea and its Legacy*, esp. 92–104.

Within the internal structure of the creed in which it is found, the ambiguity of the term's meaning as a kind of independent theological concept is mitigated by the fact that it is not actually used as such. Whatever may or may not be indicated by a doctrine of consubstantiality examined in its own right, the term's use in this creed is as *clarification of how being 'begotten' differs from being 'made'*. Here the language of the creed has to be taken beyond single terms. It confesses belief in one Son who is

> begotten of the Father, only-begotten,
> γεννηθέντα ἐκ τοῦ πατρὸς μονογενῆ,

> that is, of the *ousia* of the Father,
> τουτέστιν ἐκ τῆς οὐσίας τοῦ πατρός,

> God from God, light from light, true God from true God,
> Θεὸν ἐκ θεοῦ, φῶς ἐκ φωτός, θεὸν ἀληθινὸν ἐκ θεοῦ ἀληθινοῦ,

> begotten not made – *homoousios* with the Father [. . .]
> γεννηθέντα οὐ ποιηθέντα, ὁμοούσιον τῷ πατρί [. . .]

In maintaining the scriptural assertion that Jesus Christ is the Son 'begotten of the Father', Nicaea articulates that this begottenness equates to a relationship of *ousia*. To be begotten of the Father is equivalent to being 'of the *ousia*' of the Father. This provides the council with a means of supporting and grounding much older assertions of the Son's begottenness as relating to light drawn from light (which we have seen in Tertullian and Origen), preserving that analogy's premise that light radiating from a source is distinct from, and yet not disassociated with, the light that is the source itself. Here Nicaea can ground that analogy in a language of ontology: that which is begotten is ontologically related to its begetter, so just as we can say 'light from light', we can in this case say 'God from God' – not metaphorically, as Arius might wish, but truly (thus the more powerful restatement that follows: '*true* God from true God'); and it is in further clarification of this concept that the phrase continues 'begotten not made'. This is, as we have already noted, a deliberate refutation of Arius' conception of begetting and creation as synonymous, and a refutation grounded in the examples the creed has just cited. To be begotten is to be 'of the *ousia*' of the source, as light is from light, which is distinct from being created (*poiethenta*). How so? Here the creed's internal gloss: to be begotten does not mean simply that one is 'from' (*ek*) the *ousia* of its begetter, but that the *ousia* of the one begotten is *homoousios* with that of the begetter. The famous phrase '*homoousios* with the Father' is not so much a deliberate refutation of Arius as it is an explanation of how 'begotten not made' is the deliberate refutation of Arius. In all this, the creed carefully distinguishes between being made (i.e. defining the Son as *poiema*) and being termed 'creature' (*ktisma*), which, as Arius rightly noted, has scriptural grounding. While Athanasius would later consider the two terms as synonyms, there is no evidence that Arius did so; and while the creed anathematizes those who call the Son a *poiema*, it makes no such proclamation against the term *ktisma*. It is not the scripturally grounded vocabulary of Son as 'creature' that is rejected, but Arius' conception of creature-liness as intrinsically joined to the concept of fashioning or making, which informed his understanding of the Son's begotten relation to the Father. While, given the ease with which Arius slips between the concepts associated with each, it may be perfectly clear why Athanasius would later argue that these two terms should be treated synonymously, it is equally as clear that Nicaea itself does not do so.

The council thus rejects Arius' view, not on simple terminological grounds, but with an eye towards the question of relation they involve. Nicaea employs new terminology (*ousia*, *homoousia*) to express what it considers an ancient proclamation on the relationship of Father and Son. Terms and metaphysical constructs arising out of the third century are taken up in its mode of expression, but the task of the reader of Nicaea today is the same as that faced by the framers of the creed itself: to discover the manner in which this new mode of expression discloses longstanding confessional truths, and not some new theological vision enshrined in the novel mode of speech.

When the creed of Nicaea is read in this manner, its continuity with previous generations of thought stands out more clearly. The council's language of *ousia* and *homoousios* is not a new or novel way of conceiving God as 'relational' or nascently as 'trinity': such concepts predate the deliberations of 325 by several centuries. What is novel is the language or mode of expression used to articulate these older confessions. Whether or not the employment of *ousia*-based terminology was itself occasioned by the debate with Arius, or whether it would have arisen independently of that confrontation, remains a mystery. What is demonstrable, however, especially through a study of the anthropological language of precedent writers such as Irenaeus and Tertullian, is that the conceptuality enshrined in the *ousia*-language of Nicaea is not itself new; it follows expressions of divine reality expressed in other language centuries before. Moreover, and critically, it fails to represent fully enough the substantial expression of those earlier articulations, precisely because it is so focused on the main concern of Arius' objection: the relationship of the Son to the Father. While the language of the *homoousion* will provide an effective counter to his claims, and indeed assert more clearly than perhaps ever before the manner in which the Son is the Father's Son, and the divinity of the one God the Father also the divinity encountered in the Son, it will hardly satisfy in the largely pneumatological context of Christian thought inherited from earlier generations. Its employment in the creed of Nicaea is simply too exclusively focused on the Son's relationship to the Father. As such, Nicaea's expression of Christian doctrine could be, and was, quietly passed over in a wider frame of reference – even, for a time, by the great Athanasius. It is only when this latter comes eventually to believe that *the mode of articulation* expressed in the

Nicene creed has value for expressing the whole scope of the Church's ancient confession of God as Father with Son and Spirit, and indeed begins to suggest that it is the only suitable means for articulating properly this ancient confession, that serious consideration begins to be given to Nicaea's language in a broader arena. The main focus of this consideration then rests in two interrelated aspects: first, as is seen in the case of Basil of Caesarea among others, the matter of integrating the Christological emphasis of Nicaea into the trinitarian focus of the Church's larger confession; and second, interpreting and explaining precisely what is meant by the *ousia*-language the creed employs. As the language is new, at least in Christian discussion, attention is required (hence the complex debates of the 360s–380s) in order to ensure that it is employed in a manner that does indeed articulate the same confession as had earlier been expressed, and not something significantly novel.

A NICENE CONTRIBUTION TO ANTHROPOLOGICAL THEOLOGY?

A reading of the history of Nicaea, as well as its reception and later employment as refined at Constantinople in 381, requires that we set aside some common concerns over anachronistic usage of 'trinity', and pneumatology in particular. Examined, as it often is, from the realm of theological systematics, Nicaea seems a shot out of the blue in the landscape of the early Church: new terms, new concepts, a seemingly new focus of attention – hence the regular attention paid to it as 'first' and 'unique' and 'pivotal'. However, when it is examined as a specific instance of articulation in the long history of theological dialogue, interrelated to precedent explorations of the human person, Nicaea can be seen to stand coherently within in a lengthy tradition of consideration of the Father in relation to the Son and Spirit as the 'one God'. It is this one God who fashioned, formed and is imaged in the human formation. Further, seeing Nicaea in this framework of theology as expressed pneumatologically in preceding generations, helps explain the unusual role it plays in the progressing doctrinal project. Nicaea does not initiate a manner of envisaging God that is developed as a 'new realm' and advanced to eventual perfection at Constantinople. It attempts to articulate in new expression a longstanding conviction of the Father's relationship to the Spirit and Son, though it focuses on the latter to such an exclusive degree that it must be corrected and modified before it is ratified some 56 years later.

Nicaea can never be read as a coherent source text for Christian anthropology. Nor, in its own right as a document, does it offer much in the way of refining an anthropological approach to theology. It is a brief credo, highly situational and case-specific, focused on a narrow goal. But the creed of Nicaea is important to our understanding of theology as anthropology in the early Church for exactly these reasons. The degree of Nicaea's departure from customary expressions of theology in the first centuries, and the response of many writers in essentially ignoring the creed and carrying on with earlier approaches, demonstrates just how strongly the anthropological focus of theological expression really was. The fact that so much writing focuses on the human person, while Nicaea does not; the fact that the human as *imago* is the key to understanding the divine, while not figuring at all into the creed; the fact that antecedent authors lay critical weight on the role of the Spirit, while Nicaea doesn't; all these offer routes towards clarity over just what Nicaea was, and what it wasn't, on the immediate historical stage. It is by apprehending this interrelationship of anthropology and theology in the earliest centuries that we are most effectively able to account for the historical and doctrinal peculiarities surrounding the era of Nicaea, and to demonstrate the manner in which these peculiarities reveal the continuity between those earlier centuries and the height of the conciliar period initiated in the fourth. This sets the groundwork, in turn, for a reading of the various sources immediately to follow Nicaea. In light of what has been said in the present chapter, it cannot strike us as particularly curious that the bishop of such a central church as that in Jerusalem could, some two decades after the council, articulate his theological and anthropological understandings without it – indeed, with reference to a different creed altogether. Rather, the heavily anthropological, catechetical writings of Cyril of Jerusalem can be seen to stand in direct continuity with pre-Nicene reflection, and indeed with the implied background of Nicaea itself. His witness becomes significant because we can see within it the continuation of an earlier pneumatological focus, though in the framework of a more metaphysical construction that resonates with, but is nonetheless different from, the language employed at the council. Such an investigation of how Cyril does not use Nicaea, but carries forward the anthropological project of past centuries, will in turn give us the basis to understand how Athanasius' centralizing of the Nicene creed in the mid-fourth century is not his promotion of a new way of conceiving of God in particularly advanced trinitarian terms, but his attempt to enshrine Nicaea's new mode of expression as the most valid manner of preserving more ancient confessions. The project of refining theological articulation through anthropological considerations, so vivid in earlier writers yet so hard to discern in Nicaea, in fact forms the groundwork for the creed's eventual ratification and widespread adoption.

Chapter 4

BAPTIZED INTO HUMAN REALITY: CYRIL OF JERUSALEM

Much less is known of Cyril's contribution to post-Nicene thought than is known of many of the other figures of his age. The present chapter examines his sacramental focus as revealing a link to precedent doctrinal articulation, from the starting point of anthropological concerns. His perception of baptism as indicative of a soul-body distinction, linked by the Spirit to the incarnate Christ and becoming by participation what the Son is by nature, is the impetus for Cyril's detailed focus on the Son's relation to the Father and Spirit. His emphasis on bearing the 'image' of God, as being a participant through the Spirit in the Son's life of suffering, offering and redemption, links his definition of sacrament to his perception of 'likeness', as a making real in man of the glory of the Father.

*   *   *

Where Nicaea was insufficient, in terms of its suitability as a basis on which to ground wider doctrinal discussion, was the realm of pneumatology. The apparent 'gap' between the Spirit-orientated discussions of the second and third centuries on the one hand, and the post-Nicene fourth on the other, was the object of our consideration in the preceding chapter. Our observation there – that polemical concerns led to sustained focus on the relationship between Son and Father, and a corresponding lack of attention to the Spirit that, in addition to the novelty of language employed, added to the challenges facing Nicaea – is borne out in the immediately post-Nicene witness. The 'post-Nicene silence' from 325 to c. 350 does not imply a general theological quiet, but a lack of specifically Nicene influence and language on the continuing work of doctrinal discussion in those decades. These years mark out what is in actuality a remarkably active era, notable to our purposes inasmuch as it bears strongly the flavour and focus of the pre-Nicene period explored in Chapters 1 and 2. As ever, it is continuity and not radical change that characterizes the first half of the fourth century.

This spirit of continuity is perhaps most apparent in the witness of one of the great non-Nicene post-Nicenes, Cyril of Jerusalem. Still an understudied voice from the patristic period, Cyril's position in the intriguing quiet following the council, and his lack of substantial bearing or influence upon the debates of the second half of the century, often see him sidelined in studies of the era. He receives only passing mention in otherwise thoroughgoing monographs, and it is a rare university syllabus that dwells much on him between Nicaea and Athanasius or the Cappadocians. Cyril is a catechist, a teacher, an exponent of baptism and Christian initiation, who uses 'another creed' (i.e. not that of Nicaea) but otherwise is not heavily engaged in the expansive post-Nicene theological project.

It is, however, precisely Cyril's lack of direct engagement in those disputes that makes his witness important. His overt concern with anthropology sets him in line with earlier authors such as Irenaeus and Tertullian; and the degree to which his anthropological discussion grounds his description of divine reality, advances the project of those earlier writers. It is through the anthropological context of his teachings that Cyril refines his articulation of God, the reality imaged in the human as Father with co-eternal, naturally co-divine Son, in union with co-divine and equally eternal Spirit. In some sense, Cyril 'says the same thing' that Nicaea implies – that is, that the Father, Son and Spirit are equally divine, equally eternal, in the manner that is the implication of Nicaea's *homoousios* – but he does so specifically by means of, and through the conceptual vision provided by, his understanding of human natural reality. Cyril's trinitarian theology is wholly, and perhaps more notably than in earlier sources, theology as anthropology.

As nearly every study on Cyril begins, 'we know virtually nothing about Cyril's early life'[1]. Born c. 313, the same year Constantine issued the so-called 'Edict of Milan', Cyril was what Walker has called 'a child of the new age, who had never known an empire without a Christian on the throne'.[2] While Telfer argued for origins in Caesarea, scholars have settled on what is the more traditional view, that Cyril was born in or near Jerusalem, based in part on his knowledge of the pre-Constantinian landscape of the city.[3] He had one sister, at least; but beyond this we know nothing of any other siblings.[4] Of his parents we can only assume that they were fairly well to do, given that Cyril's position and rhetorical skill betray an upper-class education (Sozomen calls him 'among the most distinguished' bish-

---

1   E. Yarnold, *Cyril of Jerusalem* (The Early Church Fathers; London/New York: Routledge, 2000) 3.

2   P. W. L. Walker, *Holy City, Holy Places? Christian Attitudes to Jerusalem and the Holy Land in the Fourth Century* (Oxford: Clarendon Press, 1990) 31. Cf. M. Vércel, *Cyrille de Jérusalem* (Paris: Les Editions Ouvrieres, 1957) 9–25. The precise date is, as Drijvers terms it, an 'educated guess' based on Jerome's comments at *De Ill.*, 112; cf. J. W. Drijvers, *Cyril of Jerusalem: Bishop and City* (Supplements to Vigiliae Christianae, 72; Leiden/Boston: Brill, 2004) 31.

3   See W. Telfer, *Cyril of Jerusalem and Nemesius of Emesa* (The Library of Christian Classics; London, 1955); cf. Drijvers, *Cyril of Jerusalem: Bishop and City* 31, and Yarnold, *Cyril of Jerusalem* 3. For Cyril's comments on the city prior to Constantine's building project (culminating in the dedication of his great basilica in 335), see *Cat.* 14.5, 9.

4   Knowledge of his sister comes from the remark, in Epiphanius' *Pan.* 73.37.5, that bishop Gelasius of Caesarea was the son of Cyril's sister. Perhaps he was appointed by Cyril himself; cf. A. J. Doval, *Cyril of Jerusalem: Mystagogue – The Authorship of the Mystagogic Catecheses* (Patristic Monograph Series, 17; Washington, D.C.: Catholic University of America Press, 2001) 12. Yarnold's claim that Gelasius was Cyril's brother seems a simple mistake: *Cyril of Jerusalem* 6.

ops of his period, 'on account of [his] great eloquence').[5] There are traditions that he may have been a monastic in his early life, but if this is true it is not something he ever mentions to his hearers.[6]

Such is the extent of our knowledge of Cyril's early years. When he died in March 386, an old man of over 70, he had been bishop for 36 years, some 15 (or possibly 16) of which were spent in three periods of exile.[7] Only 12 years old when the council of Nicaea was held in 325, and never involved in the production of theological treatises that engage with Nicene theological terminology (the absence of the term *homoousios* from his *Catechetical orations* is noted in almost every study), Cyril would ultimately be praised by the bishops assembled in Constantinople in 381, in a letter issued after the council, as 'the right reverend and most religious Cyril [. . .] who was some time ago correctly ordained by the bishops of the province [of Jerusalem], and has in several places fought a good fight against the Arians'.[8]

'Fighting the good fight against the Arians' is a peculiar claim, given that Cyril produces a listing of notable heretics in his sixth oration, which doesn't include Arius or any 'Arians'.[9] More notable is the fact that being an 'Arian sympathiser' was a charge Cyril faced repeatedly throughout his life. The attention paid to refuting it in 381 only reinforces that the charge was widespread. If Drijvers is entirely right to note that the sources on Cyril's ecclesiastical life 'make clear that [he] was a prominent and controversial figure in his time', they also make sorting out the details of that controversy nearly impossible.[10] Ancient sources range from calling Cyril a great and noble leader to an out-and-out Arian or Macedonian.[11] The statement by the bishops in Constantinople, that Cyril was 'correctly ordained', identifies the source of the dispute in questions surrounding his consecration to the episcopacy. Having been a deacon from the first years of the 330s (ordained by Macarius of Jerusalem) and a priest from c. 343 (ordained by Maximus), Cyril was elevated to the episcopacy of Jerusalem c. 350 amidst considerable controversy.[12] While it is probable that the majority witness is

---

5 Cf. *Soz. HE* 3.14.

6 Though he praises the ascetical life in various places; see *Cat.* 4.24, 12.33–4; cf. Drijvers, *Cyril of Jerusalem: Bishop and City* 31–32.

7 The first from 357–59; the second from 360–61; the third from 367–78. See Yarnold, *Cyril of Jerusalem* 5–7; Vércel, *Cyrille de Jérusalem* 25–29; Drijvers, *Cyril of Jerusalem: Bishop and City* 65–68.

8 *Theod. HE* 5.9.

9 See *Cat.* 6.12–36.

10 Drijvers, *Cyril of Jerusalem: Bishop and City* xiv.

11 Ancient sources on Cyril's life include Jerome, *De Ill.* 112 and *Chron.* a. 348; Epiphanius, *Pan.* 73.23.7, 27.8; Rufinus, *HE* 10.24, 38; 11.21; *Soc. HE* 2.38–45, 3.20, 4.1, 5.3–15; *Soz. HE* 3.14; 4.5, 20–25; 7.14; and *Theod. HE* 2.26–7, 3.14, 5.8–9. Later sources are cited in Drijvers, xiii. I agree with Drijvers that the Armenian *Vita Cyrilli* (Vienna Armenian Codex 224, c. 1428) cannot be taken as a credible source.

12 This following Jerome, *Chron.* a. 348. See Doval, *Cyril of Jerusalem: Mystagogue* 13–17.

correct, and that Cyril succeeded his consecrator, Maximus, after the latter's death, it is not possible entirely to discount the alternative scenario recorded by both Sozomen and Socrates, especially given the long life of the controversy. These have it that Acacius of Caesarea and Patrophilus of Scythopolis conspired to have Maximus removed and Cyril elevated in his place.[13] The abiding charges of Cyril's Arian sympathies must come from the fact that Acacius was well known for his 'Arian' doctrines, as was Patrophilus. Maximus, for his part, had been a supporter of Nicaea.

The great question is just how much Cyril was a Maximus-style 'Nicene' or an Acacius-style 'Arian', and opinions in history have varied widely. Jerome clearly paints him in Arian tones, with all the distaste one would expect of such characterizations. But while Cyril's works are perhaps notable for not listing Arius as among the great heretics, they are, too, for being decidedly non- or even anti-Arian in theological scope (a point we shall address more thoroughly below). While I hesitate to follow Drijvers in asserting that Cyril adhered to a kind of 'Nicene orthodoxy' throughout his life, especially from the 350s onwards (primarily on grounds that this seems an anachronistic category, grounded in poor understandings of Nicaea's place in history, addressed in the previous chapter), it seems clear from his statements on the relationship of the Son to the Father that he was not an Arian in the way Jerome, Socrates and Sozomen thought him to be. As to the other ancient charge, his focus on the Spirit makes it certain that he was not a Macedonian.[14] But the non- or even anti-Arian focus to some of his statements should not lead us to conclude that Cyril was therefore 'Nicene'.[15]

In point of fact, Cyril was a non-Nicene, at least in creedal terms. In his instruction offered to candidates for baptism in Jerusalem, a significant portion of the Lenten catechetical programme is taken up with a commentary on 'the creed' which is to be 'committed to memory word-for-word' as a thing precious and sacred, part of the *disciplina arcani* or secret store of holy knowledge communicated only verbally, never in written form.[16] But Cyril's creed is not Nicaea's. One might

---

13 See *Soz. HE* 4.20.1; *Soc. HE* 2.38.2.

14 On the Arian question, see Drijvers, *Cyril of Jerusalem: Bishop and City* 181–86; cf. pp. 33–34 for the less problematic claim that 'from his extant writings no Arian leanings can be deduced'. This comes across more strongly in Doval's statement that 'Cyril's theological views were decidedly anti-Arian'; *Cyril of Jerusalem: Mystagogue* 23. For the charge of Macedonianism, see *Soz. HE* 4.20.

15 So see Ayres, *Nicaea and its Legacy* 153–57.

16 Cf. *Cat.* 5.12. On the timeline of catechetical instruction in Jerusalem under Cyril, see the hypotheses of J. Day, 'Lent and the Catechetical Program in Mid-Fourth-Century Jerusalem', *SL* 35.2 (2005), 129–47, esp. the table at 139–40 and 147. For notes on the concept of *disciplina arcani*, see Yarnold, *Cyril of Jerusalem* 38–40, 49–50; E. Yarnold, *The Awe-Inspiring Rites of Initiation: Baptismal Homilies of the Fourth Century* (Slough: St Paul, 1972) 50–58 [2nd ed. 1994, T&T Clark]; and J. Day, 'Adherence to the *Disciplina Arcani* in the Fourth Century', *SP* 35 (1999), 266–70. Drijvers, *Cyril of Jerusalem: Bishop and City* 89 follows Kretschmar in noting that this practice may have been somewhat fanciful, as the contents of the creed, etc., were likely widely and publicly known by the mid-fourth century; see G. Kretschmar, *Jerusalemer Heiligtumstraditionen in altkirchlicher und frühislamischer Zeit* (Wiesbaden: Harrassowitz, 1987).

(though probably shouldn't) call it 'Nicene' in scope; but the baptismal creed in Jerusalem is notable for its lack of *ousia*-orientated discussion on the relation of Son to Father. If Cyril remained faithful to Maximus, and if Maximus was indeed a 'pro-Nicene', this must have been in spirit rather than letter. More likely, Cyril and the Jerusalem creed bear witness to the fact that Nicaea was but one voice in a period of widespread consideration of trinitarian themes, and that being 'anti-Arian' after Nicaea didn't always mean being 'pro-Nicene'.[17]

The fact that Cyril's creed is employed as a functional text, rather than a dogmatic confession, is also important. In the fifth catechetical oration, candidates for baptism 'receive the creed' from the bishop as an integral part of their preparation for initiation into the life of the Church. In his exegesis of its various components in the 6th–18th orations, Cyril treats the articles of his creed as indicative of baptismal life: its elements are important inasmuch as they reveal aspects of human stature that will be fulfilled in baptismal rebirth. In this manner, his treatment of the dogmatic contents of the creed are practical in their catechetical scope: treatment of Christ as 'Son by nature' is important catechetically, inasmuch as it reveals that initiates for baptism are to be 'Sons by adoption'. The creed is taken not so much as a confessional statement *per se*, but a concise teaching on the realities of the human person and his God, as exposed and encountered in sacramental initiation.[18]

This personal nature to the creed is reinforced by the manner of its delivery and reception. Rather than a dogmatic statement, the creed is, to Cyril's mind, the capital reduction of scriptural teaching and instruction for one approaching the faith. It is delivered personally, in the Church, from elder to initiates, as an eminently practical, instructional document. There is a lovely, thought somewhat fanciful, engraving of Cyril found on the front leaf of Touttée's landmark edition of Cyril's *Catecheses*, depicting the bishop seated in his episcopal throne, instructing an enormous pool of baptismal candidates.[19] Surely Cyril's crowds would not have been this large, but the communal spirit of the engraving is in line with the spirit of the creed's presentation in the orations. It is an initiatory tradition, delivered person-to-person, on the way to baptism.

This is characteristic of Cyril's whole testimony. Though we retain part of the post-baptismal catecheses of John Chrysostom, Cyril's is the only complete set of

---

17 Reinhart Staats' comments on Cyril's role in the formation of the Constantinopolitan creed seem hard to justify; see, for example, R. Staats, 'The Eternal Kingdom of Christ: The Apocalyptic Tradition in the "Creed of Nicaea-Constantinople"', *PBR* 9.1 (1990), 19–21.

18 So P. Jackson, 'Cyril of Jerusalem's Use of Scripture in Catechesis', *TS* 52.3 (1991), 434: 'What Cyril is seeking to inculcate in the elect is a kind of experiential knowledge which presupposes assent to what they already know of the Christian faith and will deepen their faith commitment sufficiently for it to be appropriately sealed with water and the Spirit'.

19 A. A. Touttée, *S. Cyrilli archiepiscopi Hierosolymitani operae quae exstant omnia, et ejus nomine circumferuntur* (Paris: Jacobus Vincent, 1720); reproduced more recently as the frontispiece to Drijvers, *Cyril of Jerusalem: Bishop and City* x.

catechetical lectures from antiquity. This is a significant detail, as catechetical teaching is decidedly different from polemical or dogmatic, into which categories most earlier witnesses fall. Cyril's 23 pre-baptismal orations, as well as the five post-baptismal 'Mystagogics' now rightly attributed to him, represent a different approach to theological articulation than that seen in the extant writings of the second and third centuries.[20] While some documents from those earlier eras (including Irenaeus' own *Epideixis*) are often termed 'catechetical', what we most often mean by such ascriptions is 'doctrinally summary', or, more directly, non-polemical in form and character (so the *Epideixis*, written to Marcellinus to describe the 'one upward path to life' as exegeted from the scriptures by the apostles). But in Cyril we have catechesis as a proper genre, a distinct and unique approach to theological exposition. The goal of this writing is not to describe but to prepare. The discursive content offered is presented as a means of entry, of preparatory exploration of a life about to be lived (or, as in the case of the *Mystagogics*, a life recently entered into). This represents more than a simple change of audience from polemical foe to initiate or newly baptized: in his catecheses Cyril articulates the breadth of his doctrinal teaching in the context of personal appropriation. The entirety of the Christian message is explored in the first-person. Who is this 'trinity' *into whose life I am about to enter?* Who is the Spirit *who is about to wash me in the waters of baptism?* And, with no little centrality, *who am I*, who now enters into communion with this God and Church? As P. Jackson characterizes Cyril's intent: 'He thus sees his purpose in preaching on the Creed as not so much to impart information, as to enable his listeners to be so overwhelmed by the importance of what God has done in salvation history that they will want to give their lives to Him and become part of that history.'[21]

To frame discourse in the genre of catechesis personalizes the approach to theological questions, and makes their anthropological basis all the more central. The human, personal subject, the one to whom the catechesis is addressed as guide, becomes the lens through which the confessional tenets of the faith are refracted and given clarity. In its deliberate attempt to subjectify, rather than objectify, these central confessions, catechesis as Cyril employs it attempts to explore Christian truth in the realm of the person approaching entry – from the perspective of relationship and personal transformation. This leads him to develop his pastoral task along increasingly nuanced lines of personal appropriation and

---

20   On the authorship of the *Mystagogics*, see Doval, *Cyril of Jerusalem: Mystagogue*; as well as the nice summation, influenced by Doval, in Yarnold, *Cyril of Jerusalem* 24–32. Cf. E. Yarnold, 'The Authorship of the Mystagogic Catecheses Attributed to Cyril of Jerusalem', *HJ* 19 (1978), 143–61. Some still posit John of Jerusalem as author: see E. Mazza, *Mystagogy: A Theology of Liturgy in the Patristic Age*, tr. M. J. O'Connell (New York: Pueblo Publishing Company, 1989) x, 150. Despite this ascription, Mazza's text remains useful on historical questions – though in its attempt to read Cyril as a modern-day Roman Catholic, perhaps a bit too biased in interpretation.

21   Jackson, 'Cyril of Jerusalem's Use of Scripture in Catechesis', 434.

self-discovery. The context of the catecheses is progression towards the great rite of Christian initiation, which Cyril prefers to call 'the laver' of baptism. Within this context, his project advances by a series of unstated yet clear questions of preparation: *What* is about to happen to me, and why? (baptism); *Who am I* to whom this will happen? (questions of anthropology proper, on the nature of man); *How* will this mystery come about? (soteriological issues); *Who* effects it? (doctrines of God); and *what* does it mean? (redemption, eschatology). The sacramental experience of entering into the life of the Church sets the stage for the manner in which Cyril will articulate its teaching – and this personal, pastoral approach in turn effects the focus of that articulation. Put briefly, the idiocentric focus of one about to be baptized establishes the orientation of catechetical discussion as fundamentally anthropocentric and anthropological. The human person becomes, in a way even more explicit than in our earlier sources, the framework for knowing God.

This is the foundation of Cyril's approach to humanity bearing God's image. In the human creature is imaged the life of the incarnate Christ, baptized in the Jordan, who in receipt of the Spirit suffers and attains the glory of his Father – namely, the perfection of man. To be 'after the image of God' is, for Cyril, not only to be created in some semblance of the divine, but more importantly to be created for participation in the glory of the incarnate Son. As we shall see him develop at some length, Cyril sees this as the impetus for rightly defining the Son's relationship to the Father: for what the Son is to the Father by nature, the human person becomes through him by the Spirit, by participation. The human creature, baptized into the Son's life as naturally an image of the Son, comes to have a share in the Son's glory. The image is united to the one imaged, through the distinction of participation. This participation and sharing reaches its pinnacle in the union of the person to Christ in his sacrifice. Man joined to the suffering of the incarnate Son is the epitome of the natural image, realized in a true likeness.

In the present chapter, we shall look first of all at Cyril's starting point in the nature of the baptismal sacrament. It is in discerning baptism as both death and life that Cyril establishes his categories of human nature in its relationship to sin. This leads him to what will be our second section, on the nature of the soul in this relationship, and how definition of the soul as cleansed in baptism indicates a doctrine of sin as economic. A third section will investigate how this confession of an economy of sin leads Cyril to articulate redemption as adoption into the life of God, effected through the 'becoming sons' of adoption in Christ, who is 'Son by nature'. It is this context that drives Cyril to express his trinitarian conceptions as part-and-parcel of his exploration of human redemption. The Spirit unites humanity to the Son, who is able to redeem humanity by adopting it into the relationship with the Father that is his naturally and eternally. After exploring at some length how this influences the way Cyril talks about the Son and Spirit, we shall conclude the chapter with a section on the ultimate fruit of this relationship of redemption: the human person joined in imitation to the suffering of Christ, living 'in image' that which the Son is by nature.

WHAT MYSTERY IMMANENTLY COMES? BAPTISMAL DEATH, LIFE AND ENSLAVEMENT AS THE REVELATION OF HUMAN NATURE

The sacramental dimension of Cyril's approach to catechetical discussion stages his discourse in a different manner than that seen in our precedent authors. More specifically, it essentially inverts the approach used by Tertullian who had, as we have seen, considered questions of anthropology and theology from a protological perspective reminiscent of Irenaeus. In his concern over the state and effect of sin on the soul-body composite that is the human person, Tertullian had based his discourse on a reading that began with beginnings: with primal man and the economy prior to the introduction of sin. In order to understand sin and redemption, he begins with a description of the created, composite state, subsequently corrupted and later redeemed.

Cyril, on the other hand, takes from his sacramental approach the opposite tack: it is in the end, the redeeming moment of baptismal re-creation, that he finds his starting point. Rather than working from primal conditions to fallen, Cyril starts from the moment of correction and redemption of the fallen, drawing out of this act, this baptismal experience, the realities implied for original formation and full human potential. Framing his discussion catechetically as preparation for baptism, the redemptive act of correction manifests and explains corruption, which in turn reveals retrospectively the true created state of man. This will demand not only that Cyril's sacramental approach to anthropology take the Christological course of starting from the redemption offered in Christ, and from this perspective approach the realities of the created realm; but also from the first that it orientate itself centrally in the realm of pneumatology. As Cyril will discuss at length, it is the Holy Spirit who is encountered first and foremost, immediate and active in baptismal regeneration. This Spirit, which already in Irenaeus and Tertullian alike we have seen described as life and, in active receipt, the measure of full human life, will find definition in Cyril primarily through the great symbolic measure of baptism: death, which weds to life.

We ended our chapter on Tertullian with quotation of a passage calling the harmonious relationship of humanity and God a 'blessed nuptial vow' kept whole and undefiled. This language of marital union is unsurprisingly frequent in the patristic corpus, given the substantial treatment it receives in the scriptures.[22] Cyril is no exception. In setting the stage for the course of instruction to follow, he notes in his prologue to the catecheses that the goal of the baptismal mystery at which it is aimed is 'to make your soul holy for your heavenly bridegroom'.[23] In the waters

---

22 See, for example, Matthew 22.1–14; Mark 2.19; John 3.29; 2 Corinthians 11.2; Ephesians 5.22, 23; Apocalypse 19.7, 9.
23 *Pro.* 6.

that represent the tomb and death, he later reminds his flock after their reception, one sees not only these elements of death and tomb, but life and mother, for the person is thereby reborn into a new life of union with her 'new bride'.[24] Two points present themselves, each central to Cyril's teaching: first, that there is achieved in baptism a real departure and re-orientation (thus the symbolism of death and a new maternity); and second that this re-orientation of human life is one of union (represented in the nuptial imagery of the bridegroom). The 'garment' of human life that is the pre-baptismal expression of humanity, is not merely to be covered up, but cast off and changed.[25] The 'new garment' is, in turn, to be a life caught up in Christ, as fish are caught in a net – an image that conjures up both death and life. Cyril instructs his hearers: 'allow yourself to be caught; do not try to escape. Jesus is fishing for you, not to kill you, but to give you life once you have been killed'.[26]

Baptism is to be understood as death, and in that death new life. As such, Cyril's exposition of anthropology first through redemption, takes from the witness of baptism the conviction that redemption starts with cessation and death as the bridge to a new beginning. Yet baptism, while itself a type of death, is also consequent upon a death already experienced: the 'death' of sin. The 'fish' of Cyril's net analogy are already bound to death; the question is what may come of it. The analogy comes in the form of the welcome Cyril gives his hearers, whom he admits may have joined the catechetical programme for a variety of reasons, some laudable, others not.

> I accept this as bait for my hook and let you in. You may have had the wrong reason for coming, but I have good hope that you will be saved. Perhaps you did not know where you were going, or recognise the net waiting to catch you. You have swum into the Church's net. Allow yourself to be caught. Do not try to escape. Jesus is fishing for you, not to kill you but to give you life once you have been killed. For you have to die to rise again. You have heard the apostle say, 'Dead to sin, alive to righteousness' (cf. Romans 6.11, 13). Die then to your sins and live to righteousness. Make today the first day of your life.[27]

Baptism is a death that becomes a laver of regeneration, inasmuch as it restores that which was sundered by a precedent death. A developed liturgical symbolism to the plunging beneath the waters is clearly apparent, and with it a host of anthropological convictions bound up in the dying and being re-born that the sacrament effects.

---

24   See *M. Cat.* 2.4.
25   See *Pro.* 4; *M. Cat.* 2.2; cf. Matthew 22.8–13 .
26   *Pro.* 5.
27   Ibid.

Further, that which 'dies' in the baptismal mystery is not left vague: there is a manner of life, a mode of human existence, that therein meets its end. 'Die, then, to your sins'. Cyril further sees that the death to sin is a kind of second death, for this mode of life (i.e. the sinful) was antecedently the death of original life. Affirmations of these qualities to baptismal cleansing paint a vivid picture of the characteristics of the death-creating 'life' that in turn 'dies' in baptism: the life that awaits purification in baptism is a false-life; a dead life of 'spotted and stained soul';[28] of ill-will towards God and fellow creatures;[29] a life not of likeness to the divine.[30] The human condition on which baptism acts is, therefore, discerned as one of disfigurement and deformity. Sin is a 'stain' for Cyril, much as it was for Tertullian, and one that debars from proper existence.[31] This disfigurement is not restricted to the aesthetic or moral realms: it constitutes a real transformation of human potential in the cosmos. Disfigured humanity no longer has the power to wrestle with or defeat demonic foes;[32] it is made a weakling, incapable of a self-attainment of righteousness, inasmuch as it has been 'grievously wounded' beyond its power to heal.[33]

All this is evidenced, for Cyril, in the very fact of baptism as authentic death. That condition which so defeats true life must itself suffer death in order to free the defeated, the 'polluted', from bondage and re-initiate it in the context of authentic living. Baptism is therefore seen as 'the divine source of life', that which God effects through death to the old self, in order to impart his proper life to the creature.[34] Yet in the midst of this death which gives rise to life, Cyril is clear that what dies is not the nature of humankind, which needs rather to be altered or transformed in order authentically to live, but the mode of life 'spattered with the mud' of sin and soiled by the same. In short, that which dies in baptism is a type of actualized 'life' that is in fact death: the very means of cessation of life. It is a death of death: the false-life of corrupt living.

Such an entrance into anthropological discourse through the death (and new life) of baptism, allows Cyril to frame in his discussion in a retrospective or backwards-looking manner. If it is 'death', or false-life, that is killed in the baptismal regeneration, the initiate's interest then becomes the nature and character of this false-life that must be cast off. By looking backwards from baptism, Cyril can base his deliberate anthropological discourse in the interrelation of composition and disfiguration the sacrament presupposes. To this end, it is again in his reflections on the sacrament proper that Cyril finds the staging ground for a discussion

---

28   *Cat.* 3.2.
29   *Pro.* 4; *M. Cat.* 5.23.
30   See *M. Cat.* 3.1.
31   Cf. *M. Cat.* 5.23.
32   See *Cat.* 3.13, 14. *Cat.* 12.7.
33   *Cat.* 12.7.
34   *M. Cat.* 1.1.

on matters specifically anthropological. In a passage on the twofold nature of
the baptismal mystery as spiritual yet material (as effected by water), Cyril finds
corollary to the composition of the human person:

> For since human beings have a double nature and are composed of soul and
> body, the purification is twofold also: immaterial for the immaterial, bodily
> for the bodily. The water cleanses the body, and the Spirit seals the soul, so
> that we can approach God with hearts sprinkled and bodies washed in pure
> water. (cf. Hebrews 10.22)[35]

Though his starting point is sacramental, Cyril here adopts the same bi-partite
conception of human nature found in Tertullian. The human person is 'twofold',
of body and soul, each fashioned by God.[36] This is revealed above all in the
twofold nature of the sacrament, the material and the immaterial (which Cyril is
happy to use as broad descriptors for body and soul respectively); and the act of
identifying these constitutive anthropological elements *from a sacramental context* indicates for Cyril the abiding and eternal character of the same. Water
cleanses body and Spirit soul, and 'both are needed in order for you to be made
perfect'.[37] As baptism redeems, as it is the divine source of renewed life, so the
elements of human creature redeemed in baptism are confirmed as integral to
authentic human existence.[38]

Cyril explores the character of humanity's two constitutive elements along
these lines. The body cannot be viewed as an 'alien container', foreign to God or
wanting in dignity, any more than can the water that is used sacramentally to
cleanse and refurbish it.[39] Cyril exegetes the Old Testament at length in defence
of the sanctity of water, going so far as to claim that in the human economy 'wher-
ever a covenant is made with anyone, water is to be found there'.[40] But his focus
on water, which is directly intended to counter potential discomfort at so simple
an element being used for Christianity's chief initiatory mystery, informs his
cosmology – and in turn anthropology – *writ large*. Matter, and most importantly
the matter of the human body, cannot be declared void of dignity *qua matter*.
Dignity rests in usage, not substance. What ought to be of concern to the human
person is not her corporeality, but her employment of that corporeality to virtue or
vice. The body must be kept pure for the Lord, and for Cyril there is nothing in its
corporeality that would prevent this.[41] He is convinced, as were both Irenaeus and

---

35 *Cat.* 3.4; tr. E. Yarnold, p. 90, with minor modifications.
36 Cf. *Cat.* 4.18; on bi-partite elements in Tertullian, see above, pp. 64–69.
37 *Cat.* 3.4.
38 Cf. *M. Cat.* 1.1.
39 Cf. *Cat.* 4.22.
40 *Cat.* 3.5.
41 See *Cat.* 4.26.

Tertullian, that creation into a material, temporal realm demands mutability, and mutability in time mandates growth from imperfection to perfection; and this necessity is seen as part of the design of creation and not a flaw of form. So he instructs his catechumens in a comment that will have implications later in his discussions on the nature of the Son, and which gives clear evidence already of his anthropological framing-in of theological concepts:

> The generation of bodies requires the intervention of time, though no time intervenes for the generation of the Son from the Father. In this world a being is begotten in an imperfect state; but the Son was already perfect when begotten by the Father. He was begotten from the beginning, just as he is now. In our begetting, we change from the ignorance of a child to rationality. Your own generation was imperfect, my friend, for your development requires gradual advance. But do not imagine it was the same with the Son [. . .].[42]

While Cyril wishes to ensure that his hearers do not envisage the Son's begetting anthropomorphically (and he insists on this point only a few lines later[43]), it is nonetheless the image of human begetting that serves as the boilerplate for his discussions on the language of begetting with regard to divine relation. The starting point here is Cyril's confession that all begetting 'in this world' is temporal, and thus begotten creatures must develop and grow. In common with earlier writers, the mutable, developmental characteristics of created natures imply a need for growth from imperfection to perfection. Cyril's unique usage of this point, which itself he simply accepts as the common heritage of Christian anthropology, is in taking it up as the context for understanding, by contrast, the eternal nature of the divine Son. There is, in this, further affirmation of the value of the created, material realm, since it becomes the effective starting point for accurate theological perception.

His comments on materiality, and the body in particular, are not without nuance; and Cyril readily speaks of the flaws and deficiencies of the flesh. But, like others before him, Cyril exegetes Paul's words at Romans 7.5 ('when we were in the flesh, the sinful passions which were aroused by the law were at work in our members to bear fruit to death') so as to find in the term flesh (*sarx*) not reference to the body itself, but to 'carnal actions' or, more potently, 'carnal passions'.[44] In its own right, the body can be understood only as perfectly designed – since it is a thing designed by God – and beautiful; but this body does not always exist according to his perfect and beautiful architecture.[45] The body's beauty is disfigured when it is made unclean, which is the effect upon it of the

---

42 *Cat.* 11.7.
43 See *Cat* 11.8.
44 *Hom. Par.* 17.
45 See *Cat.* 4.22.

'mud' of sin.[46] Its perfection is led captive, become a slave to the power of this disfiguring force. Nonetheless, and as such an analogy itself indicates, the enslavement of the body to sin is never to be understood as its natural state. As Cyril exhorts his hearers, 'Be leaders, not slaves!'[47] Slavery can be overcome by proper leadership, and a body 'covered in mud' and bound by the enslaving effects of sinful habits can be cleansed and set free. Yet here a paradox, for in Cyril's understanding, the body cannot lead. Indeed, to be led by corporeality is precisely to 'walk according to the flesh', the very prohibition established by the apostle. So while the body may be enslaved by sin, and so lead the person in the way of 'carnal passions and desires', a redeemed corporeality must involve the body being freed from this enslavement and led by another. Cyril speaks of this leadership in terms of a new bondage, echoing Christ's comments on discipleship as a yoke and the Pauline imagery of the disciple as a slave of Christ. The flesh is to be 'enslaved' to the immaterial reality in humanity, the soul. It is this which must lead, for the body is, properly considered, the 'instrument of the soul' – its clothing and attire.[48]

THE FUNCTION OF THE SOUL AND THE DEFINITION OF SIN

Cyril's address of the soul is nowhere near the length or intricacy of that found in Tertullian. Discovered in shorter segments in other orations (e.g. *Pro.* 9; *Cat.* 10; *Hom. Par.* 17; *M. Cat.* 1), the brunt of Cyril's address is located in the fourth baptismal lecture, under its own heading as one of the 'ten doctrines' of Christian belief. While his basic ascription of the soul/body dichotomy is located in the material/immaterial means of effect discovered in baptism, these lectures present a more refined address of the soul, its nature and its function. Importantly, it is in the soul that Cyril identifies the locus of the divine image. The soul is 'God's fairest work, formed in the image of its maker'[49] – a claim Cyril never directly makes of the body alone. This is not, however, to suggest that it is the soul's immateriality which allows it, rather than the body, to establish the image; Cyril's reflections on the body's inherent dignity stand against such a reading. It is not the immateriality of the soul that impresses Cyril as imaging the divine, but its character as life and life-giving within the bi-partite human creature. It is the soul that is 'a living, rational, incorruptible being, because of him who gave it these gifts'.[50]

---

46 See *Cat.* 4.23.
47 *Hom. Par.* 18.
48 *Cat.* 4.23.
49 *Cat.* 4.18.
50 Ibid.

This assertion lies behind Cyril's claim that the body is the soul's instrument (mentioned above), similar to Tertullian's language of the body as 'house'. Yet in making such statements, Cyril is not defaming the body as inconsequential or 'lower' than the soul (the second-century anti-'Gnostic' project had sunk in by the fourth, even if the issue was still very much in the air); rather, his comments are essentially a simple admission that the material body is not itself animative. Echoing biblical imagery, in which the body itself is lifeless dust until infused with God's breath, Cyril wishes to reinforce the essentially lifeless characteristic of body *qua* body. It is the soul that brings the body to life, constituting the living person. In a comment on the soul's share in sin, to which we will turn again later, Cyril draws attention to this animating quality unique to the soul:

> If sin is due to the body, why doesn't a corpse sin? Place a sword in the right hand of a man who has just died; no murder will take place. Whatever forms of beauty are displayed before a young man who has just died, no desire of fornication will be felt.[51]

The question of sin for the moment set to one side, Cyril's dichotomization of soul and body as animator and animated, reflects the ancient testimony of the scriptures on which he is reflecting. The relationship of the soul to the body echoes that of the 'breath of life' to the fashioned dust of Genesis 2.7. The soul gives life to the body, and without it the latter cannot be seen as the true image of its creator. The soul brings the body into the image of God, and it is this that causes Cyril to see the soul as the locus of the divine image. But it is only the locus because it is life-giving, and this life-giving aspect connects it intimately and intrinsically to the body it animates. The body is not of diminished importance on account of the soul's animating precedence: as Cyril stresses, human nature is to be not of soul, but body and soul together. The one who will stand before God at the judgement will be one of soul and body alike.[52] Cyril maintains this balance, grounded always in the notion that the soul indeed has precedence, but a precedence that only has meaning in the context of the body. Precedence does not equal extent. Cyril makes this observation direct in reminding his catechumens that, ultimately, it is not simply the soul that is God's image, but 'man' – that reality defined by neither element apart, but by the dual-presence of them both.[53]

Cyril's grounding of his anthropological discussion in a reflection on the baptismal mystery has here shaped his discourse. Baptism must be both bodily and spiritual, not like that of Simon Magus, whom Cyril claims 'was baptised but not enlightened; he dipped his body into the water, but did not enlighten his heart

51 *Cat.* 4.23.
52 See *Cat.* 4.30.
53 See *Cat.* 12.5.

with the Spirit'.[54] Further, if baptism is administered 'for the forgiveness of sins' (cf. Mark 1.4, Luke 3.3),[55] then its anthropological witness is not merely to the nature of the person who is cleansed, but also to the sin of which baptism is the laver. Here Cyril discovers further clarity on the nature of the soul, for it is, as we have already seen him proclaim, the soul that is spattered with the 'mud' of sin, which is 'dressed in avarice'.[56] To claim that sin resides in the body is to go not only against the teachings of the scriptures as Cyril reads them (hence his quotations of the Old Testament on the value of the material), but also against the witness of every-day observation. Here the direct focus of the passage cited above on the body's inanimacy: put a sword in the corpse of a man who has died (i.e. whose soul has departed) and no murder takes place; put a beautiful woman before the corpse of a dead man and there arises no lust or desire. So Cyril: 'Do not tell me that the body shares the blame for sin [. . .] the body itself does not sin; the soul sins through the body'.[57]

It is in the soul that the human person's self-determination and rational freedom reside, and so Cyril's insistence on its priority in the divine image which nonetheless is only manifest in the soul-body composite that is the full person. It is the soul that makes deliberative choices, which by those choices both soils and is soiled by the evil of its own determination.[58] The body has its own 'corruptible and defective side' – it is as Abraham said but 'dust and ashes'[59] – but this is identified by Cyril as the inherent weakness and limitation of the material, not as an objectifiable sinfulness in the human corpus. The body is itself pure and must be kept pure, though it is engaged in sin as the instrument of the sinning soul. It is not the immediate actor in the free-determination of wrong; yet, as united to the soul, it is not foreign to those acts it engenders. The soul sins through the body, and so the body, like the soul, becomes unclean and must have a share in the re-birth of baptism.[60]

Cyril makes a point of emphasizing the freedom inherent in the human soul as created after the image of God, and the presence of sin in humanity as rooted in that freedom. All souls, from Adam's to the eschaton, are alike. Whether male or female, sinner or saint, the nature of the soul is one. Its structure is uniform and similar in all, not classified by nature as just or unjust.[61] Here Cyril takes as his own a point that has been fundamental to our previous authors: the nature underlying human reality is singular, common and unchanging in its fundamental properties. For Irenaeus, this was imaged in the language of 'one race' in Adam; for Tertullian in

---

54 *Pro.* 2.
55 See *M. Cat.* 2.6.
56 *Pro.* 4.
57 *Cat* 4.23.
58 See *Cat.* 4.18.
59 See *Cat.* 6.3; cf. Gen 18.27.
60 See *Cat.* 4.23 and *Cat.* 3.4.
61 All these claims asserted in *Cat.* 4.20.

humanity's 'one blood'; and for Cyril in 'one nature' common to just and unjust alike. If this be so, then unless God himself be the fashioner of sin, the soul *qua* soul cannot, of its natural character, be held responsible for sin. Cyril is direct on the matter:

> For you are not a sinner by birth nor a fornicator by chance; nor, as some in their madness dare to say, do the conjunctions of the stars compel you to devote yourself to wantonness. Why do you avoid acknowledging your own evil deeds and cast the blame on the innocent stars?[62]

> I would have you know this, too, that before the soul enters the world is has committed no sin; but though we arrive sinless, now we sin by choice.[63]

Sin is, for Cyril as much as for both Irenaeus and Tertullian, an act and not a natural reality. It is economic, not ontological. It may corrupt and wound, but the wound is economic as much as the sin is economic.[64] The immediate testimony of baptism is that the soul, together with the body, can be and is purified of sin.[65] It may be soiled, but it can yet be made holy for its bridegroom. And when the soul thus responsible for sin is redeemed by a God-initiated departure from sin, bodily healing follows.[66] The purified soul purifies its instrument. As such, the condition of man reveals the nature of God through the sacrament. Anthropological renewal discloses the nature of the one who renews, in the one who is renewed.

WHO WORKS THIS MYSTERY IN ME? FROM AN ECONOMY OF SIN TO A CONFESSION OF REDEMPTION

So much like those before him, then, Cyril conceives of humanity's 'sinful state', its 'fallen nature', as mode or manifestation of economy. To speak so powerfully of sin as dirt, as mud that soils the soul and body, is at the same time to inculcate the potential for cleansing from such stain. The fact that baptism is so often called 'laver' is connected to Cyril's affirmation of the potential for holy, pure living – a practical extension of his anthropology, in continuity with Irenaeus' insistence that heretics should be corrected so that they may walk according to the upward path of truth, and Tertullian's obsession with the rules of righteousness of everyday living. The stain of sin can be cleansed. Christ's solemn 'Go, and sin no

---

62 *Cat.* 4.18.
63 Ibid. 4.19.
64 Cf. *Cat.* 12.6.
65 So *Pro.* 9; *M. Cat.* 1.1.
66 Cf. *Hom. Par.* 17. Cyril does note that at times bodily healing precedes the healing of the soul.

more', spoken to the healed paralytic (cf. John 5.14), is an exhortation based on genuine potential, intended to be realized by all.[67]

Yet such proclamations of hope have to be weighed against the obvious preponderance of sin in the world. They cannot be maintained credibly without asking whence such evil comes, and why its apparent universal spread. Exploration offered in Irenaeus spoke of sin's origin in infantile susceptibility to the wiles of the 'strong man' (Satan) expanding across the human race as a cloud over the earth, effecting all of Adam's race through the economy of Adam's act. Tertullian took a concordant emphasis on the influence of Satan, and explained in more compositional terms the manner in which the economy initiated by the devil led to a context of impatience, in which a consistently good nature universally gives rise to sinful, fallen human persons. The basic tenets of such lines of approach – humanity as 'imperfect' at creation, ensnared by the devil in immaturity; developmental in character, troubled in economy but not in nature – are mirrored in Cyril. What is intriguing, however, is the manner in which these concepts are explored by him catechetically within the context of the increasingly central trinitarian disputes of the fourth century. It is largely in connection to reflections on the relationship of the eternal Son to the eternal Father, driven by echoes of the challenges posed by Arius, that Cyril articulates his explanation of human redemption arising out of human nature. But where Cyril's response differs from, for example, Nicaea's, is in the manner in which this discussion of Son and Father is integrally united to a discussion on the Spirit, mandated by Cyril's sacramental focus.

We have seen already that Cyril regards baptism as effecting two connected realities: the death of a fallen mode of life (the passionate way of sin), and a union with Christ as bridegroom. This union constitutes the redemptive grounding of the new life entered into through the sacrament. The connection of baptism, which is paramountly an act of the Holy Spirit, to Christ the Son of the Father, is drawn for Cyril by way of Christ's own baptism in the Jordan. It is inconceivable that this baptism be for the pardoning of sin, for Cyril sees in Christ no sin to be pardoned. Rather, as was also the case in Irenaeus, Christ 'came to be baptised and to sanctify baptism', by that sanctification 'to confer grace and dignity on the baptised'.[68] Cyril expands on this in explicitly incarnational language:

> 'Since the children share flesh and blood, he shared them too' (Hebrews 2.14), so that by sharing in his incarnate life among us, we might share also in his divine grace; in the same way Jesus was baptised so that sharing with him we might recover both salvation and dignity.[69]

---

67 Cf. *Hom. Par.* 19.
68 *Cat.* 12.15. For Irenaeus' discussion on Christ's baptism, see above pp. 35–38.
69 *Cat.* 3.11.

Christ sanctifies the waters of baptism through his incarnate reception of the Spirit, that in dying to sin and being washed by that Spirit in baptism, all humanity might share in his incarnate existence. The grace offered in baptism is the ability to have a share in Christ's incarnate reality – to be adopted as sons of God in Christ:[70]

> For you who are candidates for baptism [. . .] are now in the process of becoming sons of God; for you are becoming sons by grace and adoption, according to the scriptural statement, 'as many as received him he gave the power to become the children of God, to those who believed in his name, who were begotten not of blood nor of the will of the flesh or the will of man, but of God' (John 1.12, 13).[71]

The Son, sons, and the Arian question

The very phrases 'son[s] of God' and 'begotten of God' could hardly be brought up – whatever the context – in the mid-fourth century without calling to mind the whole dispute over the relationship of the Son to the Father that had raged between 318/9 and 325, and which was re-emerging in the 350s as new groups and individuals continued to consider the potential ramifications of Arius' basic sentiments, together with those of his opponents. Cyril, as we have already noted, is clearly a non-Nicene, and strong evidence of the need to revise our perceptions of how Nicaea was received in subsequent generations prior to its deliberate centralization by Athanasius and others. Nonetheless, not ascribing to or otherwise employing the creed or language of the council, does not equate to a lack of familiarity with the basic and even focused situational concerns that prompted it. A familiarity with the fundamental tenets of Arius' objections is clear throughout Cyril's writings, and in its own way propels the substance of his catechetical discourse.[72] In further explaining the manner of sonship effected in humanity through being baptismally 'begotten of God' (cf. John 1.13), Cyril states summarily:

> Jesus Christ was the Son of God, but he did not preach the gospel before his baptism. So if even the master chose the time for this in the proper order,

---

70 Cf. *Cat.* 11.4.

71 *Cat.* 11.9.

72 Once again, ancient questions surrounding Cyril's involvement with Arian parties, especially those of Patrophilus and Acacius, stand in tension with what appears, in Cyril's writings, to be a deliberate anti-Arian orientation. See various quotations to this effect on p. 124. See R. C. Gregg, 'Cyril of Jerusalem and the Arians', in R. C. Gregg (ed.), *Arianism: Historical and Theological Reassessments* (Philadelphia: The Philadelphia Patristic Foundation, 1985) 85–109; and Drijvers, *Cyril of Jerusalem: Bishop and City* 182–85.

should we servants presume to act out of order? Jesus began his preaching only after 'the Holy Spirit descended on him, in bodily form like a dove' (Luke 3.22) – not that Jesus wished to see the Spirit first, for he knew the Spirit even before he came in bodily form; what he wanted was that John, who was baptising him, should see. For John said, 'I did not know him; but he who sent me to baptise in water told me, the one on whom you see the Spirit descending and remaining on him', that is he (cf. John 1.33). If your devotion is genuine, the Holy Spirit will descend on you too, and the Father's voice will resound over you; but it will not say 'this person is my Son', but 'this person has now become my son'. Over Jesus 'is', because 'in the beginning was the Word, and the Word was with God, and the Word was God' (John 1.1); over him 'is' because he has always been the Son of God. But over you 'has now become', because you do not possess sonship by nature, but receive it by adoption. He is eternal; you receive the grace as an advancement.[73]

It is the eternal relation of Son to Father that merits, in Cyril's eyes, the change in language from 'this *is* my beloved Son' spoken at Christ's baptism, to 'this person *is become* my son' that can be spoken at one's own. John 1.1 is Cyril's 'proof text' for the fact that Christ as incarnate Word has always been Son of God, and is not made so economically. His stature is his by nature, from his proper eternity as Son of the Father. This is true of his sonship as it is also of his priestly dignity, as it is also of his title 'Christ', which Cyril reads usually as 'healer'.[74] Others have been called 'christs' as types, designated priests by promotion; but the Son 'is the true Christ. He did not attain priesthood from among men by promotion, but possessed priestly dignity from his Father from all eternity'.[75]

Whether or not Arius himself ever taught that the Son was 'promoted' as such is unclear. Cyril does not explicitly name Arius or any of the so-called 'neo-Arians' as the sources of the teaching against which he here inveighs, though it seems difficult to extricate his argument from the Arian dilemma.[76] He dedicates extensive space to refuting any claims against the Son's eternal relationship in divinity to the Father:

Again, when you hear him described as 'Son', do not conceive him to be adopted, for he is the Son by nature, the only-begotten Son, without any brother.[77]

---

73 *Cat.* 3.14.

74 Cf. *Cat.* 10.13.

75 *Cat.* 11.1.

76 Based on a comparison with the dates of Athanasius' pointed attacks against Arius and 'the Arians' (which cannot be much earlier than the 340–50s), there is grounding here for resisting the assertion, put forward by some scholars, that such characterizations of Arius' thought are wholly Athanasius' invention.

77 *Cat.* 11.2.

Once more, when I tell you that he is the Son, do not take this statement to be a mere figure of speech, but understand that he is the Son truly, Son by nature, without beginning, not promoted from the state of slave to that of son, but eternally begotten as Son by an inscrutable and incomprehensible birth.[78]

So he is the Son of God by nature and not by adoption, being begotten of the Father.[79]

Cyril's focus in these sections of his eleventh oration could, in theory, be on simple doctrinal clarification – of an ancient systematics or disputational dogmatics; but this is hardly his style. Cyril's catechesis is broadly objective in its scope, but, as we have already seen, it is intentionally subjective as a means of personal preparation. It is doubtful that Cyril here segues into a specific response to Arian concerns. His invective against flawed views of Christ's eternal sonship is proffered not polemically, or at least not chiefly so, but as a type of apophatic clarification of what is *not* being attained through baptismal adoption into Christ. That which Christ effects, he so does in the divinity he has naturally and from all eternity as only-begotten Son of the Father. If such divine stature were not his naturally, Cyril suggests, he would not have had the power to overcome that mar of sin that has infected 'even his chosen people'.[80] Further, he would have been sinful in his own humanity, for we have seen Cyril maintain that the one nature of man is universally corrupted in an economy that fosters a 'life' of death, which must be killed in the regeneration of baptism. Confession of Christ's sinlessness at baptism, however, abrogates this reading. When Christ became incarnate on account of human sin (which Cyril demands is the immediate reason for the incarnation), when he assumed a humanity that 'was not an appearance only, nor an illusion', he did so as eternal Son of the Father, capable of overcoming in humanity that which the latter was incapable of overcoming in itself.[81]

The adoption realized in baptism is, then, an adoption into the life of filial relation to the Father which the Son is by nature, and which he makes available to humanity through joining human nature to himself in the incarnation – 'for if the incarnation was an illusion, so too was our salvation'.[82] Explaining this more fully, Cyril states:

The Lord took on from us a condition like ours, so that our salvation might come through humanity. He took on a condition like ours in order to supply for its defects with a greater grace, and that sinful humanity might become a

---

78 Ibid. 11.4.
79 Ibid. 11.7.
80 *Cat.* 12.6.
81 See *Cat.* 4.9.
82 Ibid.

partner of God. 'For where sin was abundant, grace was superabundant'. (Romans 5.20)[83]

Cyril calls upon his conviction that beings begotten in the world are imperfect, requiring growth, to explain that without supplying for what is wanting in that imperfection, such growth could not take place. When Cyril in another passage discusses humanity's battle against demonic and temporal foes, he reminds his hearers that a natural ability to wage such battle is not their own, not only on account of imperfection but also due to the disfiguring stain of sin. The power to defeat the enemy comes only via the grace received in the death and new birth of baptism, which order must always be preserved.[84] While the Son has divine power by nature, it is the lot of humanity to receive it by adoption, to 'receive grace *as an advancement*'.[85]

There is revealed in this a twofold character to incarnational soteriology as Cyril articulates it. On the one hand, it advances humanity to new heights of perfection, causing it to become a 'partner with God'. On the other, it meets, confronts and defeats the force of sin that hinders such advancement. Christ comes into the cosmos as human so as to enable man to 'enjoy him' by 'tempering his grace to our capacity', that the human race might more easily receive the advancement of growth into God.[86] These two aspects to the incarnational salvation offered in Christ correlate to the 'death' and 'new life' of baptism, and clarify the manner in which the new life offered thereby is one of union and participation. Christ runs the 'course of endurance' that is his incarnate life and passion, in order to unite, in his person, the imperfect nature of those who are, as generated beings, inherently imperfect and in requirement of gradual advance. These he draws to himself, he who 'was already perfect when begotten by the Father' – that is, his own nature as eternal Son of God.[87] The person 'redeemed' in baptism is the one whose temporally defined existence is united to the eternal nature of God in Christ, such that the life expressed in the person is one of authentic 'partnership' with the divine life.[88]

How this life of unitive partnership comes about is, in Cyril's presentation, bound up in the theology of the Holy Spirit that is so much at the centre of his pre- and post-baptismal catechetical projects. It is this Spirit who sanctifies the waters of the sacrament, as we have already seen him state. It is this Spirit who works the transformation from death to matrimonial new life with Christ. It is by the working of this Spirit only that one becomes, through baptism, 'true-born', and without

---

83 *Cat.* 12.15.
84 Cf. *Cat.* 3.13; *M. Cat.* 2.3.
85 *Cat.* 3.14.
86 *Cat.* 12.13, 14.
87 *Cat.* 11.7; cf. 4.13 on the 'course of endurance'.
88 Cf. *M. Cat.* 3.2.

this Spirit the most enthusiastically performed baptismal ceremony represents at best only a physical washing.[89] As to the matter of how the initiate to the mysteries – the one whom Cyril describes as 'enrolled' for enlightenment[90] – is to understand the means by which the Spirit effects such regeneration and transformation, Cyril responds with an articulation of the Spirit as personal agent of divine communication with the human individual, through means of the human soul.

THE ROLE OF THE HOLY SPIRIT: BEARING THE LIFE OF THE SON

In the first of his *Mystagogics,* already explored in brief, Cyril makes clear that the human soul, representing most basically all that is immaterial in humanity, is purified of its sins (through the means, as he states there, of the exorcisms performed prior to the immersion) and, thus purged, thereby possesses salvation.[91] Later he elaborates more fully that

> no one should imagine that baptism only confers the forgiveness of sins and the grace of adoption, just as John's baptism only conferred the forgiveness of sins (cf. Matthew 3.11; Luke 3.3). We should be clear about this: that just as baptism cleans away our sins and conveys the gifts of the Holy Spirit, so too it represents Christ's sufferings [lit. 'is the antitype of Christ's sufferings'[92]]. This is the meaning of Paul's words which you heard proclaimed just now: 'Do you not understand that we who were baptised into Christ Jesus were all baptised into his death? So we were buried with him through baptism' (Romans 6.3, 4). Perhaps in writing this he had in mind people who believed that baptism conveys forgiveness of sins and adoption, but didn't yet realise that it contains a share by imitation in what Christ suffered in reality.[93]

It is not simply through the remission of sins effected in the baptismal exorcisms and washing that the human person 'possesses salvation', but through the receipt thereby of the Holy Spirit as a 'gift', which unites the person fully to Christ – not only in life but in death and sacrifice. The Spirit brings to the personal existence and experience of the one baptized, the life-through-death of the one who is 'healer' and able to cure human deficiency.[94] It is the Holy Spirit who, in Cyril's articulation, anoints the baptized person with the life of the Son, the life of eternal

---

89   See *Pro.* 4; 22.
90   *Pro.* 1.
91   See *M. Cat.* 1.1; *Pro.* 9.
92   Cf. Yarnold, *Cyril of Jerusalem* n. 7 to p. 174.
93   *M. Cat.* 2.6.
94   Cf. *Cat.* 12.1.

and perfect relation to the Father who 'is in everything and outside everything',[95] yet whose wisdom, power and justice are ever substantial in the Son to whom the Spirit joins the person.[96] As such, the working of the Spirit in the baptismal mystery is in a direct sense 'Christoform': it is the Spiritual working in humanity's spiritual aspect (the soul) of the life, death and resurrection of Christ. This is made explicit in Cyril's explanation of chrismation with oil after the baptism proper:

> These rites [the anointing of Solomon by the high priest, cf. 1 Kings 1.38, 39] were performed for them as a prefiguration (*typikôs*), but for you not as a pre-figuration but in reality, because your salvation began with the one who was anointed in reality by the Holy Spirit. For he is truly the firstfruits and you are the whole lump (cf. Romans 11.16). If the firstfruits are holy, it is clear that the holiness will spread to the whole lump.[97]

The salvation received through the anointing with chrism is, for Cyril, the salvation of the one whose anointing was of the Spirit not conveyed in oil, but descending in the form of a dove (cf. Matthew 3.16; Luke 3.23). The Spirit by whom the person is sealed at chrismation is received in likeness to the incarnate and baptized Son.

Cyril expresses the receipt of new life in baptism as the purifying of the soul of its sin, by which the soul is made 'heavenly', reflecting the sinlessness of God. This 'making heavenly' of the soul is followed by the in-dwelling of the Spirit, not just in the person's soul, but in the whole of her being – body and soul together. For 'if the body co-exists with a holy soul, it becomes the temple of the Holy Spirit'.[98] This lot, of being a temple in receipt of the holiness conveyed by the in-dwelling of the Spirit, is a requirement for the fullness of life, 'for every rational creature needs the holiness that comes from him'.[99] Drawing out an explicit liturgical connection, Cyril emphasizes that it is only in such a state of received holiness that there is authenticity to the bishop's words in the Liturgy, 'the holy things are for the holy', for 'the offerings are holy, since they have received the descent of the Holy Spirit, and you are holy too, because you have been granted the Holy Spirit'.[100] Predictably, it is not a 'generic holiness' that is imparted to the person in receiving this 'gift of the Spirit', but the holiness of the life of the Father's Son. Cyril makes quick to point out that this liturgical proclamation by the bishop is met with the people's response, 'One is holy, one is Lord: Jesus Christ',

---

95   *Cat.* 4.5.
96   See *Cat.* 4.7.
97   *M. Cat.* 3.6.
98   *Cat.* 4.23; cf. 1 Corinthians 6.19.
99   *Cat.* 4.16.
100 *M. Cat.* 5.19.

for truly there is one who is holy, holy by nature; for though we are holy, we are not so by nature, but by participation and discipline and prayer.[101]

It is the holiness of the one, and one alone, who is 'holy by nature' that is imparted to the person 'by participation' through receipt of the Holy Spirit. It is in the 'putting on' of Christ that comes by the Spirit in baptism and anointing, that those 'shaped to the likeness of Christ's glorious body' at last become fully the living images of the Son of God.[102]

JOINED TO THE SUFFERING OF CHRIST

In stating that the 'sufferings of Christ' are represented (typified) in baptism, along with the remission of sins and impartation of the divine life of the Spirit (see again *Mystagogic* 2.6), Cyril has framed his discussion on personal communion with the Son in the specific context of coming to be co-sufferer with the incarnate Christ. Here we have a development in articulation that has little explicit precedent in earlier authors, at least as concerns exegesis of the working of the Spirit in divine-human communion. Since Paul's own writings (cf. Romans 8.17) – on which Cyril is in this context reflecting – the idea of being joined to the sufferings of Christ was current in Christian consciousness; but Cyril is not merely repeating the comments of earlier writers. His consideration of personal co-suffering with Christ is framed specifically through his elaboration of the role of the Spirit, and once again in the sacramental context of baptism (*Mystagogic* 2, from which this principal quotation is drawn, is Cyril's most succinct extrapolation of the baptismal rite and its significance, delivered to the newly illumined shortly after their reception). It is not merely that one is to embrace and emulate Christ's longsuffering sacrifice, and so be joined to him in commonality of will, that excites Cyril's catechetical enthusiasm; but that in the Spirit the human person is, in soul and body, united to him who suffered. The life of the Suffering One becomes, by the indwelling in soul and body of the Holy Spirit, the life of the one joined to his suffering. So writes Cyril:

> Christ was really crucified and really buried and literally rose again, and all of this he did for our sake, so that by sharing his sufferings in imitation, we might gain salvation in truth. What unmeasured love this showed for humankind! Christ received the nails in his pure hands and experienced pain, and grants me salvation through sharing his experience without the pain and the toil.[103]

---

101 Ibid. The phrase occurs in the Byzantine Liturgy at the conclusion of the Anaphora.
102 See *M. Cat.* 3.1.
103 *M. Cat.* 2.5.

It is clear that Cyril here speaks of emulation – one shares in Christ's sufferings 'in imitation', much in the manner of speaking of previous writers. The same is repeated only a few lines later.[104] Yet we must carefully define what Cyril means by 'imitation' (*mimesis*), for it is not simple re-enactment or emulation.[105] The one who 'imitates' Christ 'shares the experience' of the one of whom he 'contains a share by imitation'. There is in Cyril's utilization of the term a kind of mirror to the older theological language of 'likeness', taken as relating to the actual iconic representation or manifestation of the image bound up in the human 'image and likeness' of God. Cyril's reading of human 'likeness' to God is not simply a similarity by external emulation, but a reality of anthropological relation to the 'glorious body' of the incarnate Son by the power of the Spirit.[106] Cyril's definition of 'imitation' follows this understanding, connecting it explicitly to the language of 'likeness' later in *Mystagogic* 2. That passage warrants reproduction in full:

> It was to teach us that what Christ suffered 'for us and our salvation'[107] truly and not in make-believe, and that we have become sharers in his sufferings – it was for this reason that Paul declared with such clarity, 'for if we have been planted with him in the likeness of his death, we shall be planted with him also in the likeness of his resurrection' (Romans 6.5). The expression 'planted with him' is well chosen, for it is here [i.e. in Gethsemane, on Golgotha at the site of the crucifixion] that the true vine was planted, and we have been planted with him through sharing in the baptism of his death. Concentrate all your attention on the apostle's words. He did not say 'if we are planted with him in his death', but 'in the likeness of his death'. It was a real death that Christ really experienced, for his soul was separated from his body; and his burial was real, for his holy body was wrapped in a clean winding-sheet, and everything was done for him in reality. For us, however, there is the likeness of his death and his sufferings, but of salvation not the likeness but the reality.[108]

One does not participate or have a share in 'the reality' of Christ's passion, for neither are a given catechumen's hands pierced with nails, nor is he buried in the tomb. But the baptized person has, through the communion with the Son effected in that baptism by the Spirit, the *likeness* of those sufferings – a 'share' in them by the imitation of personal communion, which joins him to the 'reality of salvation'.[109]

---

104   Cf. ibid. 2.6.

105   For a good, if brief, treatment of the general concepts of imitation and reality in Cyril, see Mazza, *Mystagogy* 154–58.

106   See *Cat.* 4.18; *M. Cat.* 3.1; etc.

107   This a curious quotation: the phrase 'for us and our salvation' is found in the creed of Nicaea, but it is clear from a synthesis of quotations that Cyril is not employing the Nicene creed in his catechesis. The phrase's presence here is something of a mystery.

108   *M. Cat.* 2.7.

109   See Mazza, *Mystagogy* 158.

This language of 'the real' resonates throughout Cyril's teaching on the incarnate Son, and specifically as relates to his sufferings and resurrection. 'His passion was real, for he was really crucified'.[110] The reality of Christ's passion is given such weight in Cyril's catechesis because, in his own words, 'I know the resurrection – for if he had remained crucified, perhaps I would not have affirmed the cross; perhaps I would have concealed it, and my master too. But since the cross was followed by the resurrection, I am not ashamed to affirm it'.[111] The passion is known from the reality of the resurrection, the cross is seen from the reality of the empty tomb. The death of the incarnate Son is known from the vantage point of the 'resurrection' of baptismal re-birth; and even as that latter resurrection to new life is of no effect if there has not antecedently been a death to the false 'life' of sin, so the resurrection of Christ cannot be seen, says Cyril, as the inauguration of human salvation unless there is a death to human death, realized by the one later raised. Death must be overcome in Christ in order for 'the mystery [to be] fulfilled, scripture [to be] fulfilled, and sins redeemed'.[112] Cyril offers a lengthy quotation of Hebrews 9.11-14 ('he entered once for all into the holy place through his greater and more perfect tent not made with hands, that is, not of this creation [. . .], through his own blood to obtain eternal redemption'[113]), precisely to show that it is the Son's divinity, as eternal and natural Son of the Father, that makes his death salvific, 'for it was not a common man who suffered, but God made man, competing in the contest of endurance'.[114] Cyril's insistence on the Son's divine status, explored already in this chapter, here has direct soteriological bearing. Moreover, that bearing is described in incarnational terms:

He stretched out his hands on the cross to encompass the ends of the world. [. . .] He who set the sky in place with his spiritual hands stretched out human hands. They were fastened with nails for this purpose: that when the humanity which bore the sins of humankind had been fastened to the wood and died, sin might die with it, and we might rise again in righteousness. For since death came through one man, life too comes through one man (cf. Romans 5.12–18), the one man who as Saviour voluntarily accepts death. Remember what he said: 'I have power to lay down my life, and I have power to take it up again'. (cf. John 10.18)[115]

It is in his humanity that the divine Son of the Father offers up the fallen life of human sinfulness: through the death of his human body, and thus his human life

---

110 *Cat.* 13.4.
111 Ibid.
112 *Cat.* 13.32.
113 Quoted fully in *Cat.* 13.32.
114 *Cat.* 13.6.
115 *Cat.* 13.28.

(Cyril extrapolates, as we have seen, that on the cross Christ's soul departed his body unto death) the false-life of death is itself put to death. In his humanity he rises from the dead, restoring that humanity to life.

It is precisely here that Cyril's language of participation, likeness and imitation discovers its full force, summarized in his language of 'partnership' with God in Christ:

> Just as Christ was truly crucified and buried and rose again, while you are privileged in baptism to be crucified, to be buried and to rise again in him with likeness, so it is with the anointing with chrism. [. . .] You were anointed with *myron* and became partners with Christ, and began to share with him.[116]

The human person, receiving the Holy Spirit in baptism and chrismation as a sacramental realization of the anointing received by Christ in the Jordan, becomes thereby partner with him and shares with him in the life of incarnate union with the Father. By being anointed in Spirit *via the body* with oil, the person becomes a 'sharer in Jesus Christ', the true olive tree into which one is thereby grafted.[117]

SACRAMENT AND IMAGE: THEOLOGY ENCOUNTERED ANTHROPOLOGICALLY

The final fruit of the baptized life is, for Cyril, union with Christ in his suffering, which is union with Christ in his work of salvation. That imitation of Christ's sacrifice, which by one analysis might seem superficial (for one's hands are not pierced, one's body not buried), is nonetheless 'real' inasmuch as it accomplishes in reality the fruit of the prototypical suffering of the Son: true death to sin, true resurrection into new life. Human likeness to Christ is realized in this sacramental imitation and participation in his life, which causes the person to image the Son through union with him.

The grounding for 'image' as perceived in this manner is the authentic relationship of the Son to the Father. What one becomes through union with the Son by imitation in baptism, has meaning for Cyril only if the Son's relation to the Father is *not* one of similar progression or advancement. The Spirit's work in baptism is to unite one to the Son, that who and what the Son is naturally, the person becomes through participation, through adoption. As such, it is the nature of the Son into which the nature of man is grafted when realizing the divine image. If this is but another nature in need of advancement into God, then the fruit of such grafting is hardly a thing at which to marvel; but 'he is the Son of God by nature and not by

---

116   *M. Cat.* 3.2.
117   *M. Cat.* 2.3; cf. Romans 11.24.

adoption, being begotten of the Father', and thus union with him is salvific.[118] Likeness to the Son is understood as being adopted into all that the Son is: so the Father can say to the recently baptized, 'this person has become my son'; and the bishop to his flock 'the holy things are for those who are holy', while the people respond 'one is holy, Jesus Christ'. What the Son is, his creatures have become; yet never naturally, for the human person is holy only ever inasmuch as he participates in the life of the Son who does not participate in holiness, but is holy by nature as eternal Son of the Father.

This is, as we have seen, the work of the Spirit in the rite of baptism: to effect the participation in the Son that unites humanity to the Father. Through the Spirit's work in making the person actively an icon of Christ, so that one encounters in the person Christ himself, the subjectivity of Christian experience – which drives Cyril's whole catechetical project – reaches its highest degree. Not only can the Father look on the baptized person and declare that he 'has become my son', but the initiate can in a new way look to the Father, through his participation in the Son, and say 'my Father'. We have seen both Irenaeus and Tertullian comment on the prayer of Christ in manners linked to their conception of image and likeness in trinitarian contexts, but Cyril addresses this prayer in greater length than either.

> [We entitle] God our 'father' and say, 'Our Father, who art in heaven'. O most surpassing loving-kindness of God! On those who revolted from him and were in most extreme misery has he bestowed such a complete forgiveness of evil deeds, and so great a participation of grace, that they should even call him father. 'Our Father, who art in heaven': for they are a heaven who bear the image of the heavenly, in whom is God, dwelling and walking in them.[119]

It is in bearing the image of the heavenly, of the Son, that the human person, through 'so great a participation of grace', stands before the Father and speaks to him in terms proper to the Son himself.[120] Here Cyril has almost echoed the thought of Tertullian, who similarly had claimed that in one's relation to Christ 'the model', attributes proper to Christ become, through the Spirit, attributes proper to man.[121]

*   *   *

It is impossible to locate, in Cyril, any substantive distinction between theology and anthropology as subjects of address. His articulation of a doctrine of God

---

118 Cf. again *Cat.* 11.7.

119 *M. Cat.* 5.11.

120 Cyril's commentary on the Our Father is interesting in a number of other respects. *M. Cat.* 5.15 in particular translates τὸν ἄρτον ἡμῶν τὸν ἐπιούσιον not as 'our daily bread' but as 'our substantial bread', since it is 'appointed for the substance of the soul'.

121 See above, p. 71.

is distinctly trinitarian, and to a developed degree; but is in some sense it is an ancillary topic to the question of economy in baptism. Yet ancillary may be the wrong word, for that human economy is perceived as the working out of a human nature which has definition only in its iconic connection to God who is Father with his Son and Spirit. In the end, it is not that either realm – theology or anthropology – precedes the other, but that they are inextricably bound one to the other. A theology grounded in 'image', approached by means of an exploration of the sacramental rite of initiation, requires that this theology be anthropological from the first.

In this, Cyril demonstrates well the connection of mid-fourth century thought to that of earlier centuries. Even at the height of post-Nicene Arian concerns, the discussion that propels Cyril's interest is not discordant with those that long pre-date the highly metaphysical framework of his period. Cyril is an important witness precisely because he shows how continuous the anthropological-theological discussion was across these early centuries, and right through the pivotal rise of conciliar dogmatics in the fourth. The council of Nicaea may have been a watershed, but broader theological focus carried on in continuity with past conversations. More than this, that continuity was finding new modes of expression in the fourth century, and not simply in terms of pro- or anti-Nicene language. Cyril's commonality with earlier writers, coupled with his own advances in terminology and non-Nicene ways of addressing the same questions considered by the council, evidence the variety of articulative frameworks present in the fourth century. Perhaps more significantly, his writings demonstrate the degree to which concerns over the Son–Father relationship could be grounded in a pneumatological context. Again, Cyril is not new here (Irenaeus had already linked human participation in the Son's relation to the Father to the Spirit's anointing in the Jordan); but he shows how even discussions on eternal sonship, generation, participation and the like could be grounded in considerations of the Spirit's role in uniting humanity to Christ.

Despite the unique nature of his testimony, in the reception of fourth-century ecclesiastical history Cyril has nonetheless traditionally sat somewhere in the sidelines, almost wholly eclipsed by the giant figure of Athanasius. If scholars have long struggled to place Cyril into the clear-cut camps of 'Arian' or 'Nicene', with his Alexandrian contemporary there has never been any question. But Athanasius, who so enthusiastically embraces the Nicene creed, who energetically argues for the centralization of its theological framework, presents a puzzle all his own. Few would deny his success in bringing Nicaea to the fore; but whether the resultant 'Athanasian trinitarianism' maintains a real connection to the articulation of those before him – or even contemporaries such as Cyril – has been open to much debate. While critics readily attack him as inventing an orthodoxy all his own, or at the very least re-aligning traditional Christian discussion to metaphysical constructs and principles, the question to drive the final chapter of our study must be this: how does the anthropological context for articulating theological doctrine, which had dominated the early centuries of the Church, ground Athanasius' promotion of Nicaea?

Chapter 5

MOVING INTO BEING:
ATHANASIUS OF ALEXANDRIA

This final chapter will investigate the anthropological grounding of Athanasius' discourse, particularly in the *Contra Gentes – De incarnatione*, but with reference also to his later, and more specifically anti-Arian works. Beginning with his views on creation revealing its creator, it will explore Athanasius' categories of dependent creation, in the context of corruption and incorruption, and the way in which he uses this to ground discussion of humanity's relation to God as participatory, the Son's as non-participatory. This is worked out in reflections on the nature of the human person, and in particular the contemplative power of the soul, which Athanasius sees as linked to the presence of the Spirit. Christ's defeat of death and renewal of the image, as himself true Image, grounds Athanasius' dogmatic assertions on the nature of Father, Son, and to some extent Spirit, and establishes the basis of his objections to Arius and promotion of Nicene vocabulary.

*   *   *

The dominance of Athanasius of Alexandria on the mid-fourth-century landscape is undeniable. A 'great pivotal figure' in the development of Christian doctrine, current scholarship on Athanasius has started to take attentive note of both the positive and negative effects this position has had on the study of his thought over the centuries.[1] Unlike Tertullian, support for whom has ebbed and flowed considerably in various eras, Athanasius has by and large been upheld as a great teacher and theologian until the past century, when support in some circles began to give way to critical re-interpretations of his life and influence.[2] In the twentieth and

---

1   The title is from a prime example of such good scholarship: K. Anatolios, *Athanasius: The Coherence of His Thought* (London: Routledge, 1998) 1.

2   On the positive assessment of Athanasius dominant until the twenty-first century, see Behr, *Nicene Faith* 164–66; T. G. Weinandy, *Athanasius: A Theological Introduction* (Aldershot: Ashgate, 2007) 7–9. Weinandy cites, as examples of the positive assessments of Athanasius that were at their height in the nineteenth century, E. Gibbon, *The Decline and Fall of the Roman Empire* (vol. 2; London, 1897) 362; J. A. Moehler, *Athanase le Grand et l'église de son temps en lutte avec l'arianisme* (Paris, 1840); and J. H. Newman, *Select Treatises of Athanasius in Controversy with the Arians* (London, 1881).

early-twenty-first centuries, assessment of Athanasius in scholarship has swung to extremes: either great saint, or egoistic propagandist. Some of the recent tendency towards a more critical engagement with the Athanasian legacy is welcome – for example, in a more open reflection on his demonstrably complex personality, the nature of his many exiles, his ability to make enemies in at least equal measure to friends, etc. However, some has gone too far, pressing certain arguably negative traits into a position of centrality that shoves aside a great body of historical evidence on others.[3] It is hard, on an open reading, to see Athanasius as particularly more or less embroiled in the controversial political and social issues than others of his era: an age when Church and state were at the full flowering of their new interrelationship, with all the benefits, but also all the troubles and conflicts, this could bring. It was an age in which, as the historical evidence makes very clear, articulation of doctrine was hammered out as often in crowds and riots as in gentle discussions, and the preservation of certain points from oblivion often led to radical partisanship, intrigue and political manoeuvring. Athanasius may appear more entwined in the power play than some, and it is true that past scholarship has tended to gloss over certain troubling aspects of his involvement and behaviour; but discovery that Athanasius did not shy away from the intrigues and political machinations of current Church-state intrigues, that he was indeed right at the heart of them, in the end makes him less a 'gangster' to be singled out, than a fairly representative man of a new age in ecclesiastical life.[4]

Born c. 296 to a family of middle means that, if perhaps Pagan at the time of his birth, was baptized into Christianity while Athanasius was still a child, the future bishop of Alexandria was integrated into the heart of the Church there from a young age.[5] It is likely the case that Alexander, the bishop who would evoke the reaction of Arius c. 318, was Athanasius' instructor in the faith from his youth (so the traditional story of him finding the young Athanasius on a beach as a boy, and

---

3 Such characterizations emerged most notably in the mid-twentieth century, for example, in E. Schwartz, *Zeitschrift für die neutestamentliche Wissenschaft* (34; Berlin, 1935) and E. Schwartz, *Zur Geschichte des Athanasius* (GS, 3; Berlin, 1959); cf. Weinandy, *Athanasius* 8. But it has been the work of Barnes that more recently, and more vehemently, considered Athanasius in almost exclusively negative terms: see his *Athanasius and Constantius*, which opens (p. v) with a quotation of W. Whiston's comment, 'Athanasius was plainly a violent Party-Man, and the known Head of a Party [. . .] and I need not tell the Honest and Impartial, especially in this Age of Division and Faction, how little Regard is to be given to such Testimonies'. Barnes' own preface identifies his aim as the probing of 'Athanasius' misrepresentations, many of which have held sway for centuries' (p. ix). Cf. also his *Constantine and Eusebius* (Cambridge, MA: Harvard University Press, 1981), where he characterizes Athanasius as the head of an 'ecclesiastical mafia' (p. 230).

4 The characterization of Athanasius as 'like a modern gangster' is famously Barnes': *Constantine and Eusebius* 230.

5 The date of Athanasius' birth is disputed, on grounds of a disparity between his age at consecration as bishop in 328 (he was likely only just 29, if the charges of being too young, raised in the *Festal Index*, are accurate). For a detailed treatment, see Barnes, *Athanasius and Constantius* 10–11.

receiving him as a pupil, would have it) – a youth spent, according to the reflections of Gregory the Theologian, in some classical learning, but more centrally in
developing a focus on the scriptures 'with a depth such as none else has applied
even to one of them'.[6] This focus on the scriptures served him well in later life,
and his writings show a tendency to focus on scriptural language and imagery
even after adopting the non-scriptural *homoousia*-based language of Nicaea.

Athanasius had been ordained deacon by the time of the synod in 325, and was
in attendance at Nicaea with Bishop Alexander, perhaps as his secretary. As but a
deacon, he will have had little (or more likely no) part in the proceedings of the
council itself, but it is clear that its deliberations had a formative effect on him.[7]
When Alexander died in 328 and Athanasius took up his see, the policies against
Arius and 'Arianism' forged by his predecessor in the midst of the Nicene
disputes were made Athanasius' own. Not only did this stir the emotions of
those who were already opposed to him on grounds of what they termed a faulty
ordination (part of the ongoing Meletian disputes, which the Nicene council
had attempted to redress), but his forging ahead with the policies of Alexander –
such as refusal to re-admit Arius to communion, even in the face of imperial
pressure[8] – ensured that he also found strong opposition in those whose emotions
were still raw as a consequence of the council. When Eusebius of Nicomedia
accused him of plotting the murder of a Meletian bishop Arsenius, it took nothing
less than Athanasius physically producing the same Arsenius (alive and well,
having been in hiding) to have the charges dropped.

This type of intrigue was to characterize the whole of Athanasius' episcopal life.
From 335 to 337 he was exiled in Gaul, largely on charges posed by Eusebius
about anti-Meletian activities, together with accusations of manipulating com-
merce traffic in Alexandria. In 338/339 he was charged in Antioch with embezzlement and promoting riots, deposed, and sent into a period of exile in Rome.
An attempt by the pope to have Athanasius reinstated was rejected by much of
the east (given that the statement also supported Marcellus), and it was not until
346 that he was able to return to his see (after a period of intense disputes). A third
exile followed from 356 to 362, at the instigation of the emperor Constantius,
during which Athanasius spent much of his time in the desert in fervent writing.
Allowed to return to his homeland during the general reclamation of deposed
bishops by Julian in 362, Athanasius was in Alexandria only 8 months before
the same Julian determined he was too influential to remain in the city, or even the
country. He departed into a fourth exile in the desert. He found favour under the

---

6   Gregory of Nazianzus, *Oration* 21.6; cf. Weinandy, *Athanasius* 1. The emphasis was clearly on
religious, rather than classical, learning, as Gregory's panegyric notes. Barnes takes this to mean
Athanasius did not closely study classical texts: Barnes, *Athanasius and Constantius* 11–12. This is
balanced by A. Pettersen, *Athanasius* (London: Geoffrey Chapman, 1995) 4.

7   See *Soc. HE* 1.8.13; *Soz. HE* 1.17.7; cf. Pettersen, *Athanasius* 7–8.

8   On the details of this episode, see Barnes, *Athanasius and Constantius* 17–18 and esp. n. 75
to p. 18.

next emperor, Jovian, in 363; but he reigned (and indeed, lived) only a year before Valentinian came to the throne, accompanied by a brother called Valens whom he appointed governor of the eastern territories, and who systematically demanded the exile of all bishops supportive of Nicaea. Athanasius fled his church in time to escape being arrested by Valens' troops, and remained in exile a few months. He returned later that year (364), at last to stay in Alexandria until his death in 373.[9]

Seventeen years in exile during a 46-year episcopate, having been accused of rioting, embezzlement, illegal trade embargoes, murder, defying imperial decree, anti-Meletian scheming – it is not difficult to see why some have characterized him harshly. Yet this same Athanasius evoked deep respect, and often public out-pourings of joy, amongst the inhabitants of his see;[10] forged lasting relationships with western bishops and the Roman pope; was beloved and held in high esteem by the young monastic communities of the Egyptian desert; was regarded as a defender of the faith even in his own lifetime. In a time of turmoil – and the fourth century was as tumultuous an era as they come – being the recipient of aggressive accusations was hardly abnormal, and marks out most major figures in the Church. This is all the more true in the case of the bishop of a see of particular national and international significance, and which had been at the centre of polarizing disputes for at least a quarter-century. Receiving the adulation so great a number, despite such contexts, that by the end of the century he was taken as a father figure of the faith, and by the next as one of its most stalwart defenders, is, however, something unusual. Athanasius, whatever may have been the complex dimensions of his character, was a man who spoke in words that would come to define Christian articulation of doctrine for centuries after his death.

For our purposes in this study, it is those words that are most significant. Despite the complexities of his personal situation and the changing landscape of ecclesi-astical politics and doctrinal debate in the post-Nicene era, Athanasius framed his theological writings in a manner marked out by its continuity with past genera-tions. This is most true in his earliest major work, the double *Contra Gentes – De incarnatione*, written during the early years of his episcopacy, sometime in the early 330s.[11] Here, more explicitly than anywhere else, Athanasius is able to

---

9   This overview of the intricacies of Athanasius' career is necessarily brief. For a good summary in more detail, see Pettersen, *Athanasius* 1–18. His excessively negative characterizations notwithstand-ing, there is an abundance of useful historical facts and figures on the historical aspects of Athanasius' life and times in Barnes, *Athanasius and Constantius* 1–164.

10   See *Historia Arianorum ad Monachos* 25; cf. Weinandy, *Athanasius* 4.

11   Barnes would locate the date for the work between the usually promoted early dates of c. 318 and later dates of c. 335/6, arguing that the text was composed between 325 and 328 as a '*specimen erudi-tionis* to demonstrate to the world that the young deacon who was clearly being groomed as the next bishop of Alexandria deserved his place at Alexander's side' (Barnes, *Athanasius and Constantius* 12; cf. 13). There seems little to support this directly, especially when the theological content is taken more fully into consideration. In general I agree with the later dating of the treatise, rather more dominant in scholarship today, reflecting the type of doctrinal text relevant to and expected of an early episcopal career. See Anatolios, *Athanasius* 26–30.

present the core of this theological exposition in his own terms, mindful of the issues at stake at the Nicene council that had been held a few years before, but not yet wholly bound up in the disputes that would demand a polemical and often highly contextual shape to his later texts. The *CG-DI* is Athanasius at his least case-specific. He argues against the general practice of idolatry, but is not yet in disputes with single persons, perceived camps, or over specific terminologies; and this text, more than any of his others, articulates doctrinal theology through an anthropological perspective. As idols are wrong images of the divine, Christ is the true Image, and humanity after his image; so in rightly perceiving the human, one rightly perceives Christ, and so knows the Father.[12]

In what follows, we shall focus primarily on Athanasius' discussions in the *Contra Gentes-De incarnatione*, making comparison throughout to his later works, in which he regularly refines his discussion with reference to increasingly Nicaea-specific terminologies. At the end of the chapter we shall look more directly at Athanasius on the concerns of Nicaea and the post-Nicene disputes. Throughout, it will be clear that the anthropological framework for theological discussion of the preceding centuries is borne out fully in Athanasius' writings, even as the focus begins to change and those frameworks begin to be altered.

INCORRUPTION, CORRUPTION, INCORRUPTION

For Athanasius, Christ reveals the nature of creation. Put another way, the incarnate Word reveals, in a new way, the starting point of the creature in creation. The creature is the Word's, for the Word is the fashioner of creation; and the Word is immanent in creation, since it is fashioned by him directly. This establishes a series of basic doctrinal observations for Athanasius: first, creation as the working of God in the Word, is a thing that reveals its creator, for it is fashioned by one who is himself Image of the Father. More than this, the chief of creation, the human handiwork, discloses the reality of God in a unique way as directly after the image of this Image. The creature's temporal and participatory relationship to the Son reflects – precisely by being distinct from it – the Son's eternal relationship to the Father. Second, the imaging of the Word, taking place in the corruptible creature that is the human, discloses a relationship of incorruption and corruption and lays the groundwork for refining the distinction between God and man from this vantage point of corruptibility. Third, the relationship of the incorruptible God to his corruptible creation is perceived in the participatory life of the human person, and

---

12 Given its arguments against idolatry and in defence of the incarnation and cross, the *CG-DI* is often characterized as apologetic, or more specifically an *apologia crucis*. However, it is not apologetic in an entirely standard sense: there are broader doctrinal issues being articulated by Athanasius, and the volume serves, in Anatolios' words, as 'a fairly comprehensive little catechesis' (Anatolios, *Athanasius* 30). On the nature of the treatise, see Behr, *Nicene Faith* 168–71.

in particular through the function of the soul, which unites the body to the life of the Word through the Spirit.

The starting point: creation reveals the creator

In the *Contra Gentes-De incarnatione*, Athanasius orientates his theological exposition around the centrality of creation. While it is in the incarnation that the Word's salvific power is demonstrated, and it is therefore this that gives the perspective necessary to understand the Word's relation to creation, it is nonetheless the act of creation that discloses the eternity and power of the Word-made-flesh. Athanasius grounds his thought in the assertion that creation is a composite organism, with many parts interacting and depending on one another for their own being and sustenance:

> If a man take the parts of creation separately, and consider each by itself – as for example the sun by itself alone, and the moon apart, and again earth and air and heat and cold, and the essence of wet and of dry, separating them from their mutual conjunction – he will certainly find that not one is sufficient for itself, but all are in need of one another's assistance and subsist by their mutual help. For the sun is carried round along with, and is contained in, the whole heaven, and can never go beyond his own orbit, while the moon and other stars testify to the assistance given them by the sun: while the earth again evidently does not yield her crops without rains, which in their turn would not descend to earth without the assistance of the clouds; but not even the clouds would ever appear of themselves and subsist without the air.[13]

Athanasius' point is not simply to declare an intentional harmony to the created order (and one which, as the larger body of *CG* 27 explains, hymns and praises God through its order), but to show that all creation is dependent creation.[14] With regard to these natural elements of sun, moon, wind, etc., there is an obvious interdependence and interaction. Athanasius uses these examples, then, to go further, to the dimension of dependent being as an ontological category:

> Seeing then all created nature, as far as its own laws were concerned, to be fleeting and subject to dissolution, lest it should come to this and lest the universe should be broken up again into nothingness, for this cause he [the Father] made all things by his own eternal Word, and gave substantive existence to creation. Moreover, he did not leave it to be tossed in a tempest in the course

---

13 *CG* 27.5.
14 See also *CG* 35, 36.

of its own nature, lest it should run the risk of once more dropping out of existence, but, because he is good he guides and settles the whole creation by his
own Word, who is himself also God, that by the governance and providence
and ordering action of the Word, creation may have light, and be enabled
always to abide securely. For it partakes of the Word who derives true existence from the Father, and is helped by him so as to exist, lest that should come
to it which would have come but for the maintenance of it by the Word –
namely, dissolution – 'for he is the Image of the invisible God, the firstborn of
all creation, for through him and in him all things consist, things visible and
things invisible, and he is the head of the Church' (cf. Colossians 1.15, 16), as
the ministers of truth teach in their holy writings.[15]

Athanasius sees, in the interdependence of the various elements of creation, an
image of the dependence of creation as a whole on the sustaining power of the
Word. As creation was brought forth out of nothing and is inherently unstable,
prone to dissolution[16] (an understanding of the consequences of creation *ex nihilo*
that Athanasius shares with his predecessors, going back, as we have seen, at least
as far as Irenaeus[17]), it requires the power of one who is not bound by such instability to foster its ongoing existence. For this reason, Athanasius places substantial
emphasis on the distinction between the things of creation and their creator, the
Word: 'they are made out of nothing, while he is unmade'.[18] The relevance of
the distinction is not so much to demonstrate the infinite power of the Word (as it
had been in Irenaeus), but rather to ground statements on the Word's ability to
grant to creation what it cannot obtain for itself: the stability that comes from an
existence which has no beginning, no coming-into-being, and thus no necessary
movement towards an end.

   The pattern that Athanasius has established – of creation revealing its creator,
and more than this, its relation to its creator – proves central to his whole theological approach. Creation is an image of the one who created it, such that 'by looking
up to the heaven and seeing its order and the light of the stars, it is possible to infer
the Word who ordered these things';[19] but this imaging is only the beginning of the
relevance of the relationship. As the Word's *relation* to creation is imaged in creation's interdependence (thus he is sustainer because he has not come into being),
so what is seen of the Word through creation is *his relation* to his Father – for it is
this that establishes his unique stature in and for the created order. So while contemplation of creation discloses the Word, this in turn leads one to 'behold also

15   *CG* 41.3.
16   See Anatolios, *Athanasius* 55–56.
17   See the comments of Pettersen, *Athanasius* 22–23 on the developments of a doctrine of creation
ex nihilo in Athanasius.
18   *CG* 35.1.
19   *CG* 45.1.

God his Father, proceeding from whom he is rightly called his Father's interpreter and messenger'.[20] The ultimate fruit of contemplation of the created order, is contemplation of the relationship of Word and Father.

It is in the connection of imaged *relations*, not simply imaged beings, that Athanasius can find creation's potency in revealing the nature of the Word of the Father. It is because creation is finite and temporal – that it is 'living and contingent' in the Logos, as Pettersen characterizes it[21] – that its sustenance in the Word reveals him as infinite and eternal. As creation receives its eternity through participation in the Word's eternity, so the Word must be understood as possessing this attribute in a manner that is not participatory – else he would be in the same state as transient creation itself. The 'proof' that this cannot be so is found, for Athanasius, in the very fact of creation's ongoing existence. Its failure to go the way of all temporal things, that is, into non-existence, proves its participation in that which, as a consequence, cannot be conceived as bound by the same finite limitations.[22] So the Word must be understood as eternal precisely because creation is temporal, and infinite precisely because creation is finite, yet on neither account is it lost to corruption. The interdependency of creation, which is sustained in being by participation in eternal being, discloses the Word's non-participatorial relationship to the Father:

Being present with him as his Wisdom and his Word, looking at the Father he fashioned the universe, and organised it and gave it order; and, as he is the power of the Father, he gave all things strength to be, as the saviour says: 'Whatever things I see the Father doing, I also do in like manner' (cf. John 5.19). And his holy disciples teach that all things were made 'through him and unto him' (Romans 11.36); and, being the good offspring of him that is good, and true Son, he is the Father's power and Wisdom and Word, not being so by participation, nor as if these qualities were imparted to him from without as they are to those who partake of him and are made wise by him, and receive power and reason in him; but he is the very Wisdom, very Word, and very power of the Father, very light, very truth, very righteousness, very virtue, and in truth his express Image, and brightness, and resemblance (αλλ' αὐτοσοφία, αὐτολόγος, αὐτοδύναμις ἰδία τοῦ Πατρός ἐστιν, αὐτοφῶς, αὐτοαλή θεια, αὐτοδικαιοσύνη, αὐτοαρετὴ, καὶ μὲν καὶ χαρακτὴρ καὶ ἀπαύ γασμα καὶ εἰκών). To sum it all up, he is the wholly perfect fruit of the Father

---

20 Ibid.

21 Pettersen, *Athanasius* 26.

22 In the vocabulary of his later anti-Arian writings, Athanasius says this explicitly: 'What help then can creatures derive from a creature that itself needs salvation? [. . .] A creature could never be saved by a creature' (*Ad Adelph.* 8); cf. *C. Ar.* 1.29. On creation participating in the Word, forming a 'participation model' for doctrinal discussion, see the excellent treatment in Anatolios, *Athanasius* 50–53.

(καρπὸς παντέλειος τοῦ Πατρὸς ὑπάρχει), and is alone the Son, and unchanging Image of the Father (εἰκὼν ἀπαράλλακτος τοῦ Πατρός).[23]

It is revealing that Athanasius places the emphasis of a doctrine of the 'image of God' on the Son, rather than *per se* on the human creature that bears God's image. Later in the double work, he will note with particular care that humanity is created only 'after' the image, whereas – as here – the Son is himself the 'unchanging Image of the Father'.[24] It is clear what are the implications of this distinction. As true and unchanging image, the Son is, without receipt of these characteristics by participation, ever the possessor of those attributes which are the Father's. He is not simply light and truth, but the *very* light (αὐτοφῶς) and *very* truth (αὐτοαλήθεια) of the Father.[25] It is this which makes him categorically different from 'those who partake of him and are made wise by him, and receive power and reason in him'; and this distinction is important precisely because it grounds a relationship. As creation 'receives power' and the other attributes of ongoing existence, so that receipt is made potent by being received from one who is not simply receiving these also from another. The fact of creation's existence 'in him' makes it an image of the Son's being as Image of the Father. The very fact that the relation gives eternal life to temporal creation through participation, discloses that the relationship of Son to Father cannot be similarly participatory.[26]

The chief example of creation revealing, or imaging, its creator is found in the human person, which fact gives a priority to anthropology over cosmology more generally.[27] Like all of creation, the human is created *ex nihilo*, which for Athanasius means the same implications of finitude and temporality apply to it. Nonetheless, it is this creature in particular that is given to be 'after' the Image in a unique way. The human creature is fashioned 'after his own Image', and consequently able to see and know the reality of the Word 'by means of this assimilation to himself'.[28] To be particularly after the image means that man is able to behold, in his own relationship to the Word whose image he bears, the nature of the Word as Image of the Father. In man is seen 'a participation in the Son's archetypal relationship of similitude to the Father'.[29] Moreover, because this relationship is (again, mirroring all creation) one of participation, humanity as 'after the image

---

23   *CG* 46.7, 8.
24   See *DI* 13.7; cf. *C. Ar.* 1.22.
25   It is possible that this is a more or less direct allusion to the language of Nicaea's creed: 'God from God, light from light, true God from true God . . .'.
26   So *C. Ar.* 1.15: 'If, as they say, the Son is from nothing and was not before his generation, he of course, like others, must be called Son and God and Wisdom through participation only. For thus all other creatures exist and by sanctification are glorified'; see also 1.16, 26.
27   On this relationship of anthropology and cosmology, see Anatolios, *Athanasius* 32–35.
28   *CG* 2.2.
29   Anatolios, *Athanasius* 56.

of the Image' participates in the Word in a unique way, such that the attributes of the Son become the attributes of the human person.[30] The participatory image of humanity in the Word, brings to humanity the power of the Father, which the Word has eternally as his own characteristics. So man 'has also God's own power from the Word of the Father', and so it is his lot to 'rejoice and have fellowship with the Deity, living the life of immortality unharmed and truly blessed'. In this Athanasius stands together with each of our three previous authors. Participation in the Son draws humanity into a relationship with the Father that unites them in communion and fellowship.[31] What is unique in Athanasius is the manner in which he sees this human participation in God as disclosing, to a degree far greater than in our other writers, the intricacies of the relationship of the Father and Son.

The key to this nuance is humanity created after the Image: the Son. For Athanasius, this means that what is seen in all creation is seen most potently in the human creature; namely, the true reality of the Word-in-relation. But perception and comprehension of this Word, imaged in the person, is possible only through a right knowledge of what it means to be human. It is man's frailty, his corruptibility, his temporality, seen together with his received eternity and transformation into incorruption, that gives theological power to a doctrine of the image.

Corruption and the incorruptible Word

If revelation of the Word's nature (and thus the Father's nature, of which the Son is Image) is found in humanity as created after the Image's image, then a right perception of human nature is critical to right theological vision. This is precisely why Athanasius' early writings are so cosmologically and anthropologically orientated. It also proves to be, as we shall see, a key ingredient in his opposition to Arius.

By the time of Athanasius' writing in the early- to mid-fourth century, many of the anthropological maxims of the earlier centuries were now standard. Themes that consumed the attention of Irenaeus or Tertullian to an almost infinitesimal degree, which required substantial justification and apology, could simply be reiterated by Athanasius. So a bi-partite anthropology is just stated, rather than argued, and the basic characteristics of each aspect given brief, if succinct, treatment. The human creature is a reality of body and soul, the soul sometimes called

---

30 Cf. the discussion of G. Dragas, *Saint Athanasius of Alexandria: Original Research and New Perspectives* (New Hampshire: Orthodox Research Institute, 2005) 8–9 for a treatment of the dimension of 'theological becoming' related to 'creaturely becoming' in Athanasius. Full human personal reality is described as 'a dynamic gift maintained by the Creator Logos', linked specifically to 'transmission of the power of the Logos' through the image in man (p. 9). See also C. Kannengiesser, 'Athanasius of Alexandria and the Foundation of Traditional Christology', *TS* 34 (1973), 103–13.

31 See above, p. 155 on the Father as 'our' Father.

'spirit' and clearly perceived as the immaterial element in man. The creature is 'embodied spirit', much as for Tertullian it was a 'housed soul'.[32] The soul may be heavenly and immaterial, but it is still a created thing; and its creation, like that of the body, is *ex nihilo*, from nothing.[33] Thus man is 'naturally mortal', given to the instability of all things that come into being and so are bound to go out of it. It is the presence of the Word, and this presence alone, that sustains the existence of what creation itself requires to be finite.[34] Precisely because God knew this limitation of matter, he created humanity after his own image – giving a glimpse of the participatory nature of 'after the image' we have already discussed.[35]

This natural limitation of creation is visible first in its material nature, for 'all bodies are liable to the corruption of death'.[36] And yet, it is not tied up in materiality alone. Athanasius may call the soul 'immortal', given that it is not bound to the same physical corruption and corruptibility as the body;[37] but its natural immortality is nonetheless conditioned by its creation *ex nihilo*. That which has a beginning in being, which comes into being from non-being, is always effected by the impermanence of that creation (Athanasius, as we shall see in the next section, sees the primary effect of this creation on the soul as its 'mobility' or motion). So the soul, together with the body, fashion a person that is essentially impermanent. There is a 'weakness of their nature; for, unable to continue in one stay, they are dissolved with time.'[38]

Athanasius' preferred characterization of this weakness is corruptibility. Should the human creature depart from the presence of the Word, it will incur the 'corruption that is his by nature'.[39] That is, apart from its union with the life-sustaining Word of the Father, the human moves towards corruption and death, intrinsic in its own nature as created reality. What is critical in this is the understanding of corruptibility as a natural condition in man, but the *actual corruption* of the human being as a *process*. Corruption is an end, a *telos*, towards which all created things will naturally move. But the human person has been created in communion with the Word, who grants incorruption. Man is made to 'abide in incorruption',[40] to derive his ongoing existence 'from God who is'.[41] Athanasius thus speaks of the created human condition in distinctly participatorial terms. The human person is

---

32   See *DI* 4. Cf. Tertullian, above, pp. 65–66.
33   See *DI* 4.5, 5.1.
34   See *DI* 5.
35   See also *DI* 12.
36   *DI* 8.4.
37   So in *CG* 33.4.
38   *DI* 21.4.
39   Cf. *DI* 3.4, 5.
40   *DI* 4.4.
41   Ibid. 4.5.

fashioned to 'remain' (μένειν) in communion with the Word, and by so remaining, to have ongoing being.[42] Should this communion be broken, then

> just as they have had their being out of nothing, so also, as might be expected, they might look for corruption into nothing in the course of time.[43]

The key to this notion of corruption as a process in which the human creature engages through a turning from the Word, lies in the fact of creation itself. Everything created is transient; therefore ongoing existence for a creature must involve being joined to a source of life that is not bound by created limitations. Athanasius' insistence that the Son has not been brought into being by the Father, so much the focus of his later arguments against Arius, rests here on distinctly anthropological grounds. A created Son, a Word that has come into being, could not be the source of limitless life for the rest of creation. Because humanity, created after the image of the Word, receives eternal existence by imaging in itself the eternal existence of the Word of the Father, that Word can only be conceived in terms that disclose a fully uncreated stature.[44] And it is worth reminding ourselves that this emphasis on the Son as non-created, by which we mean not brought-into-being, is made by Athanasius on wholly anthropological grounds, without reference specifically to Arius or an Arian argument – indeed, without reference to any dogmatic assertions whatever.[45] Because the human creature is created, yet through participation in the Word does not move towards the naturally corruptible lot of all created things, the Word must be confessed as uncreated. While the human creature may be 'after' the image, inasmuch as it images God by participation in the Son, to be *truly* the Image of the Father is to be, as Athanasius says, his very truth and very power, 'not being so by participation, nor as if these qualities were imparted to him from without'.

Before we come to address how this anthropological grounding relates to the dogmatic disputes in which Athanasius was involved, and in particular how it involves a developed doctrine of the Spirit, it is necessary to note that Athanasius further develops this anthropological articulation of the Word's relation to the Father with reference to the nature and function of the soul in man. The 'mobile soul' is a necessary ingredient in the human creature's imaging of the Son's relationship to the Father.

---

42   The significance of 'remaining' is drawn out excellently by Anatolios, *Athanasius* 35–37, and in several places throughout his volume. See also Behr, *Nicene Faith* 175–77.

43   *DI* 4.4.

44   See Weinandy, *Athanasius* 29.

45   All the more interesting an observation, given the post-Nicene dating of the text (addressed above). Arius is clearly in Athanasius' mind as he writes, as would have been the council; yet he approaches the topic first and foremost in this distinctly anthropologically orientated manner.

Imaging the Word: the instrument of the soul

In our three previous authors, the place of the soul in the human composition
proved essential in understanding the human as united to God, and in that union
imaging the God after whom it was created. The same proves true with Athanasius, though his treatment of the soul is certainly less extensive than either Tertullian's or Cyril's. Further, a persistent fascination with questions over whether
Athanasius believed Christ to have a human soul (i.e. in relation to concerns over
Apollinarianism), has often led scholars to abstract the question from that of his
perception of the soul in general. It is encouraging that the most important recent
studies have begun to look at Athanasius' understanding in more detail, but there
is still much ground to cover.[46] Given, as we have already begun to see, that
Athanasius frames his doctrinal assertions on God's nature squarely through his
anthropological reflections, the nature of the soul and its function in man are of
critical importance to his larger thought.

Like Tertullian, whose comments on the soul often described it in terms of
its guiding power over the body, Athanasius asserts the soul's primary function
as direction or governance. While the soul and body together form the human,
it is the soul that is the guiding force in human life. To put it in the terms of
Weinandy's recent study, the soul is 'like a charioteer':[47] it guides the body, either
towards the good or towards the bad. By Athanasius' time, this is long since an
axiomatic anthropological concept. The body, as a thing corporeal, is governed
by an incorporeal reality. But Athanasius does not simply re-state this common
position. In his reflections on the nature of the soul, he links it directly to the body
in terms of the corporeal senses. The body is not described only as physical construct, but as sensory agent; and the soul is that which directs not just the body
generally, but the bodily senses inw particular. So he writes:

> Hence, because it is distinct, it acts as judge of the senses, and while they
> apprehend their objects, the intelligence distinguishes, recollects, and shows
> them what is best. For the sole function of the eye is to see, of the ears to hear,
> of the mouth to taste, of the nostrils to apprehend smells, and of the hands to
> touch. But what one ought to see and hear, what one ought to touch, taste and
> smell, is a question beyond the senses, and belonging to the soul and to the
> intelligence which resides in it.[48]

The soul is the governor of the sensory power of the body, and that by which
the bodily senses can be used to direct the person either towards evil or good.[49]

46　For recent assessments of the soul in Athanasius, see Anatolios, *Athanasius* 53–67; Pettersen,
Athanasius 40–44; Weinandy, *Athanasius* 19–21.
47　Weinandy, p. 15; echoing Athanasius' own use of the imagery at *CG* 5.2.
48　*CG* 31.3.
49　Cf. *CG* 4.4; see Pettersen, *Athanasius* 42–44.

Athanasius' nuance here is important. By focusing on the body as sensory, interacting with the cosmos through the usage and manipulation of its physical senses, he connects it to the soul in more than a generalizing manner. The soul is not simply a 'life force' or an 'immortal element', but that which moves the bodily senses towards right focus, perception and action. On this account the soul is intimately connected to the intellect (νοῦς), which Athanasius has identified as 'residing in it'[50] – its deliberative, discerning power. The *nous* is the means by which the soul guides the bodily senses towards things divine rather than things base; and it is able to do this because the soul itself is also a sensory agent. It, like the body, senses things apart from itself, yet because it is distinct from the body, it senses different things. In particular, the soul, as 'immortal' and 'spiritual', senses things of immortality and spirit – namely, things divine.[51] It moves the bodily senses towards God because it senses and communicates with God in a unique manner. This is the focus of Athanasius' discussion at a critical passage of the *Contra Gentes*, to which we have already made mention. His precise wording is important:

> This is the reason why the soul thinks of and bears in mind things immortal and eternal; namely, because it is itself immortal. And just as, the body being mortal, its senses also have mortal things as their objects, so, since the soul contemplates and beholds immortal things, it follows that it is immortal and lives for ever. For ideas and thoughts about immortality never desert the soul, but abide in it, and are, as it were, the fuel in it which ensures its immortality. This then is why the soul has the capacity for beholding God, and is its own way thereto, receiving not from without but from itself the knowledge and apprehension of the Word of God.[52]

This rich passage reveals a number of important elements in Athanasius' understanding of the soul. First, he notes that the soul, given its nature distinct from the body, is able to comprehend the things of God in a different manner. Second, this comprehension is described in terms of 'contemplation': of ideas and thoughts 'abiding in' the soul through its natural sensory power. Third, and perhaps most significantly, the soul's immortality and eternity arise from this contemplation of God's immortality and eternity. It is the 'fuel' which ensures its own immortality, and which gives to the soul a knowledge of the Word. More than this, the apprehension of the Word, as arising out of this divine contemplation, can be said to come 'not from without', but from the soul itself.

---

50 For a good treatment of the νοῦς in Athanasius, see Anatolios, *Athanasius* 61–67.

51 See Dragas, *Athanasius: Original Research* 30–31 for further discussion on this anthropological distinction, including its linkage to the notions of mobility and immobility, which we shall treat below.

52 *CG* 33.4; cf. *C. Ar.* 2.80.

Athanasius has painted a picture of the human person that identifies the source of divine communion as the soul – much as in Irenaeus, Tertullian and Cyril. Yet he has done so in a manner that refines the soul's communicative power. *How* the soul communicates to the person the attributes of God is clearer here than in any of our previous sources. The soul's natural sensory power, sensory of the immaterial as it itself is immaterial, provides it with the means to contemplate God through the directive power of the *nous*; and this contemplation, as a spiritual communion with God's own being, causes the soul to well up in itself – and communicate to the body – the eternal attributes of the divine life.[53] The soul's contemplation is the very means of participation that defines human existence as being after God's image, which is the working of God's grace in the human creature.

Athanasius has not broken entirely new ground in articulating the soul in this way. There are clear hints of the same in Tertullian's *Testimony of the soul*, which describe the communion of the soul with the Holy Spirit as causing it to utter divine things as of 'a nature congenital to it'.[54] There, as here, the soul's communion with God brings divine attributes into the first-person of the whole human being, soul and body together. Nonetheless, Athanasius has given new definition to the soul's ability to serve the human creature in this way. The soul is the body's 'governor' or 'charioteer' because it contemplates, through its immaterial senses, divine things, and so participates in them through that contemplation. Thus the human person, if properly employing the *nous* to orientate its life around the soul's communion with God, bears in itself God's life, eternity, immortality, wisdom, strength, truth, etc. When Athanasius writes of his great hero of the desert, St Anthony the Great, he takes care to note that the hermit's renowned spiritual insight is given to him 'from his soul'; and that the monk's soul, when 'in its natural state' of divine contemplation, is able to see with clear sight, with God's own vision, further than even the demons.[55]

The soul's contemplation grounds man's participation in God. As we have already seen, this participation in God is the very focus of humanity as after his image, which therefore places the soul as a central ingredient in man 'after the image of God'. Yet because the soul, like the body, is created, it cannot be reduced simply to an ongoing element of divine communion in the person. It must be understood as bound to the same impermanence and motion towards an end as the body (since it is not the body's materiality, *per se*, that gives rise to these, but its created nature, which the soul shares). The instability of the soul is reflected in what Athanasius terms its 'mobility' (εὐκινησία). It is, through the functioning of the *nous*, deliberative. It can move towards heaven or towards earth, but what remains consistent is that it *does* move, and therefore it is involved in the fact of

---

53 See Anatolios, *Athanasius* 61–62.
54 *De Test.* 5; cf. above, p. 71.
55 See *VA* 5.5, 34.2.

human existence always being a process, an economy – whether into corruption or incorruption.[56] It can move towards the natural objects of its immaterial senses (the attributes of God's divine life), or it can move towards baser and less noble things. And just as contemplation of God brings to the soul the attributes of God, namely life and eternity, so contemplation of the baser things of the earth brings to the soul the attributes of those created realities, namely finitude, corruptibility and death. So Athanasius says of this soul:

> Having departed from the contemplation of the things of thought, and using to the full the several activities of the body, and being pleased with the contemplation of the body, and seeing that pleasure is good for her, she was misled and abused the name of good, and thought that pleasure was the very essence of good: just as though a man out of his mind and asking for a sword to use against all he met, were to think that to be soundness of mind. But, having fallen in love with pleasure, she began to work it out in various ways. For being by nature mobile, even though she has turned away from what is good, yet she does not lose her mobility. She moves (κινεῖται) then, no longer according to virtue or so as to see God, but imagining false things, she makes a novel use of her power, abusing it as a means to the pleasures she has devised, since she is after all made with power over herself (τὸ ἑαυτῆς δυνατὸν μεταποιεῖ). For she is able, as on the one hand to incline to what is good, so on the other to reject it; but in rejecting the good she of course entertains the thought of what is opposed to it, for she cannot at all cease from movement, being, as I said before, mobile by nature (παύσασθαι γὰρ καθόλου τοῦ κινεῖσθαι οὐ δύναται, τὴν φύσιν οὖσα, ὡς προεῖπον, εὐκίνητος).[57]

Motion towards 'pleasure', understood here as a debased usage of the bodily senses, causes the soul to contemplate, and thus manifest in itself, all the aspects of those pleasures – not simply the transient joy that comes from them, but the very fact of transience itself, which is intrinsic to all created things, sensible to the body. The soul ceases to be (or, is lessened in being) a means of participation in God, and becomes instead only another means of fulfilling the potentials of created nature. The soul ceases to cause the person to image the Word, since it no longer realizes, through contemplation, a participation in divine life. It is for this reason that Athanasius will assert, in speaking of Christ's incarnation, that through it 'the soul is created anew in God's image'.[58] This is not to say that the soul alone, rather than the whole of the human person, is implicated in the *imago Dei*; rather, it is to reflect the fact that it is through the soul's contemplative participation in

---

56 See *CG* 4.2, 3.
57   *CG* 4.1–3.
58   *DI* 14.2.

God that the entire human person participates in him, and thus images the Son. When the soul is 'defiled' through turning from God, the whole man ceases to be after the image of his maker.[59]

THE SOUL'S MOVEMENT INTO NON-EXISTENCE: SIN AS TRANSFORMATION

Sin as movement

Conception of the soul's 'mobility' (εὐκινησία), and its charge to 'remain' (μένειν) in its created state of contemplation of divine things, grounds Athanasius' articulation of the by-now common perception of sin as act. Rather than something ontological, sin is defined as a movement, held in opposition to stability, or 'remaining', in the contemplation of (and participation in) God.[60] Like those we have explored before him, Athanasius stresses that 'from the beginning (ἐν ἀρχῇ), evil did not exist', and as such must not be perceived as constituting a nature in itself.[61] Rather, it is a movement, effected by a perversion of the soul's natural contemplation, such that the intellect (νοῦς) follows the bodily senses. The whole human person, like the full human community, thus comes to turn away from the participatory contemplation of God, 'seeking in preference things nearer to themselves'.[62] It is the sensory power of the soul, the very thing that enables the human creature to participate in the life of God and thus image the Son, that also allows – through its perversion – the creature to be led away from this same participation. And as the soul distorts its rose as 'charioteer' of the body, this lusting after baser things effects the body: 'the soul sees that she can move the body also in an opposite way; and so, instead of beholding the creation, she turns the eye towards lusts, as she has the power to do'.[63]

Sin is therefore understood by Athanasius as movement – away from the sensory contemplation of God (sensibly accessible to both soul and body), towards the sensory contemplation of finite creation. As we have seen, Athanasius understands contemplation as involving a drawing into one's self of the attributes of the thing contemplated, which is why contemplation of God involves a movement into the fullness of divine life. Similarly, though to the other extreme, contemplation of finite realities implies an ever greater participation in all the attributes of that

---

59 Cf. *DI* 11.3–7. See the summary remark of Anatolios, *Athanasius* 65: '[. . .] we can speak of the relation with God as constitutive of the human person in Athanasius's [sic] anthropology.'
60 Cf. Ibid. 35–37.
61 *CG* 2.1; cf. 6.2–5, 7.3. See Weinandy, *Athanasius* 13, 15–16.
62 *CG* 3.1.
63 *CG* 4.4. And so humans are, in the words of Pettersen, 'self-shaping beings' (*Athanasius* 53).

finitude, namely corruption and death. It is this dual notion of motion towards/ participation in, that grounds Athanasius' famous language on the human condition in the *De incarnatione*, when he comes to consider the 'divine dilemma' and God's response to the state of man. He describes the condition of humanity in dynamic terms, indicating motion and transformation: man 'is perishing', this chief work of God is 'on the road to ruin';[64] the creator is faced with the 'dehumanising of making';[65] and, perhaps at his most poetic, 'Man [. . .] was disappearing, and the work of God was being undone'.[66] Athanasius stresses the economic quality of sin, which propels the human person away from 'what is' towards what 'is not' through misuse of the soul's contemplative power.[67]

Speaking of a motion towards what 'is not' (εἰς τὰ μὴ ὄντα) is significant, as it reinforces Athanasius' notion of participation in divine life as the intended state of human existence. Only God eternally is, as we have explored above. All else subsists only through participation in God's existence, since all else is created and thus bound to corruptibility. Sin cannot be a binding to some evil thing, since it is an error 'of the Greeks' to ascribe to evil 'a substantive and independent existence'.[68] Athanasius' economic articulation of sin and evil reinforces his notion of creation requiring subsistence in God's own nature, the nature of 'the one who is'. To be created after the image of the Son is to be created for participation in what he possesses naturally: the very eternity of the Father. To turn from this participation is to reject a likeness to Christ, bowing down to the pleasures of the moment rather than the nobler calling of the image.[69] And if one does not attempt to live after the likeness of the Word, one cannot hope to image the Word's relation to the Father. So it is the acts of man that effect his likeness to the Son, and the likeness to the Son that draws him into the Son as Image of the Father.

To act in a manner that does not reflect the Son's likeness is to move towards 'non-being', to engage in the process of 'perishing' that leads the human to become little else than 'brute beasts, rather than men'.[70] The person, breaking from communion with divine life, is returned to the natural conditions of created nature. Athanasius' insight, in describing this condition of movement as brought about through a misuse of the senses, is in giving effective explanation to the pervasiveness of such movement throughout the whole of the human economy. As the fulfilment of a sensory perversion, sin becomes a self-perpetuating attraction. The soul, as the body, comes to desire ever more strongly the pleasures of those things 'closer to itself', and becomes habituated to the attempt to satisfy these

---

64 *DI* 6.1, 7.
65 *DI* 13.1.
66 *DI* 6.1.
67 See *CG* 4.3.
68 *CG* 6.1.
69 So stated by Athanasius at *DI* 12.6.
70 Ibid.

desires. As Athanasius writes, in a passage exploring sin in relation to Adam and Eve:

> As is apt to happen, having formed a desire for each and sundry, they began to be habituated to these desires, so that they were even afraid to leave them; whence the soul became subject to cowardice and alarms, and pleasures and thoughts of mortality. For not being willing to leave her lusts, she fears death and her separation from the body. But again, from lusting, and not meeting with gratification, she learned to commit murder and wrong.[71]

While earthly lusts are never fully gratified, they nonetheless consume the desire of the soul and body. The person 'falls in love with pleasure'.[72] It is on this account that sin, as motion into non-being and away from participation in God, comes to have so universal a sway over humanity. Athanasius understands humankind to be a race in solidarity[73] – following the assertions we have seen in Irenaeus, Tertullian and Cyril that humanity is one race, one blood, one nature – and so this habituation towards lustful misuse of the senses takes on cosmic dimensions. Rather as Irenaeus had conveyed the advance of sin through the imagery of a great cloud spreading out over the whole earth, so Athanasius states that

> corruption ran riot among [men] and held sway over them to an even more than natural degree, because it was the penalty of which God had forewarned them for transgressing the commandment. Indeed, in their sinning they had surpassed all limits [. . .].[74]

There is a 'universal liability to death' amongst humankind, because the power of the senses, misused, draws the whole race under its sway.[75] This is linked to the natural power of the senses, but also to the power of natural corruptibility – a reality that leads all created things towards dissolution and death, as God had forewarned Adam and Eve in Eden. And so, like others before him, Athanasius is able to speak of humanity as held at 'ransom' to the 'debt' of sin. Even though this is connected to the 'penalty of which God had forewarned' the race, it is not the infraction, nor a punitive response to it, that so binds humanity to its end. Rather, it is the natural power of death itself (i.e. corruption) in the created order. Having fallen to corruption through a movement away from participation in God, humanity is bound to death; the 'debt' man owes is to the created order itself, 'for, as

---

71   *CG* 3.4.
72   *CG* 4.2.
73   See *DI* 9.2–4.
74   *DI* 5.2.
75   See *DI* 8.2.

I said before, all were due to die'.[76] Just as participation in God establishes within the human person the attributes of God's eternity, so participation in death draws death into the person. So Athanasius describes the condition: 'death was within the body, woven into its very substance and dominating it as though completely one with it'.[77] It is for this reason that the human person cannot free itself from this debt of death. Even if man were to repent fully of his transgressions, the fact would remain that his condition is not simply of trespass, but of corruption.[78] The corruption would remain, even if sin were abolished. The person is held in ransom to death. God, who is chiefly known as saviour, is perceived through the lens of this condition.

Image, reason, vision: seeing the incarnate Word

Athanasius assumes that the groundwork for a right understanding of divine doc- trine – of God as Father with a Son, of the Spirit, of salvation – resides in this right understanding of the created order, and chiefly the human creature. It is for this reason that his first major theological work, which remains in some manner his most robust, is structured in the way it is. The *CG-DI*, which as a whole is about refuting false perceptions of God imaged in the world, orientating the reader instead towards the true Image, the Word of the Father (first by commenting on false idols, and then on the incarnation), sets the groundwork for its 'theological' subjects (the Son's relation to the Father, his incarnation, the nature of the salva- tion he offers) through a detailed address of the human person: the nature of the body and the soul, of living after the image and the movements of sin. It is the constitution of the human being, rightly understood in the full measure of its created nature, that enables a proper understanding of the God who both sustains it and, when that sustaining power is forfeit to corruption through the soul's per- version of the senses and their contemplation, is able to redeem it. And, as has been intimated from the beginning of this chapter, it is precisely in this anthropo- logical perspective that Athanasius forges his key dogmatic assertions on the nature of God. That the Son of the Father must be distinct in being from all created things, inasmuch as all created things have a beginning in being and thus move naturally towards an end of being, is an observation taken from the anthropo- logical testimony of human existence, not from a pre-determined metaphysical understanding of God. Athanasius' eventual embrace of the term *homoousia* to define the relationship of the Son to the Father, is an outgrowth of the assertions we have already seen: that the Son must possess naturally, *without receiving them by participation*, the attributes of God the Father – else that in which the human

---

76 *DI* 20.2.
77 *DI* 44.5.
78 See *DI* 7.

person participates is no more a source of sustenance and life than the corruptible human himself.

Athanasius' focus on the senses, both of the body and the soul, frames in his anthropological vision of the person as acting agent. Senses ground determinations, and so the person is a being in constant motion: either into the infinite God, whose infinity and eternity thus become its own life, or into the finite creation, whose finitude thus defines its existence. It is because Athanasius focuses so heavily on the human as sensing being, that he is able to describe the reality of relation to God, of participation in God, in essentially sensory terms. One contemplates, in the uncreated and 'eternal' senses of the soul, the divinity of God, and thus participates in it. This contemplation guides the senses of the body, so that they turn towards higher things and, with the soul, engage in the 'sensing' of God himself – through creation, through revelation. So ultimately, Athanasius can describe the participatory relationship of man to God in sensory terms: chiefly vision and knowledge. The human person 'rightly sees' God through contemplation in the soul, through right vision and rational understanding of the created order, and thus lives in union with him. So when Athanasius comments on rationality as part of the image of God in which man has a share, it is not simply an indication that since God is rational, so humanity must also be in some sense rational. Rather, this rationality is part of the participatory nature of humanity existing in union with the Word. It is only in a right 'knowledge of his maker' that man possesses reason: it is not an independent attribute of the creature, but a result of participation in God's rationality through the intellect, given as an 'extra grace' by God to man.[79] When the human person rightly contemplates the Word, rightly 'sees' God in the vision of the senses, the person then sees with the Word's proper vision. The person then has a 'share in the Image' who is the Word himself; he is a creature 'sharing the nature of the Word'.[80] The rationality of the human is 'a portion of the power of the Word: free and blessed reason',[81] brought into his or her personal existence by the 'vision' of God through the senses of soul and body. The being who is *after* the image, *senses* the Image, and thus *participates* in the Image and is imbued with the Image's reason, eternity, power, strength and life.

This is the anthropological context that forms the immediate stage for Athanasius' consideration of Christology proper. Who Christ is, is understood from the perspective of this human reality. It is the Word as saviour, who redeems humanity *known to be limited and hindered in this way*, that is met in the incarnate Christ, and so these aspects of the human condition speak to the nature of the one who so redeems.

---

79   See *DI* 11.2–7; on 'extra grace' and 'extra gift' see *DI* 3.3; cf. Pettersen, *Athanasius* 27–29.
80   See *DI* 13.2.
81   *DI* 3.4.

Image Renewed: Christ, the Spirit and the Sensibility of Salvation

If sin is a movement into corruption, salvation is a movement into incorruption. This simple statement belies the complexity so often assumed of Athanasius' theology. The salvation offered in Christ is a salvation of redirection: it is the Word's response to the moving-into-non-being of his creation, redirecting it through his own being into life and eternal existence. 'His it was once more [. . .] to bring the corruptible to incorruption',[82] and this is both his intention and his unique power, as the one who first fashioned man. As creator, 'it belonged to none other to bring man back from the corruption which had begun, than the Word of God, who had also made them from the beginning'[83] – since the creator, rather than the created, is not bound by the limitations of created nature. So the Word is uniquely able to effect redemption, and that position rests in his eternity as one not-brought-into-being. Similarly, the Word's nature allows him to meet humanity's sin at the level of the senses, where it had first arisen, and work redemption in the same, precisely because he is un-created in being; and it allows the defeat of death in humanity to be a cosmic reality, effecting the whole of the race in his singular person, through the Spirit.

Making redemption sensible

As it is the misuse of the senses that causes the soul to move towards the earthly, and thus contemplate and participate in finitude rather than God's eternity, redemption must consist in the re-orientation of the senses around the contemplation of divine things.[84] Athanasius insists that the created order itself should have sufficed, of its intended design, to inspire right contemplation in the human creature; but senses that have succumbed to the 'lust' of pleasures begin to see awry even what is intrinsically good. In a passage that is redolent of Irenaeus' comments in *Refutation* 4.28–29, Athanasius writes:

> For as a kind teacher who cares for his disciples, if some of them cannot profit by higher subjects, comes down to their level, and teaches them at any rate by simpler courses, so also did the Word of God. It is as Paul says: 'For seeing that, in the wisdom of God, the world through its wisdom did not know him, it was God's good pleasure, through the foolishness of what was preached, to

---

82 *DI* 7.5.

83 *DI* 10.3. Cf. Weinandy, *Athanasius* 34.

84 On the incarnation effecting a reorientation of humanity towards remaining in (and participating in) God, see Anatolios, *Athanasius* 37.

save them that believe' (1 Corinthians 1.21). For seeing that men, having rejected the contemplation of God, and with their eyes downward, as though sunk in the deep, were seeking about for God in nature and in the world of sense, feigning gods for themselves of mortal men and demons; to this end the loving and general saviour of all, the Word of God, takes to himself a body, and as man walks among men and meets the senses of all men halfway – to the end, I say, that they who think that God is corporeal may from what the Lord effects by his body perceive the truth, and through him recognise the Father. So, men as they were and human in all their thoughts, on whatever objects they fixed their senses, there they saw themselves met halfway, and taught the truth from every side.[85]

Athanasius speaks in didactic terms. Humanity is 'taught the truth from every side', with the divine reality of the Word given physical shape to confront their senses. He can even speak of this as the Word 'disguising himself', that he may live among man and cause them to 'centre their senses on himself'.[86] Yet, the Word's coming into the realm of all man's senses – those of the body as well as those of the soul – is not solely a didactic measure. The human race is more than taught by the experience of the Word in the flesh. In his most famous single paragraph situated towards the end of the *De incarnatione*, Athanasius repeats his statements on divine pedagogy (the Word takes flesh that man 'may know and apprehend Him from His works', etc.), but goes on to link this directly to anthropological transformation through the incarnation:

For he was made man, that we might be made God; and he manifested himself by a body, that we might receive the idea of the unseen Father; and he endured the insolence of men, that we might inherit immortality.[87]

Receiving the 'idea' of the unseen Father is pedagogic; but it is clear that Athanasius is speaking in terms beyond rational comprehension. Reception of the 'idea' is united to 'becoming God'; learning of Christ's suffering correlates to 'inheriting immortality'. Following from his anthropological convictions of contemplation forging participation, Athanasius indicates the participatory reality inaugurated by the incarnation. The Word becomes accessible in a new way to the senses, and in that becoming, the senses are brought into contemplation of God himself so that they may participate in God himself, and so bring the human person into fuller union with the divine.

What makes the incarnation a uniquely life-giving event for humankind is its dual aspect: presenting the uncreated God to the race, and presenting it directly

---

85 *DI* 15.1–3.
86 See *DI* 16.1.
87 *DI* 54.3.

and accessibly to the race in an unmediated fashion. The end result is eternal life and a movement from non-being into true being, because one comes to contemplate and participate in the reality of the divine Word; but this result is accessible to the human person because the Word has become intimately associated with the person herself. Christ becomes a 'peer' to the human race, so that what is contemplated is not external to the race, but bound to its very nature.[88] The Word comes to man *as man*, and thus brings to man the fullness of his divinity. The creator's work continues: it is the power of the creative Word that re-fashions man into communion with himself – a reality possible only to the divine creator, and given surety only by his truly human engagement with the race.[89] Seeing redemption in re-creative terms, affords Athanasius the language to express it as directly connected to the initial creative design after the image. Redemption consists in the Image re-kindling in the human race an existence that images his own, wrought by the full Image becoming present in humanity, 'creating man afresh after the image'.[90] And, just as man being created 'after the image' at the first meant participation in God after the manner of the Son's eternal existence in the Father (possessing through participation that which is the Son's naturally), so this redemption through the Word gives rise to a newfound participation in the Son. The human person is, in the incarnation, 'wound closely to Life',[91] and 'knit into the Word from heaven, that it might be carried to heaven by him'.[92] Or, to take Athanasius' strong words in the *Life of St Anthony*, the Word 'assumed a human body so that, having participated in human nature, he might make us humans participate in the divine and spiritual nature'.[93] The nature of human existence as essentially participatory – a foundational anthropological principle for Athanasius – finds itself directly mirrored in his conception of salvation. Christ perfects human participation in the Father.

Defeating death

The specific 'how' of this salvation – namely, participation in the Word's eternal life – sets up the contours of Athanasius' articulation of the Word's redemptive

---

88 On the language of 'peers', see *DI* 20.4; cf. Weinandy, *Athanasius* 32–34.

89 See *DI* 20.1.

90 *DI* 13.7. Similar anthropological and Christological conclusions are reached, though through use of different vocabulary, in Dragas, *Athanasius: Original Research* 38–40.

91 *DI* 44.6.

92 *C. Ar.* 3.33.

93 *VA* 74.4, tr. T. Vivian and A. N. Athanassakis, *The Life of Anthony: The Coptic Life and the Greek Life* (Kalamazoo, MI: Cistercian Publications, 2003) 213. This is according to the Greek version. The Coptic reads that the Word 'assumed a human body in order to bring good to us, sharing a human birth so we humans could participate in the nature of divinity made visible' (ibid. p. 212). The concept is tied in to Athanasius' firm belief in the unchanging nature of the Son, which remains in the incarnation; see *C. Ar.* 2.6.

nature. The fact that the whole human person, not simply soul but body also, is redeemed in the Son, further clarifies this articulation. The body's material corruption, its debt to death, if it is genuinely defeated in the Word, thereby gives the absolute context of the Word's non-created status. He is, as Athanasius says, moved by compassion for the limitations of 'his Father's handiwork',[94] and so takes to himself a body, that a body united to himself might partake of one who had no limitation. The defeat of *bodily* death demonstrates, to a degree beyond any other example, the nature of the Word as eternally imaging the Father in a manner not of participation, but in which others may participate. This is Athanasius' focus in an important passage:

> For the Word, perceiving that in no other way could the corruption of men be undone save by death as a necessary condition, while it was impossible for the Word to suffer death, being immortal and Son of the Father, to this end he takes to himself a body capable of death, that it, by partaking of the Word who is above all, might be worthy to die in the stead of all, and might, because of the Word which was come to dwell in it, remain incorruptible; and that thenceforth corruption might be stayed from all by the grace of the resurrection. Whence, by offering unto death the body he himself had taken, as an offering and sacrifice free from any stain, straightway he put away death from all his peers by the offering of an equivalent.[95]

The incarnate Christ gives his body to death 'in the stead of all', since all have a share in the bodily nature of humanity; and so all have a share in the nature of the incarnate Son.[96] More than this, Christ's particular body comes to the whole race: all die in him, and are quickened from death in him, through 'the appropriation of his body'.[97] In the incarnate Christ, the Word becomes accessible to humanity not *only* through contemplation, but through bodily appropriation. So when the Son takes a human body, he takes one real and mortal like all others, since it is this finite creation that needs to be united to the eternity of the Word. This union 'loosed it from its natural liability, so that corruption could not touch it',[98] thereby bringing about, in Athanasius' description, a twofold miracle. First, the death of all is consummated in the Lord's body; and second, since it is the body of the eternal and incorruptible Word, death and corruption are themselves destroyed in the same act.[99] The 'debt' owed by humankind to death is paid, since death itself is

---

94   See *DI* 8.1–4, at 2.   .
95   *DI* 9.1.
96   See *C. Ar.* 3.20.19; cf. 3.22.27.
97   Cf. *DI* 8.4.
98   *DI* 20.4.
99   See *DI* 20.5, 6.

defeated. In his sacrifice, Christ 'accomplished not his own death, but the death of all mankind'.[100]

This is the framework within which Athanasius perceives the full meaning of Christ's sacrifice on the cross. As a debt was owed by the whole race, Christ entered into the full existence of the race so as to offer his human existence in response to that debt. Hence Athanasius' great focus on Christ's *body* in the scope of the passion and resurrection. There is little attention paid to the question of a human soul in Christ in this context, because Athanasius' anthropology understands the 'debt' of death chiefly as the *bodily* burden of corruptibility and defeat. At the same time, the body is so bound to death only because of the soul's misuse of the senses; and so the soul, with its intelligence, must figure into Christ being 'truly man' – a point Athanasius stresses in the famous seventh chapter of his *Tome to the Antiochenes*.[101] While his comments there may not constitute an entirely satisfying response to questions over *how* the human soul of Christ, with its deliberative *nous*, is to be understood in relation to the Word's eternal and immutable will (in which contexts the passage is most regularly cited), it nonetheless confirms his anthropological vision as reflected wholly in the incarnate Christ, body and soul. And precisely in this context, it is the effects of the soul on the body – namely that it has turned from communion with the sustaining Word to dissolution in material death – that give the offering of Christ's human body such significance. Being made afresh the object of the soul's sensory contemplation, Christ's bodily offering defeats the 'curse' of death by entering into and becoming that curse (cf. Galatians 3.13[102]). Life being united to death, death is destroyed. It has become a thing 'tread down with Christ's own body, and brought to nought'[103] – a reality fully disclosed in the resurrection. The bodily reality of human nature, which in the incarnation has become Christ's own body, has succumbed to death,

> but it was impossible for it to remain dead, because it had been made the temple of Life. Whence, while it died as mortal, it came to life again by reason of the Life in it.[104]

---

100 *DI* 22.3.

101 *To the Antiochenes*, 7: 'it was not possible, when the Lord had become man for us, that his body should be without intelligence: nor was the salvation effected in the Word himself a salvation of body only, but of soul also'.

102 Raised in *DI* 25.

103 *DI* 30.2.

104 *DI* 31.4; cf. *De Decr.* 14: 'As we, by receiving the Spirit, do not lose our own proper substance, so the Lord, when he became man for us [. . .] was no less God; for he was not lessened by being enveloped in a body, but rather deified it and redeemed it immortal'. See also his comments at *C. Ar.* 2.8, on Christ's taking a body as a priestly robe for the work of redemption.

Christ is risen in his human body, and death is destroyed by that death and rising. The question, though, remains, how does Christ's human death and resurrection equate to the salvation of the whole human race? It is in this context that Athanasius' anthropology takes on directly pneumatological tones. The human participates in Christ's life and resurrection through a union wrought by the Holy Spirit.

Wrought in the Spirit

It is a much commented on fact that Athanasius' *Contra Gentes-De incarnatione* makes very little of the Holy Spirit; and we have raised in previous chapters the questions this poses of Athanasius' continuity with previous generations. The anthropological discussions of Irenaeus, Tertullian and Cyril make little sense at all without the Spirit being given central significance in human existence, yet Athanasius appears to argue the brunt of his anthropology with almost no mention of him. This is compelling evidence in support of the later dating of the *CG-DI* that scholarship now by-and-large accepts: I am inclined to think that a pre-Nicene text would have borne more of an emphasis on the Spirit, in continuity with earlier writings (including those of Irenaeus, with which Athanasius was clearly familiar[105]). Athanasius' presence at the Nicene synod, and subsequent years of reflection on the ongoing debate engendered by both Arius and the council, have clearly shaped his focus in this work, even if he does not yet employ the council's language or formulations. He presents an anthropology that is resonant with earlier writers, but with a narrower focus (namely, on the nature of the Son as true Image of the Father) that is current in his age. It is impossible to know quite how Athanasius would have framed in his anthropological theology if the disputes with Arius had not been current, though it remains a perennial temptation to speculate.[106] What can be known, however, without speculation, is how Athanasius understood the Spirit as bound up in human redemption. His comments on the Spirit's work in uniting man to Christ, and thus to the Father, are central to articulating how the Son's incarnation and sacrifice are redemptive to the whole race, and reveal the Spirit both as integral to human existence and as co-active and co-ordinate to the Father and Son.[107]

---

105 See Anatolios, 'Influence', 463–76.

106 Two standard works on the Spirit in Athanasius are T. C. Campbell, 'The Doctrine of the Holy Spirit in the Theology of Athanasius', *SJT* 27 (1974), 408–40; and C. Kannengiesser, 'Athanasius of Alexandria and the Holy Spirit between Nicea I and Constantinople I', *ITQ* 48 (1981), 166–80. To these we can add the more recent Weinandy, *Athanasius* 103–19; and Pettersen, *Athanasius* 183–89.

107 My observations here are in line with those of Anatolios, who notes that while the substance of 'trinitarian' issues is not obvious on the surface of this text, 'it is nevertheless integral to his presentation, and the very casualness by which it is repeatedly enjoined makes it in some way all the more striking' (Anatolios, *Athanasius* 44; see more broadly 44–47).

Athanasius' most potent comments on the Spirit come in the volumes against the Arians, and in his letter to Serapion. Unsurprisingly, and very much in line with earlier writers (as well as his contemporary, Cyril), the main context of such discussion is baptism. Like Cyril, Athanasius frames comments on the Spirit in baptism from the perspective of Christ's baptism in the Jordan, noting that Christ's reception of the Spirit there is fundamentally an act not for himself, but for the whole human race. 'When he is anointed in his human respect, it is we who are anointed; when he is baptised, we are baptised; [. . .] he sanctifies himself for us, that we might be sanctified in him'.[108] So Christ's reception of the Spirit is part of the communicative, participatory reality of the incarnation. As humanity is to participate in the Word through the incarnation, Christ receives the Spirit humanly, that the incarnation may become, too, an encounter with the Spirit sent by the Son. And it is ultimately this communion in the Spirit that is central to Christ's offering of redemption to the whole race, for it is the Spirit who is able to draw all human-kind into participation with Christ's humanity.[109] This is the point that Athanasius wishes to emphasize in two closely connected passages that, while lengthy, must be printed in their entirety:

Therefore because of the grace of the Spirit which has been given to us, in him we come to be, and he in us; and since it is the Spirit of God, therefore through his becoming in us, reasonably are we, as having the Spirit, considered to be in God, and thus is God in us. Not then as the Son in the Father, so also we become in the Father; for the Son does not merely partake of the Spirit, that therefore he too may be in the Father; nor does he receive the Spirit, but rather he supplies it himself to all. And the Spirit does not unite the Word to the Father, but rather the Spirit receives from the Word. And the Son is in the Father, as his own Word and radiance; but we, apart from the Spirit, are strange and distant from God. By the participation of the Spirit we are knit into the Godhead, so that our being in the Father is not ours, but is the Spirit's which is in us and abides in us [. . .].[110]

The saviour, then, saying of us, 'As thou, Father, art in me, and I in thee, that they too may be one in us' (John 17.21), does not signify that we were to have identity with him; for this was shown from the instance of Jonah; but it is a request to the Father, as John has written, that the Spirit should be vouchsafed through him to those who believe, through whom we are found to be in God, and in this respect to be conjoined in him. For since the Word is in the Father, and the Spirit is given from the Word, he wills that we should receive the

---

108   *C. Ar.* 1.48.
109   On the changes in humanity's condition wrought by this participation, see Pettersen, *Athanasius* 97–107.
110   *C. Ar.* 3.24.

Spirit, that, when we receive it, thus having the Spirit of the Word which is in the Father, we too may be found on account of the Spirit to become one in the Word, and through him in the Father.[111]

Athanasius stresses the role of the Spirit in bringing man into communion with the Father through the Word. It is the Spirit's sanctifying power that is the 'how' behind Christ's incarnational sacrifice being effective for all: the full reality of the incarnate Word is that into which the human race is 'knit' through the Spirit's sanctifying presence.[112] Not only does the anthropological framework that grounds Athanasius' articulation of salvation thus frame in the Holy Spirit as integral to the redemption offered in the Word, it also establishes the divine nature of the Spirit – for all that is true of the Son as uncreated and eternally divine, must be true too of the Spirit, if this Spirit is to be life-giving and the conveyor of divine nature to the human race. So with Athanasius, like the others we have examined, it is ultimately the condition of the human creature redeemed in the Word that grounds doctrinal assertions that man must be saved by Father, Son and Spirit; that the Father, Son and Spirit are distinct, with interrelated roles in human existence and redemption; that God is, in all respects, known and articulated as this trinity.[113]

It remains the case that Athanasius speaks far less of the Spirit than do others; yet it is noteworthy that when he does speak of the Spirit, he does so within an anthropological context, much as is the tradition of preceding generations. It is this context that gives him the means to articulate the Spirit's significance to the human condition and its redemption, as well as the Spirit's identity as revealed in humanity's imaging of the Son.

Becoming Sons and Gods: Athanasius on the Concerns of Nicaea

In the above, it will have become clear that Athanasius' articulation of doctrine, his discussions of God and divine nature, are resonant with earlier eras while shaped by the contours of his own. This can hardly surprise: it is very much the way of patristic reflection. Still, the apparent shift in doctrinal focus that comes about with the Nicene council, and Athanasius' strong support of it later in

---

111   *C. Ar.* 3.25; cf. 3.26.
112   On this, see Dragas, *Athanasius: Original Research* 9, 45. So also Athanasius' words at *Ad Serap.* 1.30: '[The baptised person] can have no communion in the gift [of God's grace] except in the Spirit; for it is when we partake of him that we have the love of the Father and the grace of the Son, and the communion of the Spirit himself.'
113   See *Ad Serap.* 3.5. For further on the Spirit in Athanasius, see Behr, *Nicene Faith* 231–49.

his life, too often cause him to appear, too, as 'different' from past theologians. Seeing the basis of his doctrinal vision in an anthropological context, however, rather than in the dogmatics of an *ousia-* and *homoousia*-based theological dispute, demonstrates the marked continuity of his perception with those who had gone before him. In the same way, this approach helps discover common ground with contemporaries, such as Cyril, who are less-directly embroiled in the Arian controversies and less (or not) informed by Nicaea.

Athanasius' dispute with the thought of Arius had little to do with a metaphysical declaration of God as *ousia* defined in any one way or another, nor *per se* with a fear that calling the Son a 'creature' (*ktisma*) pitted him against the Father's *ousia*. Rather, Athanasius' concern centred in the participatory nature of human existence: one that has to participate in divine life in order to overcome the limitations natural to a being that has been brought into existence. If the Son saves this creature, understood in this way, then the Son *cannot* himself be 'life' in only a participatory sense. The Son must be understood to *be* life, not to receive life, since it is by participating in the Son's life through the Spirit that man is united to life's power over death and corruption. Because participation in the Son causes the human person to live, the Son is known to be the very Life of the Father – a life that is the Son's own without participation. For this reason, Athanasius is insistent, not that the Son cannot be referred to by the generic term of 'creature' (*ktisma*) as representing a distinct being and reality (as it is used of the Word, for example, in scripture), but that the Son must not be considered a thing *made* (*poiethenta*) – a thing brought into being.[114] This is not primarily on grounds of dignity or power, but because everything that is brought into being has an end in being, and subsists in life only through participation in life. And since the Son is known anthropologically as one who does not participate, but in whom creation participates and receives life, the Son can never be understood as one of the things made – as a 'creature' in the sense that both Nicaea and Athanasius stress. Arius' error is not that he did not believe the Son was divine; clearly he did. Athanasius sees his error as residing in a basic anthropological impossibility. However divine a created Son may be, he will always be divine by participation, life by participation. But the testimony of the human condition is that the Son does what no creature can: give life rather than receive it.

The same is emphasized in Athanasius' usage of image. To place such emphasis on the Son as Image, and humanity as after the image of the Image, is to draw out this distinction between participation and eternal being. Humanity is *after* the Image inasmuch as it images the Father by participation; whereas the *true* Image images the Father in a unique manner. Eventually, Athanasius applies Nicaea's *homoousion* to this distinction as an exact means of definition. Yet it is clear that

---

114   On the vocabulary at stake, see Dragas, *Athanasius: Original Research* 55–58.

language of *homoousia* reflects a position that, for Athanasius, is grounded first and foremost in the anthropological testimony of the divine image.[115]

Difficulties remain with Athanasius' articulation of the Spirit. Part of this situation will always be ascribable to the context of the early-fourth-century debates, which in general focused on the Spirit to a far lesser degree than past generations; but even within this narrower focus, certain issues stand out as challenging. His description of the Spirit as an image of the Image, that is, an image of the Word, is perhaps the most pronounced, and has recently been given some substantial consideration.[116] There is a real question as to whether this does not pose challenges not only of a hierarchicalization of the Father, Son and Spirit, but also to the very notion of image and participation that is so key to Athanasius' anthropological perception. It is unlikely, however, that much new ground can be covered in the realm of Athanasian pneumatology, unless some lost text is discovered that might shed more light on it. But what is of relevance to our study is the significance that Athanasius *does* give to the Spirit, not simply as 'there because the scriptures say he is there' and thus somehow needing to be included in a discussion on the Father and Son, but as an integral reality of human existence, participating in God. The Spirit may not be as central to Athanasius' discussions as he was in the writings of Irenaeus, Tertullian and Cyril; but in common with those authors, Athanasius discovers in the human creature a lens on the nature of God in which the Spirit plays a significant, unique and defining role. As man struggles towards his maker, as he moves from non-being into being, it is the Spirit that unites him to the Son, and the Son that brings him to the eternity of the Father.

*   *   *

We have, in St Athanasius, the testimony of a theologian at the end of our period of interest who, despite the dramatic changes taking place in the landscape of fourth-century theological discussion, grounds his theological articulation in a framework that is distinctly harmonious with earlier writers. Even amidst the rapid shift towards metaphysical language and contextual debates that would often see discussion begin and be carried out almost exclusively in the realm of *theotes*, of 'godhead', Athanasius himself, when he sets about presenting a concise theological vision, frames it anthropologically. It is only when the ongoing disputes after 335 force his direct engagement with other terminologies and frameworks, that he begins to move away from the anthropological context of the *CG-DI*; but even then, his comments in those later texts hark back to fundamental theological positions he has clearly established in anthropological terms.

---

115   On Athanasius' minimal use of *homoousios*, even in his later works, see Pettersen, *Athanasius* 146–60.

116   See, for example, his comments in *Ad Serap.* 1.20 on the Son being imaged in the Spirit in the same way the Father is imaged in the Son. For recent treatment, see Weinandy, *Athanasius* 103–11.

The emerging complexities of the post-Nicene era, tying themselves ever more explicitly to Nicene terminologies after the synod at Constantinople in 381, do mark a transition in Christian theological discourse. It becomes more and more common to address theological questions in isolated contexts – to discuss, in a kind of semi-exclusion, the Trinity, Christology, Pneumatology. The anthropological context in which doctrine had been forged over the past three and a half centuries does undergo a shift. Yet Athanasius remains a potent reminder that it is a shift, not a break. The very man who exercised such influence in bringing the Nicene definition to ecclesiastical centrality, did so in the conviction that it gave concise testimony to doctrinal articulations rooted in anthropological contexts. While he, like others of the fourth century, may have made less of the Holy Spirit than previous writers on account of the debates of the era, and so been happy to endorse Nicaea even with its weak comments on the Spirit (which Constantinople would rectify), the anthropological basis of his own writings makes clear that the Spirit was critical to his theological vision. In the incarnate Word, humanity sees God his Father; and in the offering of this incarnate Son, is joined to the Father through the Spirit. The creature and its creator meet in Christ, 'through whom and with whom be to the Father himself, with the Son himself, in the Holy Spirit, honour and might and glory for ever and ever'.[117]

---

117 *DI* 57.3.

CONCLUSION

The progression of theological discussion from the second to the fourth centuries is marked out by a remarkable spirit of continuity, even as it embraces profound change. While conversations taking place in the mid-fourth century amongst such theologians as Cyril and Athanasius involved metaphysical language that would hardly have been conceivable to second-century writers like Irenaeus or Tertullian, the basic contours of their arguments and articulations are profoundly similar. Situational contexts might demarcate lines of emphasis between a Tertullian and an Irenaeus, or an Athanasius and a Cyril; but these varying approaches, once studied carefully, only emphasize the common roots that ground them. There is, in Irenaeus' emphasis on creation, Tertullian's emphasis on conduct, Cyril's emphasis on baptism, Athanasius' emphasis on incorruption, a unifying core of focus that makes the diversity of their approaches part of a common heritage.

This unifying core is the human person. More specifically, it is the manner in which the human creature forms, for all our authors, the framework for articulating theology – whether theology informing cosmology, behaviour, sacramentalism, dogmatic trinitarianism or any other arena. The incarnation of the Son forms the whole basis for Christian theologizing, which conceives of the project of theology as the articulation of the God encountered in the human. And so it is in and through the human, the *anthropos* in which the eternal Son is known, that God is disclosed to the creature, and by which the creature comes to know his God. This ties 'theology' and 'anthropology' together at the most fundamental level. A genuine engagement with the incarnation means that theology *is* anthropology, since the *Theos* reveals himself *as anthropos*, and it is in the human that man sees and knows God. This is first and foremost in the human Jesus Christ, confessed as at one and the same time eternal Son of the Father; but it is true also of all human nature and existence, since humanity is created after the image of this Son, and in its rightly lived existence discloses a created manifestation of God's eternal and uncreated nature. This does not mean, however, that it is only in an unmarred economy that the human might image its maker. It is precisely in its condition effected by sin, that humanity finds further disclosure of God's nature and salvific action; for in its sinful condition, humanity sees in itself the deficiencies requiring redemption, and so finds the contours of God's nature as redeemer. The one race of Adam sees humanity in itself, and in Christ, and in seeing the nature of the fallen and the redeemer, finds grounds for articulating doctrines of God and man. This focus is rooted in the experience of the incarnate Son of the Father; but, grounded in the nature of humanity as physical as well as spiritual, sees the role of the Spirit as fundamental to theological discussion from the very first. God, with his two hands, calls his creature to himself.

The present volume set out with three aims in mind: to explore the connection of an anthropology of the divine image to the developing articulation of God as trinity; to present the beginnings of a reading of the history of the second to fourth centuries, grounded in this relationship; and through this to begin to explore the thought of our early patristic sources outside the bonds of categorizing and classifying systematizations that have predominated in the past century of patristic scholarship. It will have been successful if, here at its end, the patristic emphasis on discerning God through and in the human, has made clear the degree to which theology in the period is *theology as anthropology*, straight across the board. The one is the context and core of the other. When this is realized, we are compelled to see the dialogue of early doctrinal discussion in clarified terms: terms that will not allow a chronology of doctrinal development – moving from apologetic to binitarian to trinitarian to Christological – to stand unchallenged. Language may develop and modes of articulation may undergo refinement, but there is a fully trinitarian vision of God as Father with Son and Spirit present in nuanced, careful discussion well before the 'trinitarian era', grounded in the human person imaging its maker.

The creature, made 'a little lower than the angels', is given honour and glory in the Son, drawing its whole reality into the mystery of man's engagement with God. This is, in St Paul's words, the mystery present before all ages, made known by the apostles through the Spirit (cf. Ephesians 3.5): that 'our Lord Jesus Christ, through his transcendent love, became what we are, that he might bring us to be what he is himself.'[1]

---

1 Irenaeus, *Ref.* 3.Praef.

BIBLIOGRAPHY

ANCIENT AUTHORS

For the primary texts of the main authors studied, I have provided reference to the original text as well as available English translations. In keeping with the format of the book, I have presented the principal sources in the order of the chapters of the volume.

Irenaeus of Lyons

Ref. *Refutation and Overthrow of Knowledge Falsely So-Called* (often abbreviated *Against Heresies*[1]). The standard edition is Rousseau, A. et al., *Irénée de Lyon: Contre les hérésies*, text and translation in SC:

    I: 263, 264 (1979): A. Rousseau, L. Doutreleau
    II: 293, 294 (1982): A. Rousseau, L. Doutreleau
    III: 210, 211 (1974): A. Rousseau, L. Doutreleau
    IV: 100, in 2 vols (1965): A. Rousseau, B. Hemmerdinger, L. Doutreleau, C. Mercier
    V: 152, 153 (1969): A. Rousseau, L. Doutreleau, C. Mercier

    Tr. Roberts, A. and Donaldson, J. (eds.), *The Writings of Irenaeus*, ANF 1.

Epid. *Epideixis*, or *The Demonstration of the Apostolic Preaching*; K. Ter-Mekerttschian and S. G. Wilson, with Prince Maxe of Saxony (eds./trs.), Εἰς ἐπίδειξιν τοῦ ἀποστολικοῦ κηρύγματος. *The Proof of the Apostolic Preaching, with Seven Fragments,* PO 12 (1917; repr. Turnhout: Brepols, 1989); J. Behr, *St Irenaeus of Lyons: On the Apostolic Preaching – Translation and Introduction* (New York: St Vladimir's Seminary Press, 1997).

Tertullian of Carthage

Ad Mart. *To the Martyrs*, CPL 1 (CCSL 1, CSEL 76); ANF 3.
Ad Scap. *To Scapula*, CPL 24 (CCSL 2, CSEL 76); ANF 3.

---

1 On my reasons for using *Ref.* rather than *AH* for Irenaeus' longer work, see above, p. 21 n. 17.

Adv. Herm.	*Against Hermogenes*, CPL 13 (CCSL 1, CSEL 47); ANF 3.
Adv. Marc.	*Against Marcion*, CPL 14 (CCSL 1, CSEL 47); ANF 3.
Adv. Prax.	*Against Praxeas*, CPL 26 (CCSL 2, CSEL 47); ANF 3 and E. Evans, *Tertullian's Treatise Against Praxeas* (London: SPCK, 1948).
Apol.	*Apologeticum* (The Apology), CPL 3 (CSEL 69, LCL 250); ANF 3.
DA	*On the Soul*, J. H. Waszink, *Quinti Septimi Florentis Tertulliani De anima* (Amsterdam: J. M. Meulenhoff, 1947), and CCSL 2; ANF 3.
De Bapt.	*On Baptism*, CPL 8 (CCSL 1, CSEL 20); ANF 3.
De Carn.	*On the Flesh of Christ*, CPL 18 (CCSL 2, CSEL 70); ANF 3.
De Cens.	*De censu animae*, lost work; attributed fragments in A. von Harnack, CCSL 2.1331–6.
Fug.	*On Fleeing Persecution*, CPL 25 (CCSL 2, CSEL 76); ANF 4.
De Or.	*On Prayer*, CPL 7 (CCSL 1, CSEL 20); ANF 3.
De Paen.	*On Repentance*, CPL 10 (CCSL 1, CSEL 76); ANF 3.
De Pat.	*On Patience*, CPL 9 (CCSL1, CSEL 47); ANF 3.
Praes.	*On the Prescription of the Heretics*, CPL 5 (CCSL 1, CSEL 70); ANF 3.
Pud.	*On Modesty*, CPL 30 (CCSL 2, CSEL 20; SC 394, 395); ANF 4.
De Res.	*On the Resurrection of the Flesh*, CPL 19 (CCSL 2, CSEL 47); ANF 3.
Spec.	*On Public Spectacles* (or *On the Games*), CPL 6 (CCSL 1, CSEL 20); ANF 3.
De Test.	*On the Testimony of the Soul*, CPL 4 (CCSL 1, CSEL 20); ANF 3.

Cyril of Jerusalem

Pro.	*Prochatechesis*, W. K. Reischl and J. Rupp, *S. Patris Nostri Cyrilli Hierosolymorum Archiepiscopi Opera quae supersunt Omnia* (Munich, 1848–1860); E. Yarnold, *Cyril of Jerusalem* (The Early Church Fathers; London/New York: Routledge, 2000).
Cat.	*Catechetical Orations*, Reischl/Rupp, ibid.; LCC 4.; E. Yarnold, ibid.
Hom. Par.	*Homily on the Paralytic*, Reischl/Rupp, ibid.; E. Yarnold, ibid.
M. Cat.	*Mystagogical Catecheses*, SC 126; E. Yarnold, ibid.

Athanasius of Alexandria

Ad Serap.	*To Serapion*, PG 26; C. R. B. Shapland, *The Letters of Saint Athanasius Regarding the Holy Spirit* (London: Epworth Press, 1951).
C. Ar.	*Orations against the Arians*, Metzler/Savvdis, *Werke* I/I; NPNF II.4.

CG-DI	*Against the Nations – On the Incarnation*, R.W. Thompson, *Contra Gentes and De Incarnatione* (Oxford: Clarendon Press, 1971).
De Decr.	*On the Decrees of Nicaea*, Opitz, *Werke* II/I; NPNF II.4.
De Syn.	*On the Councils of Ariminum and Seleucia*, Opitz, *Werke* II/I; NPNF II.4.
VA	*The Life of Anthony of Egypt*, SC 400; T. Vivian and A. Athanassakis, *The Life of Anthony: The Coptic Life and the Greek Life* (Kalamazoo, MI: Cistercian Publications, 2003).

Other principal ancient sources

Ap. John	The *Apocryphon of John*, NHC II,1; III,1; IV,1 and BG 8502,2.
De Haer.	Augustine of Hippo, *De haeresibus ad Quodvultdeum*, CCSL 46; L. G. Muller, *The 'De haeresibus' of Augustine* (Patristic Studies 90; Washington, D.C.: Catholic University of America, 1956).
Ex. Theod.	Clement of Alexandria, *Extracts of Theodotus*, GCS 17; ANF 2.
Pan.	Epiphanius of Salamis, *Panarion*, GCS 25, 31, 37; P. R. Amidon, *The Panarion of Epiphanius of Salamis: Selected Passages* (Oxford: University Press, 1990).
Eus. HE	Eusebius of Caesarea, *Ecclesiastical History*, K. Lake, LCL, 2 vols. (Cambridge, Mass: Harvard University Press, 1989).
Vita Const.	Eusebius of Caesarea, *Life of Constantine*, GCS I/I; A. Cameron and S. G. Hall, *Eusebius: Life of Constantine* (Oxford: Clarendon Press, 1999).
Ep. Caes.	Eusebius of Caesarea, *Epistula ad Caesarienses*, PG 20.
De Synod.	Hilary of Poitiers, *On the Synods*, PL 10; NPNF II.9.
De Ill.	Jerome, *On Illustrious Men*, PL 33; NPNF II.3.
Chron.	Jerome, *Chronicle*, M. D. Donalson, *A Translation of Jerome's Chronicon with Historical Commentary* (Mellon University Press, 1996).
Dial.	Justin Martyr, *Dialogue with Trypho the Jew*, PTS 47; ANF 1. New critical tr. as T. B. Falls, T. P. Halton, M. Slusser, *St. Justin Martyr: Dialogue with Trypho* (Washington, D.C.: Catholic University of America Press, 2003).
1 Apol.	Justin Martyr, *First Apology*, PTS 38; ANF 1 and L. W. Barnard, *St Justin Martyr: The First and Second Apologies*, ACW 56 (NY: Paulist Press, 1997).
Sole Gov.	Pseudo-Justin, *On the Sole Governance of God*, ANF 1.
Comm. Jn.	Origen, *Commentary on John*, SC 120, 157, 222, 290, 385; R. E. Heine, *Origen: Commentary on the Gospel According to Saint John* (Washington: Catholic University of America Press, 1989/1993).
Oxyrh. Pa.	The *Oxyrhynchus Papyri*.

De Conf. Ling.	Philo of Alexandria, *On the Confusion of Tongues*, F. H. Colson, G. H. Whitaker, LCL *Philo* 4 (Cambridge, Mass.: Harvard University Press, 1932).
De Op. Mu.	Philo of Alexandria, *On the Account of the World's Creation Given by Moses*, F. H. Colson, G. H. Whitaker, LCL *Philo*, 1 (Cambridge, Mass.: Harvard University Press, 1991).
Herm.	The *Shepherd of Hermas*, K. Lake, LCL *Apostolic Fathers*, 1 (Cambridge, Mass.: Harvard University Press, 1976).
Soc. HE	Socrates, *Ecclesiastical History*, PG 67; NPNF II.2.
Soz. HE	Sozomen, *Ecclesiastical History*, GCS 50; NPNF II.2.
Theod. HE	Theodoret, *Ecclesiastical History*, GCS 44; NPNF II.3.
Ad Autol.	Theophilus of Alexandria, *To Autolycus*, R. M. Grant, *Theophilus of Antioch – Ad Autolycum* (Oxford: Clarendon Press, 1970).

Other ancient sources, employed less frequently, are cited in the notes.

Secondary Sources

d'Alès, A., 'La date de la version latine de Saint Irénée', *RSR* 6 (1916), 133–37.

Alexandre, J., *Une chair pour la gloire – L'anthropologie réaliste et mystique de Tertullien* (Paris: Beauchesne, 2001).

Anatolios, K., *Athanasius: The Coherence of His Thought* (London: Routledge, 1998).

—, 'The Influence of Irenaeus on Athanasius', *SP* 36 (2001), 463–76.

Andia, Y. D., *Homo vivens: Incorruptibilité et divinisation de l'homme selon Irénée de Lyon* (Paris: Etudes Augustiniennes, 1986).

Ayres, L., *Nicaea and Its Legacy: An Approach to Fourth-Century Trinitarian Theology* (Oxford: Oxford University Press, 2004).

Bacq, P., *De l'ancienne à la nouvelle alliance selon s. Irénée: unité du livre IV de l'Adversus Haereses* (Paris: Editions Lethielleux, 1978).

Barnes, T. D., *Tertullian, A Historical and Literary Study* (Oxford: Clarendon Press, 1971/1985).

—, *Constantine and Eusebius* (Cambridge, MA: Harvard University Press, 1981).

—, *Athanasius and Constantius: Theology and Politics in the Constantinian Empire* (Cambridge, MA: Harvard University Press, 1993).

Bauer, W., *Orthodoxy and Heresy in Earliest Christianity*, tr. R. Kraft (Philadelphia: Fortress Press, 1971).

Behr, J., *On the Apostolic Preaching* (New York: St Vladimir's Seminary Press, 1997).

—, *Asceticism and Anthropology in Irenaeus and Clement* (Oxford: The University Press, 2000).

—, *The Formation of Christian Theology, vol. 1: The Way to Nicaea* (New York: St Vladimir's Seminary Press, 2001).

—, *The Formation of Christian Theology, vol. 2: The Nicene Faith* (New York: St Vladimir's Seminary Press, 2004).

—, *The Mystery of Christ: Life in Death* (New York: St Vladimir's Seminary Press, 2006).

—, 'Scripture, the Gospel, and Orthodoxy', *SVTQ* 43 (2001), 223–48.

Beinert, W. A., 'Sabellius und Sabellianismus als historisches Problem', in Hanns Brennecke, Ernst Grasmück and Christoph Markschies (eds.), *Logos: Festschrift für Luise Abramowski zum 8 Juli 1993* (Berlin: De Gruyter, 1993).

Bilde, P., 'Gnosticism, Jewish Apocalypticism, and Early Christianity', in Karl Jeppesen, Kirsten Nielsen and Bent Rosendal (eds.), *In the Last Days: On Jewish and Christian Apocalyptic and its Period* (Denmark: Aarhus University Press, 1994).

Bousset, W., *Jüdisch-Christlicher Schulbetrieb in Alexandria und Rom: Literarische Untersuchungen zu Philo und Clemens von Alexandria, Justin und Irenäus* (Göttingen: Vandenhoeck und Ruprecht, 1915).

Braun, R., *Deus Christianorum. Recherches sur le vocabulaire doctrinal de Tertullien* (Paris, 1962).

Bray, G. L., *Holiness and the Will of God – Perspectives on the Theology of Tertullian* (London: Marshall, Morgan and Scott, 1979).

Campbell, T. C., 'The Doctrine of the Holy Spirit in the Theology of Athanasius', *SJT* 27 (1974), 408–40.

Chadwick, H., 'The Origin of the Title Oecumenical Council', *JTS* NS 23 (1972), 132–35.

Crouzel, H., *Origen* (Edinburgh: T&T Clark, 1989).

Daley, C. B., *Tertullian the Puritan and His Influence: An Essay in Historical Theology* (Dublin: Four Courts Press, 1993).

Daniélou, J., *Origène* (Paris: La Table Ronde, 1948).

—, *The Origins of Latin Christianity*, tr. John A. Baker and David Smith (The Development of Christian Doctrine Before the Council of Nicaea, 3; London: Darton, Longman & Todd, 1977).

Day, J., 'Adherence to the *Disciplina Arcani* in the Fourth Century', *SP* 35 (1999), 266–70.

—, 'Lent and the Catechetical Program in Mid-Fourth-Century Jerusalem', *SL* 35.2 (2005), 129–47.

Dodd, C. H., 'Man in God's Design According to the New Testament', *Studiorum Novi Testamenti Societas* (1952).

Donovan, M. A., *One Right Reading? A Guide to Irenaeus* (Collegeville: The Liturgical Press, 1997).

Doval, A. J., *Cyril of Jerusalem: Mystagogue – The Authorship of the Mystagogic Catecheses* (Patristic Monograph Series, 17; Washington, D.C.: Catholic University of America Press, 2001).

Dragas, G., *Saint Athanasius of Alexandria: Original Research and New Perspectives* (New Hampshire: Orthodox Research Institute, 2005).

Drijvers, J. W., *Cyril of Jerusalem: Bishop and City* (Supplements to Vigiliae Christianae, 72; Leiden/Boston: Brill, 2004).

Dunn, G. D., *Tertullian* (London: Routledge, 2004).

—, 'Tertullian's Scriptural Exegesis in De praescriptione haereticorum', *JECS* 14.2 (2006), 141–55.

Edwards, M. J., 'The Arian Heresy and the Oration to the Saints', *VigChr* 49 (1995), 379–87.

Evans, E., *Tertullian, Adversus Marcionem*, 2 vols. (i, books i–iii; Oxford: Oxford University Press, 1972).

Fantino, J., 'Le passage du premier Adam au second Adam comme expression du salut chez Irénée de Lyon', *VigChr* 52.4 (1998), 418–29.

Farrow, D., 'St Irenaeus of Lyons: The Church and the World', *PE* 4 (1995), 333–55.

Fossum, J. E., 'The Origin of the Gnostic Concept of the Demiurge', *ETL* 61.1 (1985), 142–52.

Fredouille, J. -C., *Tertullien et la conversion de la culture antique* (Paris: Etudes Augustiniennes, 1972).

Frend, W. H. C., 'Heresy and Schism as Social and National Movements', in D. Baker (ed.), *Schism, Heresy and Religious Protest* (Cambridge: Cambridge University Press, 1972).

Gibbon, E., *The Decline and Fall of the Roman Empire* (vol. 2; London, 1897).

Grant, R. M., 'The Problem of Theophilus', in Robert M. Grant (ed.), *Christian Beginnings: Apocalypse to History* (London: Variorum Reprints, 1950/1983).

—, *Irenaeus of Lyons*, ed. Carol Harrison (The Early Church Fathers; London: Routledge, 1997).

Gregg, R. C., 'Cyril of Jerusalem and the Arians', in Robert C. Gregg (ed.), *Arianism: Historical and Theological Reassessments* (Philadelphia: The Philadelphia Patristic Foundation, 1985).

Gregg, R. C. and Groh, D. E., *Early Arianism: A View of Salvation* (Philadelphia: Fortress Press, 1981).

Gunton, C., 'And in One Lord, Jesus Christ . . . Begotten, Not Made', in Christopher R. Seitz (ed.), *Nicene Christianity: The Future for a New Ecumenism* (Grand Rapids, MI: Brazos Press, 2001).

Gwynn, D. M., *The Eusebians: The Polemic of Athanasius of Alexandria and the Construction of the 'Arian Controversy'* (Oxford: Oxford University Press, 2006).

Haas, C., 'The Arians of Alexandria', *VigChr* 47 (1993), 234–45.

Hanson, R. P. C., *The Search for the Christian Doctrine of God – The Arian Controversy 318–81* (Edinburgh: T&T Clark, 1988).

Harnack, A. V., 'Zur Chronologie der Schriften Tertullians', *ZK* 2 (1878).

—, *Philotesia zu Paul Kleinert zum LXX – Geburtstage dargebracht* (Berlin, 1907).

Hitchcock, F. R., *Irenaeus of Lugdunum: A Study of His Teaching* (Cambridge: University Press, 1914).

Houssiau, A., 'Le baptême selon Irénée de Lyon', *ETL* 60 No. 1 (1984), 45–59.

Jackson, P., 'Cyril of Jerusalem's Use of Scripture in Catechesis', *TS* 52.3 (1991), 431–50.

Jenkins, D. E., *The Glory of Man: Bampton Lectures for 1966* (London: SCM Press Ltd., 1967).

Jenson, R. W., 'For Us . . . He Was Made Man', in Christopher R. Seitz (ed.), *Nicene Christianity: The Future for a New Ecumenism* (Grand Rapids, MI: Brazos Press, 2001).

Jonas, H., *The Gnostic Religion: The Message of the Alien God and the Beginnings of Christianity* (Third edn.; Boston: Beacon Press, 2001).

Kannengiesser, C., 'Athanasius of Alexandria and the Foundation of Traditional Christology', *TS* 34 (1973), 103–13.

—, 'Athanasius of Alexandria and the Holy Spirit between Nicea I and Constantinople I', *ITQ* 48 (1981), 166–80.

Kelly, J. N. D., *Early Christian Creeds* (3rd edn.; London: Longman, 1972).

Knox, R. A., *Enthusiasm: A Chapter in the History of Religion* (London: Collins, 1950/1987).

Kretschmar, G., *Jerusalemer Heiligtumstraditionen in altkirchlicher und frühislamischer Zeit* (Wiesbaden: Harrassowitz, 1987).

Lawson, J., *The Biblical Theology of Saint Irenaeus* (London: The Epworth Press, 1948).

Leal, J., *La Antropología de Tertuliano – Estudio de los trados polémicos de los años 207–12 d.c.* (Rome: Institutum Patristicum Augustinianum, 2001).

Logan, A. H. B., 'Marcellus of Ancyra (Pseudo-Anthimus), "On the Holy Church": Text, Translation and Commentary', *JTS* NS 51.1 (2000), 81–112.

Lonergan, B., *The Way to Nicaea* (London, 1976).

Loofs, F., *Theophilus von Antiochien – Adversus Marcionem und die anderen theologischen Quellen bei Irenäus* (Leipzig: Hinrichs, 1930).

Markus, R. A., 'The Problem of Self-Definition: From Sect to Church', in E. P. Sanders (ed.), *Jewish and Christian Self-Definition, vol. i: The Shaping of Christianity in the Second and Third Centuries* (London: SCM, 1980).

May, G., *Creatio ex Nihilo: The Doctrine of 'Creation out of Nothing' in Early Christian Thought* (Edinburgh: T&T Clark, 1994).

Mazza, E., *Mystagogy: A Theology of Liturgy in the Patristic Age*, tr. Matthew J. O'Connell (New York: Pueblo Publishing Company, 1989).

McDonnell, K., 'Quaestio disputata: Irenaeus on the Baptism of Jesus', *TS* 59 (1998), 317–19.

Minns, D., *Irenaeus*, (ed.) Brian Davies (Outstanding Christian Thinkers; London: Geoffrey Chapman, 1994).

Moehler, J. A., *Athanase le Grand et l'église de son temps en lutte avec l'arianisme* (Paris, 1840).

Moingt, J., 'Theologie trinitaire de Tertullien', *RSR* 54.3 (1966), 337–69.

Monceaux, P., *Histoire littéraire de l'Afrique chrétienne* (1901).

Moreschini, C., 'L'*Adv. Marc.* nell'ambito dell'attività letteraria di Tertulliano', *Ommagio a E. Fraenkel* (1968).

Munier, C., *Petite vie de Tertullien* (Paris: Desclée de Brouwer, 1996).

Nasrallah, L., '*An Ecstasy of Folly': Prophecy and Authority in Early Christianity* (Harvard Theological Studies, 52; Cambridge, Mass.: Harvard University Press, 2003).

Newman, J. H., *Select Treatises of Athanasius in Controversy with the Arians* (London, 1881).

Norris, R. A., *God and World in Early Christian Theology* (New York: The Seabury Press, 1965).

O'Collins, G., *Christology – A Biblical, Historical, and Systematic Study of Jesus* (Oxford: Oxford University Press, 1995).

Orbe, A., '¿San Ireneo adopcionista? En torno a *adv. haer.* III,19,1', *Greg* 65.1 (1984), 5–52.

—, 'El Espiritu en el bautismo de Jésus (en torno a san Ireneo)', *Greg* 76.4 (1995), 663–99.

Osborn, E., *The Emergence of Christian Theology* (Cambridge: University Press, 1993).

—, *Tertullian, First Theologian of the West* (Cambridge: Cambridge University Press, 1997).

—, *Irenaeus of Lyons* (Cambridge: University Press, 2001).

Pettersen, A., *Athanasius* (London: Geoffrey Chapman, 1995).

Prestige, G. L., *St. Basil the Great and Apollinarius* (London: SPCK, 1956).

Quispel, G., *De bronnen van Tertullianus' Adv. Marc.* (Lieden, 1943).

—, 'The Origins of the Gnostic Demiurge', in P. Granfield and J. A. Jungmann (eds.), *KYRIAKON: Festschrift Johannes Quasten, 1* (1; Münster: Verlag Aschendorff, 1970).

Rankin, D. I., 'Was Tertullian a Schismatic?' *Prudentia* 19 (1986), 73–79.

—, *Tertullian and the Church* (Cambridge: Cambridge University Press, 1994).

de Riedmatten, H., 'La correspondance entre Basile de Césarée et Apollinaire de Laodicée', *JTS* 7–8 (1956–1957), 199–210 and 53–70.

Robinson, J. A., *St Irenaeus: The Demonstration of the Apostolic Preaching* (London: SPCK, 1920).

Robinson, J. M., *The Nag Hammadi Library in English* (San Francisco: Harper, 1991).

Rousseau, A., *Irénée de Lyon: Démonstration de la prédication apostolique – introduction, traduction et notes* (Sources Chrétiennes, 406; Paris: CERF, 1995).

Schwartz, E., *Zeitschrift für die neutestamentliche Wissenschaft* (34; Berlin, 1935).

—, *Zur Geschichte des Athanasius* (GS, 3; Berlin, 1959).

Seeberg, R., *Lehrbuch der Dogmengeschichte* (Second Edition edn., I; Leipzig, 1908).

Slusser, M., 'How Much Did Irenaeus Learn From Justin', *International Conference on Patristic Studies* (Oxford, 2003).

Smail, T., 'The Holy Spirit in the Holy Trinity', in Christopher R. Seitz (ed.), *Nicene Christianity: The Future for a New Ecumenism* (Grand Rapids, MI: Brazos Press, 2001).

Smith, D. A., 'Irenaeus and the Baptism of Jesus', *TS* 58 (1997), 618–42.

Staats, R., 'The Eternal Kingdom of Christ: The Apocalyptic Tradition in the "Creed of Nicaea-Constantinople"', *PBR* 9.1 (1990), 19–30.

Stead, C., 'Divine Substance in Tertullian', *JTS* NS 14 (1963), 46–66.

Steenberg, M. C., 'Children in Paradise: Adam and Eve as "Infants" in Irenaeus of Lyons', *JECS* 12.1 (2004), 1–35.

—, 'The Role of Mary as Co-recapitulator in St Irenaeus of Lyons', *VigChr* 58 (2004).

—, 'Impatience and Humanity's Sinful State in Tertullian of Carthage', *VigChr* 62 (2008), 107–32.

—, *Irenaeus on Creation: The Cosmic Christ and the Saga of Redemption* (Vigiliae Christianae Supplements; Leiden: Brill, 2008).

—, 'Scripture, *graphe*, and the Status of *Hermas* in Irenaeus', *SVTQ* (forthcoming, 2008/9).

Tanner, N. P., *Decrees of the Ecumenical Councils, vol. i* (1; London: Sheed & Ward Limited, 1990).

—, *The Councils of the Church – A Short History* (New York: Crossroad Publishing/Herder & Herder, 1999).

Telfer, W., *Cyril of Jerusalem and Nemesius of Emesa* (The Library of Christian Classics; London, 1955).

Thornton, L. S., 'St Irenaeus and Contemporary Theology', *SP* 2 (1957), 217–327.

Torrance, A., 'Being of One Substance with the Father', in Christopher R. Seitz (ed.), *Nicene Christianity: The Future for a New Ecumenism* (Grand Rapids, MI: Brazos Press, 2001).

Tortorelli, K. M., 'Some Notes on the Interpretation of St. Irenaeus in the Works of Hans Urs von Balthasar', *SP* 23 (1989), 284–88.

Touttée, A. A., *S. Cyrilli archiepiscopi Hierosolymitani operae quae exstant omnia, et ejus nomine circumferuntur* (Paris: Jacobus Vincent, 1720).

Tränkle, H., *Q.S.F. Tertullian's Adv. Ind.* (Wiesbaden, 1964).

Trevett, C., *Montanism: Gender, Authority and the New Prophecy* (Cambridge: Cambridge University Press, 1996).

Trigg, J. W., *Origen* (London: Routledge, 1998).

Ulrich, J., *Die Anfänge der Abendländischen Rezeption des Nizänums* (Berlin: De Gruyter, 1994).

Vércel, M., *Cyrille de Jérusalem* (Paris: Les Editions Ouvrieres, 1957).

Vivian, T. and Athanassakis, A. N., *The Life of Anthony: The Coptic Life and the Greek Life* (Kalamazoo, MI: Cistercian Publications, 2003).

Walker, P. W. L., *Holy City, Holy Places? Christian Attitudes to Jerusalem and the Holy Land in the Fourth Century* (Oxford: Clarendon Press, 1990).

Warfield, B. B., *Studies in Tertullian and Augustine* (Oxford: Oxford University Press, 1930).

Waszink, J. H., *Index verborum et locutionem quae Tertulliani De Anima libro continentur congessit* (Petri Hanstein, 1935).

—, *Quinti Septimi Florentis Tertulliani, De Anima* (Amsterdam: J. M. Meulenhoff, 1947).

Weinandy, T. G., *Athanasius: A Theological Introduction* (Aldershot: Ashgate, 2007).

Williams, F., *The Panarion of Epiphanius of Salamis – Books II and III* (Leiden: Brill, 1994).

Williams, M. A., *Rethinking 'Gnosticism' – An Argument for Dismantling a Dubious Category* (Princeton: Princeton University Press, 1999).

Wingren, G., *Man and the Incarnation: A Study in the Biblical Theology of Irenaeus*, tr. Ross MacKenzie (Edinburgh: Oliver & Boyd, 1959).

Yarnold, E., *The Awe-Inspiring Rites of Initiation: Baptismal Homilies of the Fourth Century* (Slough: St Paul, 1972).

—, 'The Authorship of the Mystagogic Catecheses Attributed to Cyril of Jerusalem', *HJ* 19 (1978), 143–61.

—, *Cyril of Jerusalem* (The Early Church Fathers; London/New York: Routledge, 2000).

INDEX

Abraham 36, 76, 142

Acacius of Caesarea 131

Adam 28, 30, 33, 35, 45–9, 57, 63, 68, 72, 79–81, 83, 85, 89, 97, 142, 176, 190

administrative, councils as 108–11

adoption 36, 42–3, 56, 90, 134, 145–9, 154

advancement 55, 146, 148, 154

aeons 29, 31

afflatus 77, 98

Africa 60, 104, 109, 110, 115–16

Alexander of Alexandria 109–10, 112, 119, 121, 159, 160

Alexandria 17, 104, 108, 159–60

anachronism 12, 34, 103, 107, 113–14, 126, 131

Anatolios, Khaled 184

angels 1, 6, 24–7, 32, 43, 92, 94–5

anointing 2, 34–7, 41, 43, 150–1, 154, 156, 185

Anthony of Egypt 172, 181

anthropos 2, 5–6, 8, 34, 79, 190

Apocryphon of John 31

Apollinarianism 170

apologetic 19, 20, 100–1, 162, 191

archetype 62, 167

Arian and 'Arianism' 10, 108, 111, 113, 119, 123, 130–1, 145–7, 156, 165, 169, 187

Arius 10, 104, 108–11, 113, 115–16, 119–25, 130–1, 144, 146, 159–60, 167, 169, 184, 187

Asia Minor 31

Athenagoras 17

Augustine of Hippo 18, 61, 82, 116

Augustinianism 82

baptism 9, 29, 36–8, 43, 61, 112, 129, 131–2, 134–8, 141–56, 185–6, 190

 sins committed after 57

Barnes, Timothy 58, 75, 159

Basil of Caesarea 111–13, 126

Bauer, Walter 12

begetting 120, 123–4, 139, 145, 147

'begotten not made' 122–4

Behr, John 10, 12, 23, 37, 40, 47

bi-partite anthropology 40, 64, 138, 140, 167

bitheism 119, 120

blood 45, 143

body 17, 38–41, 52–5, 62–78, 84, 86–8, 90–2, 96, 98–9, 102, 135, 138–43, 150–4, 163, 167–8, 170–7, 180–4

branch theory 10, 12

Bray, Gerald 11, 18, 56

breath 25–6, 39–40, 68, 70, 74, 76–7, 98, 141

canons 108–9, 111

Cappadocians 14, 112, 129

Carthage 17, 59, 116

catechesis 14, 127, 129, 131, 133, 135–6, 145, 151, 153, 155

children 44, 71, 83, 91, 99, 144, 145

chrismation 34, 150, 154

Christological focus 7, 9–10, 20–4, 27–8, 34, 37, 44, 106, 126, 135, 191

chronology of doctrine 3, 10, 92, 107, 115, 191

Church 4–6, 11, 19, 56–7, 76, 99, 104, 107, 109–10, 132–4, 159

Clement of Alexandria 5, 17, 104

coming-into-being 82, 123, 164, 179

communion 31, 35, 41, 45, 47–8, 52–3, 62, 88, 95, 97–9, 102, 133, 151–2, 167–8, 172, 175, 181, 183, 185–6

composition (of man) 13, 24, 38, 40, 42, 52, 61–5, 69, 77–9, 81–2, 84, 88, 100–2, 135, 137, 142, 144, 170

conciliar age 105, 109, 127, 156

Constantine 19, 109–10, 129
Constantinople 9, 14, 103, 106, 112, 114,
     119, 126, 130, 189
contemplation 164, 171–4, 177–80,
     182–3
corruption 26, 39, 62, 85, 100, 135, 142,
     162, 165, 167–9, 173, 175–7, 179,
     182–3, 187
cosmology 5, 29, 31, 42, 59, 116, 138,
     166, 190
'Council of Jerusalem' 108
creation 5, 31, 70, 120–1, 123–4, 139,
     169, 174, 190
creation *ex nihilo* 32, 67, 69, 164, 166,
     168
creed as functional text 132
creed of Jerusalem 14, 129, 131
cross 1, 3, 6, 42, 45, 48–50, 93–5, 97,
     153–4, 162, 183
Cyril of Alexandria 19

Daley, C. B. 57
Daniélou, Jean 70, 72
death 7, 11, 39, 44, 46–7, 49, 51, 61,
     65–6, 68–9, 75, 85–6, 90, 93–5, 131,
     134–7, 144, 147–9, 152–4, 168, 173,
     175–6, 179, 181–4, 187
  of Christ 3, 7
debt 49–50, 177, 182–3
defect 28, 32, 82, 86, 149
demons 137, 148, 172, 180
dependence 118–19, 163–4
development (of man) 28, 36, 38, 41, 52,
     55, 61–3, 68–9, 72–4, 78–80, 82,
     84–6, 88, 95–6, 98–9, 139, 148
  particularly of the soul 69, 71–4, 78,
     96
devil 45, 85, 95, 144
disciplina arcani 131
divinity 2, 4–7, 9, 11, 28, 31, 34–5, 39–40,
     48, 52–3, 61, 69–71, 73, 78, 97, 100,
     115, 119–21, 146–8, 151, 153, 172,
     175, 178–80, 186
  in humanity 2
doctrine 3, 5, 9, 24, 34, 61, 79, 82, 100,
     102, 105–6, 126–7, 132, 169, 177,
     186, 189, 191

articulation of 2, 6, 9, 10–15, 21–2, 53,
     56, 63, 79, 88, 100–1, 104–5,
     112–14, 116, 121–2, 125–7, 133–4,
     151, 155, 159, 161, 186, 188, 190
  development of 7, 9, 11, 13–14, 101–2,
     113, 115, 151, 158, 191
Donatism 60, 110, 116
dualism 33, 42, 54, 116
dust 22, 25–7, 38–9, 51–2, 68, 141–2
dynamic 13, 34–5, 41, 52, 54, 56–7, 71,
     86, 98–9, 101–2, 167, 175

earth 8, 21, 25–6, 32, 36, 38, 42–3, 50–1,
     90–1, 163, 172, 176
economy and history 1, 13–14, 28, 34,
     37–8, 41–4, 46, 48, 50–2, 55, 61–2,
     64, 71, 73, 77–83, 85–6, 89, 91–3,
     96–7, 102, 121, 133–5, 138, 143–4,
     147, 156, 173, 175, 190
ecumenical councils 13–14, 109, 114
Eden 20–2, 34–5, 40–1, 46, 57, 74, 79,
     85, 87, 89, 95, 97, 176
'Edict of Milan' 129
Egypt 19
emanationist trinitarianism 117–19
encounter 2–4, 6, 8–9, 11, 13, 15, 34–5,
     52, 92, 118, 125, 132, 135, 185, 190
Ephesus 110
Epiphanius of Salamis 19, 60, 111
eschatology 1, 33, 41, 42–4, 48, 51–2, 55,
     67–8, 134, 142
eternal generation 35, 118
eternity 1, 3, 5, 35, 43, 56, 71, 93, 118,
     146–7, 163, 165, 167, 171–3, 175,
     177–9, 182, 188
ethics 85, 87, 99, 101
eucharist 61, 91
Eusebius of Caesarea 19, 105, 108–11
Eusebius of Nicomedia 120, 123, 160
Eve 45, 57, 85, 97, 176
exegesis 14, 20–3, 25, 28–30, 32, 80, 88,
     132, 138–9, 151

fall 143
Father 1–4, 6, 8–11, 13, 15, 21–2, 25–9,
     32–8, 40–3, 45–7, 49–55, 62–3,
     69–71, 77–9, 84, 88–90, 93–6,

100–4, 106–7, 111, 113–26, 128–9, 131–2, 134, 139, 144–7, 150, 153–6, 162–9, 175, 177, 180–2, 184–91

fish 136

flesh 1–3, 5, 7–8, 15, 35–6, 38–9, 41, 45, 47–8, 50, 52–3, 65–6, 68, 73–4, 81, 90, 92, 98, 100, 139, 144–5, 163, 180
  as 'house' of the soul 65, 78

freedom 97, 99, 137, 140, 142, 177–8

friendship with God 89

generation 5, 35, 68, 82, 118, 120–1, 123, 139, 156, 166

genus 72, 80, 84, 100

'Gnosticism' 10, 25, 30–1, 54

'Gnostics' 17, 116

Gregory the Theologian 44, 160

habituation 176

Hands of God 1, 13, 25, 28, 32, 35, 38, 51, 54, 63, 98, 101, 113, 116, 118, 191

harmony of creation 90, 163

Hebrews 6–7, 19, 63, 138, 144, 153

Hermas 32, 87

Hermogenes 59, 97

Hilary of Poitiers 112

Hippolytus 18

homoousia 103, 114, 122–3, 125, 160, 177, 187

humanity 2–4, 6–8, 17, 25–6, 28–9, 34, 37, 41, 44–6, 48, 50–3, 58, 66, 94, 96, 101, 106, 121, 134, 137, 140, 145, 147, 153, 162, 175, 189

hypostasis 118

hypothesis of scripture 21–3, 25, 27

image of God 1, 7–9, 11, 13, 17, 24–6, 28–30, 32–5, 37–8, 41–3, 45–8, 51–5, 62–4, 69, 76–9, 84–6, 89, 98, 100–2, 127, 134, 140–2, 152, 154–5, 162, 164, 166–9, 172–3, 175, 177–8, 181, 184, 187, 190–1
  unchanging image 166

image of the Son
  Spirit as 188

imaging God 28, 43, 45, 53–4, 62, 66, 69, 71, 73, 77, 79, 84, 90, 98–100, 102, 113, 140, 151, 154, 162, 164, 166, 169, 170, 174, 181–2, 186–7, 191

imitation 31, 134, 149, 151–2, 154

immortality 39–40, 68, 70, 171, 182

impatience 62, 64, 85–9, 99, 144

incarnation 1–7, 9, 15, 21, 23, 26–9, 33–8, 40–1, 43–5, 47–52, 54, 79, 89, 91–3, 95–9, 121, 134, 144–8, 150–4, 162–3, 173, 177–86, 189–90

incarnational becoming 1, 3, 7, 44–5, 47–8, 91–2, 145, 181, 183

incorruption 45, 47–8, 140, 162, 167–8, 173, 179, 182, 190

intellect 71–3, 171, 174, 178

Jerome 56, 131

Jerusalem 1, 127, 129, 130–1

Jonas, Hans 30

Jordan 37, 134, 144, 154, 156, 185

Julian 160

Justin the Philosopher 17, 20, 40, 51, 102

ktisma 120, 124, 187

Laberius 66

light 29, 92, 99, 117–18, 124, 164–6

likeness 8, 24, 30, 32–3, 37–8, 43, 45–9, 62–3, 85–6, 98, 134, 137, 150–2, 154–5, 167, 175

Lonergan, Bernard 12

Macarius of Jerusalem 130

Macedonianism 130–1

Manichaeans 60, 116

Marcion 5, 96

martyrdom 74, 81, 97

materiality 28, 31–2, 35, 37–42, 52–3, 63–6, 70–1, 73–4, 84, 86, 91, 96, 138–40, 142, 168, 172, 182–3

mediator 22, 94

Meletius 108, 160–1

Messiah 36, 79

modalism 117

model 62–3, 79, 84–5, 89, 98, 100, 102, 155

Montanism 10, 56, 59, 60–1, 116
Mother of God 6, 35, 48
motion and movement 1, 38, 62, 164, 168, 172–6, 178–9, 181
mystery 1, 11, 13, 51–2, 93, 101, 134–5, 138, 143, 152–3, 191

Nag Hammadi Codices 29, 32
Nasrallah, Laura 75, 80
natures 2, 4, 6–8, 24, 26, 28, 34, 41, 45, 51–3, 63, 70, 72–3, 78, 80–6, 90–2, 95–6, 99–100, 117–18, 122–3, 129, 134, 137–8, 140–2, 146–7, 154, 156, 165, 167–8, 170–1, 174–6, 178–9, 181–4, 186, 190
New Prophecy 58–9, 116
Nicaea 9, 14, 103–7, 109–11, 113–15, 121–6, 128–32, 144, 156, 160–1, 186–7, 189
Nicene council
    centralization of 105, 107, 111–12, 122, 145, 156, 189
    'universal scope' 109
Nicene creed 14, 105–6, 108–13, 115, 121–2, 124–6, 145, 152, 156, 166
    punctuation of 122
'Nicene orthodoxy' 107, 131
Nicene theology 9, 14, 106, 112–13, 122, 126, 130, 156, 162, 184, 186, 189
nous 171–2, 183
nuptial imagery 100, 135, 144

obedience 34–5, 37–8, 43, 47, 49, 50–1, 74, 79, 94, 101
offering 2, 42, 45, 48–51, 91, 93–4, 98–9, 182–3, 185, 189
Origen of Alexandria 17–18, 104, 115, 117–21, 124
original sin 82
Osborn, Eric 18, 59, 83, 93
ousia 115, 122–5, 132, 187

Pantaenus 17
paradigm 29, 33, 34, 38, 45, 84, 91
participation 28, 31, 33, 37, 40, 45, 47–8, 51, 54, 61, 73, 77, 88, 118–19, 134,

148, 151–2, 154–6, 162, 165–9, 172–81, 185, 187–8
Pascha 108–10
passion 1, 5, 11, 31, 82, 139, 148, 152–3, 183
patience 62, 79, 84–5, 87, 89–91, 97–9
    of God 89–90, 99
patristic study 3–4, 13, 17, 128, 186, 191
Patrophilus of Scythopolis 131
Paul 1, 8, 46, 93–4, 113, 139–40, 151–2, 179, 191
peer, Christ as 182
Pentecost 9, 101, 106, 109
perfection 1, 30, 33, 41–4, 51–2, 55, 70–1, 85, 98, 134, 139, 148, 165
Pettersen, Alvyn 165
Philo 24–6
Plato 70
Pleroma 31, 84
pneumatology 9, 64, 103, 106, 113–15, 125–8, 135, 156, 184, 188
poiema 120, 124
Polycarp of Smyrna 18, 20, 44
post-Nicene silence 103, 111–12, 114, 128
promotion 146–7
prophecy 40, 50, 59, 71, 92
protology 21–2, 27, 29, 33, 42, 44, 55, 79, 135
Ptolemy 5, 22, 26, 29, 31
puritanism 57, 116
purity 25, 57, 83–4, 116, 137–8, 142–3
Pythagoras 66

Quartodeciman controversy 18

race 42, 45–6, 48, 52–3, 79–81, 84, 142, 176, 190
ransom 45, 49, 93–4, 97, 177
'real' in Cyril 152–4
reason/rationality 25, 38, 139–40, 142, 150, 165–6, 177–8, 180
recapitulation 28, 34, 37, 42, 44–9, 53, 79, 91, 93–4
reception (of divine qualities) 13, 41, 53–5, 64, 71, 74, 76–9, 88, 96–100, 119–20, 134–5, 149–51, 166
regula 108

relations 2, 4–5, 7–8, 10, 13–14, 21, 25–6, 29, 32, 34–5, 37–9, 41–3, 45, 47, 51–4, 61–2, 73, 75, 78, 82, 84, 86, 94, 100–2, 104, 106–7, 111, 113, 116–18, 121–2, 124–6, 128, 131–2, 134, 139, 144–7, 150, 152, 154–6, 162, 164–7, 169, 174–8
renewal 37, 64, 91, 143
resurrection 1–3, 5–8, 11, 26–7, 39–40, 42–3, 49, 51, 67, 69, 74, 89, 93, 150, 153–4, 182–4
retrospection 27, 34, 137
revelation 6, 8, 24, 50–1, 53, 63, 71, 98, 132, 162, 167, 178
righteousness 44, 46, 56–7, 79, 136–7, 143, 153, 165
Rome 18, 31, 104, 110, 160–1

Sabellius 110, 115–16
sacraments 61, 91, 99, 132, 134–8, 143–4, 148, 151, 154, 156, 190
sacrifice 3, 42, 45, 49–50, 94–5, 99, 134, 149, 151, 154, 182–4, 186
Satan 11, 28, 144
schism 56, 58–60, 108
scripture 1, 7–8, 11, 20, 22–3, 25–9, 32, 39, 51, 63–4, 68, 89, 95, 100, 106, 114, 119, 124, 132, 138, 141, 145, 153, 160, 187
    matrix of 11, 27
second nature 80, 83
Seneca 71
senses (bodily and spiritual) 170–80, 183
Simon Magus 141
simultaneous creation of body and soul 68
sin 37, 42, 46, 48–50, 57, 62, 64, 66, 79, 81–6, 88–9, 91, 94–5, 99, 100, 134–7, 139–45, 147–8, 150, 153–4, 174–7, 179, 190
    as disposition 86
    as mud 143
Sirach 8
soma 66
Son 1–4, 6–11, 13, 15, 21–2, 25–9, 32, 33–8, 40–1, 43, 45, 47–55, 62–4, 69, 71, 79, 84–6, 88–96, 98–104, 106, 113–26, 128–9, 131–2, 134, 139,
        144–56, 162, 165–7, 169, 174–5, 177, 181–2, 184–91
sonship 145–7, 156
Soranus 58, 76–7
soteriology 7, 30–1, 37, 41, 44–8, 64, 88–9, 92–3, 96, 98, 106, 121, 134, 144, 147–8, 150, 153–5, 163, 177, 179, 181, 184, 186, 190
soul 38–41, 52, 54–5, 62–78, 80, 84, 86–90, 98–100, 102, 134–5, 138, 140–3, 149–52, 154, 163, 167–77, 179–80, 182–3
    corporeality of 75–6
    divine properties 'congenital' to 71, 172
    shape of 39, 73, 75–6
    velocity of 38–9
Spirit 2, 6, 9, 11, 13, 15, 21–2, 25–9, 32, 34–8, 40–1, 43, 45–6, 51–5, 61–3, 69–71, 73, 76–9, 86–8, 92, 94, 96–104, 106, 108, 112–18, 121–2, 126–9, 131, 133–5, 138, 144–6, 148–52, 154–6, 163, 169, 172, 177, 179, 183–9, 191
    human capacity for 96–7
static 10, 13, 52, 57, 77, 98
Stoicism 70, 75
subjectivism 133, 147
substantia 77, 92, 100, 102, 115–16, 118
suffering 28, 50, 74, 134, 137, 149, 151–4, 182
systematics 126, 147, 191

theological trajectories 105
Theophilus of Antioch 17, 20, 40, 59, 104
theos 2, 5, 6, 8, 34, 190
tomb of Christ 1, 39, 51, 89, 95, 136, 152–3
transmigration of souls 66, 73
Trevett, Christine 60
triad 2, 34, 53, 100, 102–4, 113, 117
trias 104
trinitarian expression 7, 9, 10, 64, 69, 79, 87–8, 92, 99–104, 106, 114, 116, 119, 122, 126–7, 132, 134, 144, 155–6, 191
trinitarian theology 9, 13, 71, 87, 98, 107, 122, 129, 190

trinitas 61, 100, 104, 118
trinity 11, 13–15, 37, 61, 63, 102, 121–2,
    186, 191
tri-partite anthropology 40, 64
tritheism 118
'true God' 7, 25, 32, 53, 124, 166

union 2, 21–2, 35, 37, 39, 42, 48–9, 51,
    54, 62, 64–6, 68, 71, 92–100, 102,
    115–18, 122, 129, 134, 144, 148, 154,
    168, 170, 178, 180, 182, 184

Valentinianism 5, 17, 20, 22–3, 26, 28–9,
    31–2, 67, 103

Victor of Rome 18
Virgin 92
virgin birth 2, 3, 92
vision of God 9, 47, 177

Waszink, Jan Henrik 18, 75, 77
water 29, 100, 132, 138, 141, 146
Williams, Michael 30
Wisdom 25, 37, 42, 51, 165, 166
Word 3, 7, 8, 25–7, 34–6, 38, 42–3, 46,
    48, 50–1, 53, 91–2, 146, 162–71,
    173, 175, 177–83, 185–9

zeal 56–7, 59–60, 98–9, 101, 104